The Danish Army of the Napoleonic Wars 1801–1814, Organisation, Uniforms and Equipment

Volume 2: Cavalry and Artillery

David A. Wilson

Helion & Company Ltd

Helion & Company Limited
Unit 8 Amherst Business Centre
Budbrooke Road
Warwick
CV34 5WE
England
Tel. 01926 499619
Email: info@helion.co.uk
Website: www.helion.co.uk
Twitter: @helionbooks
Visit our blog at https://helionbooks.wordpress.com/

Published by Helion & Company 2021
Designed and typeset by Serena Jones
Cover designed by Paul Hewitt, Battlefield Design (www.battlefield-design.co.uk)

Cover: *Husar Premiereløjtnant* J. Ewald *c.*1814 in non-regulation service uniform

ISBN 978-1-913336-59-2

British Library Cataloguing-in-Publication Data.

A catalogue record for this book is available from the British Library.

Dedications

To my wife Josette for many years of patience

To Teddy Suren for his original inspiration and 'joie de vivre'

To Jean François Blanc for his constant encouragement.

In memoriam of my dear friend, Lieutenant Colonel Anders Lindström,
Late of the Royal Swedish Army and of Tradition of Scandinavia.
14 October 1941–3 September 2014

Contents

List of Plates

Foreword

It was four years ago, soon after I had started sculpting a Danish Napoleonic range for our company Perry Miniatures, that David contacted me. Something that often happens when you start a new range is, once it's announced or the first few figures have been shown, experts on the subject email you offering their knowledge. David explained he was writing a book on the Napoleonic Danish/Norwegian Army and offered to help with information, fantastic! David had started the project back in 2013, so he was well into the book when he made contact.

Later the same day Jørgen Larsen emailed me, introducing himself and explaining he had been researching the Danish Army for many years, not just the Napoleonic period but the later army too. He asked if he could be of assistance as he had access to huge amounts of original research material in his homeland. Double fantastic!!

I immediately introduced David and Jørgen to each other.

I thought I had a reasonable amount of information to make the range, how wrong I was!

I was blown away with the amount of information sent by both David and Jørgen over the years, from David's excellent schematics to Jørgen's source material. This of course helped me immensely with my range, but now, in book form, it can be enjoyed by everyone.

In the UK Scandinavian Napoleonic armies are probably the most difficult to find information on. It might be the language barrier but it's a rare book that even skims the surface of these north European armies, so to have a book in English dedicated to the Danish/Norwegian Army in so much detail is unique!

Alan Perry
Perry Miniatures

Preface

This is the second volume of my study, and as I have already said, this is my humble attempt to write a good working document which is as accurate as possible; this volume covering the uniforms and equipment, the cavalry and their standards, and artillery of the Danish army of the Napoleonic Wars, including the cannons, limbers and wagons. I have tried to be as thorough as possible, but although I have listed and enumerated them I was unable to draw all of the different pieces of artillery as there were just too many, so I have drawn all of the most important models and a number more will be found in the third volume.

The third volume is in preparation and will cover the Norwegian army and the Danish militias and volunteers, together with additional artillery and equipment.

Acknowledgements

A special mention must be made to Jørgen Koefoed Larsen, without whose precious help this work would not have achieved the degree of authenticity that it has. I must also mention his patience with my very poor Danish and supplying me with many extraordinary documents and putting them into their context and correcting my errors along the way.

Also I would like to extend my thanks to the following researchers for their kind and irreplaceable help and encouragement that they have given me over the years on Danish and Norwegian uniforms.

Torstein Snorrason, for his kindness and patience with me and his gift of rare books stands out.

Knut Erik Strøm, who has helped me with the least-known aspects of one of the least-known armies of this period outside of Norway, and his personal work on the Norwegian militia and volunteers.

Erik C. Aagaard, who pointed my research in the right direction and provided a vast number of documents describing the Norwegian infantry colours.

I must also mention Ola Jonsgaard Möen and Trond Bækkevold, who helped me to start this project many years ago.

Dr Peter Bunde, who has supplied me with copies of his illustrations based on his own research on this army.

Mr Karsten Skjold Petersen, senior researcher of Tøjhusmuseet in Copenhagen.

Peter Kristiansen, Curator of Castle Rosenborg Copenhagen.

Thank you all so much.

1

The Danish Regular Cavalry

Introduction

The Danish cavalry had been heavily reformed and reorganised in 1792–1803, receiving new and more modern organisation and training, modernised and standardised uniforms, saddlery and arms. Also a number of new cavalry schools, for training recruits, and schools for training NCOs had also been formed. This ensured a firm foundation for the cavalry in the period to come. In general the cavalry were very well trained in the use of the sabre and straight-sword, in standard cavalry drill and riding in formation. They were mostly mounted on strong horses from Holstein and Jutland, which were generally well tended and cared for.

The men were trained to live in the open and bivouac in the rough with a minimum of rations. These young men displayed a great deal of bravery and talent for reconnaissance and movement in rough terrain. It was these combined factors which inspired awe and fear among their enemies. Although they lacked combat experience, the majority had received five to 10 years of training before the war and they were used to living and working together as a unit.

Horses

The Jutland breed of horse has been known since the time of the Vikings and has been used as a war horse ever since.

It is a fairly sturdy rustic horse, compact and muscular with low withers and a muscular chest, some of which were crossed with the Frederiksborg breed in the eighteenth century. The Frederiksborger was an even more ancient breed, if somewhat less numerous, being seen as a luxury breed during the eighteenth century. They are a close relation to the shire horse with the same good temperament.

Today the Jutland breed is seen as typically having a chestnut coat, but originally they could equally be blacks, bays, greys or roans as well. These horses were the mainly used by the light dragoons and hussars.

The heavy cavalry and artillery preferred the famous Holsteiners, which were medium-framed horses averaging between 16 to 17 hands (64–68in, 163–173cm) at the withers. Traditional Holsteiners were dark coloured (black, dark bay, and brown) and minimally marked.

Both horse breeds were also exported in large numbers as warhorses. France and the German states bought large numbers from 1797–1813, and in 1813 nearly the whole French Guard cavalry were remounted on Danish horses. Another large customer was the Saxon cavalry which exclusively rode Holsteiners.

Harness and Shabraques

All the Danish cavalry used their version of the Hungarian harness made of black leather, and a Hungarian saddle. The hussars, light dragoons and the Livgarde added throat decorations and the officers could have cowrie shells stitched on to the head stall and breast strap.

By this time all virtually all the Danish shabraques were made in the 'hussar' style. These Shabraques were supposed to last for a period of between 16 and 24 years, so most of the cavalry, with a couple of exceptions, used the shabraques of the 1802-issue model right through the war. As they were relined regularly, the actual shape and possibly the piping may have varied a little over time.

Basic Tactics

The heavy cavalry (*Rytter-Regimenterne*) were trained to perform massed cavalry charges to maximise the effect of their heavy horses and heavy swords. They were mainly trained to fight on horseback unlike the light cavalry regiments. The regiment would deploy its squadrons in lines and approach the enemy. The speed would move from trotting to running, ending in a gallop. But reforms made in 1792–1800 meant that they were made 'lighter' (losing their cuirass, heavy boots and heavy saddles etc.) and were also trained in providing their own security by being able to send out skirmishers, scouts and flank guards. This made them more manoeuvrable, independent and more flexible on the battlefield, but being 'bigger men on bigger horses', they retained the strength of heavy cavalry.

During the reform of the cavalry from 1792–1800 the traditional 'dragoon' regiments also changed radically. The previous concept, that the dragoons could fight on horseback but also dismount and engage the enemy on foot if needed, was abolished (except in Norway, where this

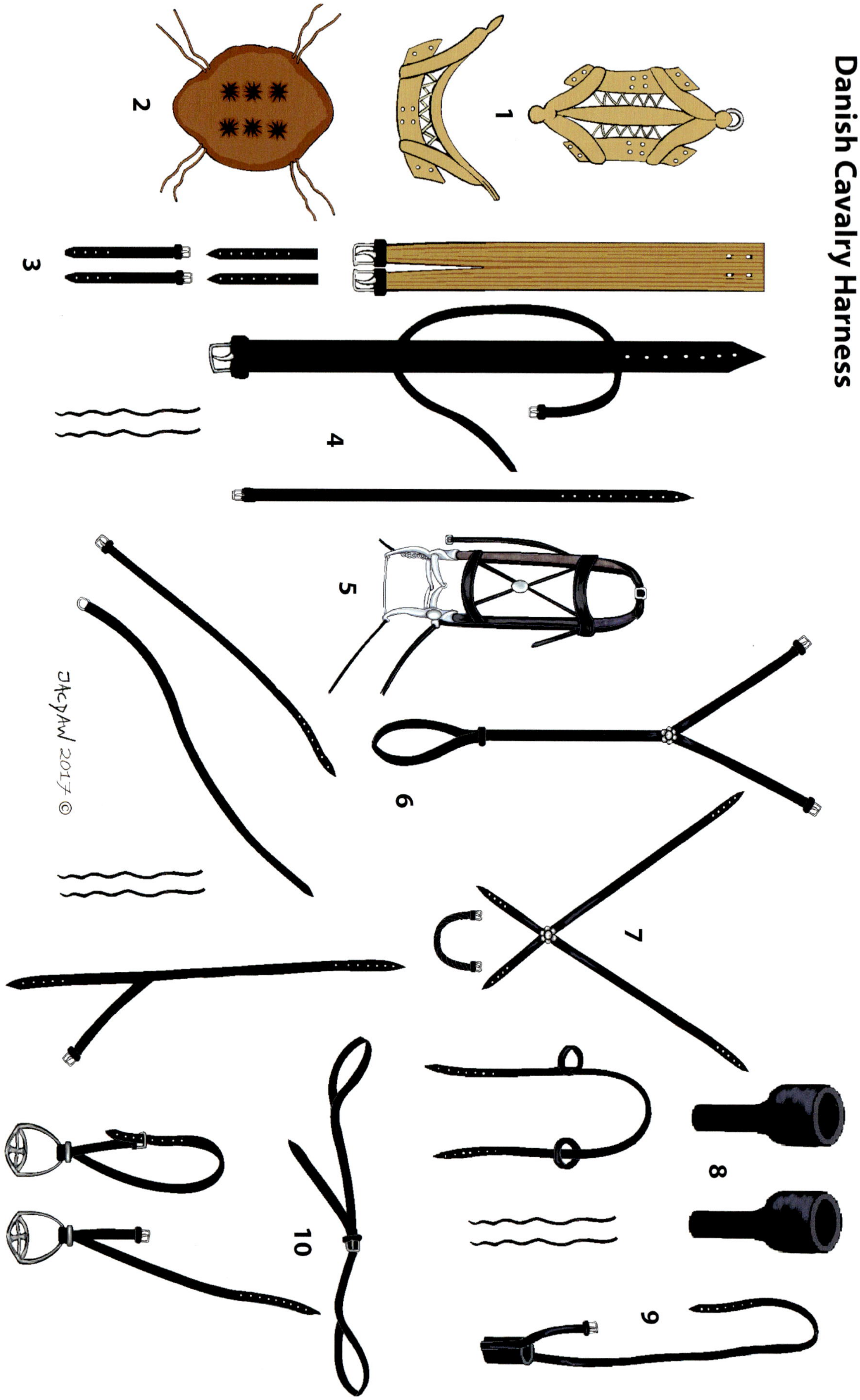

Danish Cavalry Harness

Plate 1. Basic Danish Cavalry Harness

1. Saddle tree
2. Leather seat
3. Surcingle
4. Saddle strap
5. Bridle and head stall
6. Breast strap
7. Crupper straps. Below, holster straps to breast straps
8. Holsters and straps
9. Carbine bucket
10. Stirrups and stirrup straps

Source: an original drawing conserved in the Tøjhusmuseet, now called the Krigsmuseet.

ability was still seen as an asset), as they proved to be much more effective when fighting on horseback.

The light dragoons were meant to be used mainly as a fast reconnaissance and escort force. They were to be used as scouts and were trained to fight in small combat units as it was expected that they would clash with enemy patrols. They also received extensive training in fast raids on shaken and surprised enemies. However, if needed they also had the ability to attack in close order, and so formed they had a flexible 'in between' role of heavy and light cavalry.

The original concept was that the dragoons could dismount and engage the enemy on foot, but this system had been abandoned before the Napoleonic wars.

The Danish hussars functioned like all other light cavalry of its day. The hussars were trained like the light dragoons as scouts and frequently functioned in a supporting role of the infantry. Like the light dragoons, the hussars would be used to shield friendly infantry from enemy cavalry during major engagements.

The lancer squadron of the hussar regiment were based on the Prussian Bosniak doctrine, and although they were basically for show, during the war they were used to patrol and guard the coastline.

Only the artillery and infantry received any approbated patterns or orders to change to the new system of NCO distinctions in 1789 (or later), not the cavalry, hussars, Guides and particularly the Livgarden til Hest. Therefore they continued to use the 'old' 1774 type of distinctions until 1812. The reason why the cavalry never changed their distinctions is that they never had sword/carbine belts over their left shoulder, only the cartridge pouch, held by a narrow shoulder strap referred to as a 'dragon' of twisted cord, not unlike an NCO's distinction, but without the fringe, so it was decided that there was no need to change their distinctions before 1812. The Guard (and possibly the hussars as well) had even retained the use of extra silver lace on their collar and cuffs, as part of their NCO distinctions.

The officers of the hussars and Royal Horse Guards had special cuff distinctions from 1802 on their kollets and dolmans (they were also allowed to wear the M1802 'epaulettes' on their other uniforms, as they 'should be carried by all officers of the army').

This was completely changed for the cavalry, hussars and Guides in 1812, as well as for the Guards, both the horse and foot, but both these units were allowed to retain some silver lace on their uniforms. The exact details for the use of the new NCO distinctions for the Horse Guards were not clearly detailed, and although it is intended that they also should have new cuff distinctions, 'but at a later date' at the 'next uniform change', in fact they may have kept their old distinctions for a while longer than the rest of the army.

Another thing one must remember is that so many old uniforms were intended to be worn until they were worn out, so many units continued to use old uniforms until the end of the war, sometimes modified by the regimental tailors or the men themselves.

The 1812 change in the form of distinctions and the form of the cuffs seems to have been applied to the officers, NCOs and trumpeters, but generally not to the troop, many having the older form of cuff right up to 1815. To this one must add non-Danish items purloined from allies or enemies, in particular foul weather items which were popular acquisitions due to the climate. Cloaks of French origin have been noted as being used and appear in a few contemporary illustrations.

Some mention must be made of the French *Général de Brigade* Charles Lallemand, who was detached to command the Danish avant-garde or Light Brigade which he led until January 1814 with great zeal and bravery, notably at the battle of Sehestedt. He was noted as shouting '*Vive l'Empereur, Brave Danois allons allons!*' He was easily recognised by waving his red polish field cap. He wore a general's version of a dark blue hussar uniform with silver lace and buttons, with a general's waist sash, all under a dark blue cavalry cloak.

2

The Royal Horse Guards, Den Kongelige Livgarden til Hest

The Royal Horse Guards was a small unit mainly charged with escorting the King and his family in the royal residence in Copenhagen, and by this time no longer fought on the field of battle, with the exception of the defence of Copenhagen in 1807. A letter from the Danish Chancellery dated 15 August 1801 stipulated that the enrolled Guards should be 'beautiful and well-formed people' and in any case they must not be redheads as they were regarded at the time as being uncouth. They should be literate as well.

The regiment was composed of volunteers from all over Denmark (including Norway, Holstein and the Isle of Bornholm), and once accepted into the regiment they served continuously, but six years was the basic period of service in the unit. The 'Guardsmen' had a higher status than ordinary line cavalrymen (an 'ordinary' Guardsman was equal to a vice corporal), and their uniforms were made of finer cloth, and they received new issues more frequently than ordinary soldiers.

This was a regiment which was now composed of only two small squadrons. The first was called the Liv Eskadron and the second was simply known as the 2nd Eskadron.

The regimental staff of the Livgarden til Hest was composed of a colonel (*Oberst*; this was always the king in person), a lieutenant colonel (*Oberstløjtnant*), a major, an ADC (a second lieutenant), a quartermaster sergeant (*Kvartermester*), a senior juridical officer (*Auditor*), a surgeon (*Feltskærer*), and an assistant surgeon (*Underkirurg*), a master of horse as in instructor (*Berider*), an assistant squire (*Assistent*), a blacksmith or farrier (*Fanesmed*), a saddler (*Sadelmager*), a kettledrummer (*Pauker*) and five trumpeters (*Trompetere*) and two squadrons of Livgarden til Hest. The first squadron had an establishment of four officers, five NCOs and 60 Livgarden til Hest, the second squadron had the same but without the kettledrummer. The horses of the Liveskadronen were dark brown bays, those of the second squadron were black.

Uniforms of the Livgarden til Hest

The Livgarden til Hest had a lacquered black leather M1798 helmet with a crest which had white metal reinforcing bands, there was a black fur caterpillar over the top and a black horse mane, and it had a scarlet cloth turban with three silver chains each side. The helmet had a pointed uplifted lacquered black leather peak with white metal edging. The crown of the helmet was made from a single piece of leather and was reinforced with a metal strip on both sides and a white metal bar and diamond on the front of the base of the crown above the peak. Originally the helmet had a black leather chin strap.

In 1808 detachable white metal chin scales were added to this leather chin strap, for parades and field service.

On left side there was a white brushed woollen plume which had a red tip for the 1st Squadron, the Liveskadron or Life Squadron, and a light blue tip for the 2nd Squadron.

These helmets were supposed to last for 12 years. In 1801 the horsehair mane or tails was quite thin and short and the plume was made of three bunches of cock's feathers and was shorter and wider. During their period of service these helmets were maintained, and they acquired new feathers, comb and tail, as these were renewed every four years. In 1810 new helmets were due, according to clothing terms. There is reference in a letter from the Danish war department to the Horse Guards, dated 17 January 1810, that 'new helmets are being made and will be delivered to the Horse guards…' later the same year. Also, '[the] same helmets are allowed a new and more expensive type of plume also, if that plume cannot be found cheaper…' This new helmet, although clearly based on the former model, was somewhat different in form/shape. For reference we refer to it as the M1810, although this was not an official reference. On the front there was a large silvered brass plate bearing the crowned arms of Denmark with supporters, all within a wreath (the same shield as that worn on the Royal Foot Guards' bearskins). There was a wide silvered metal band around the base and the turban appears to have been crimson red for both troops. The type of cloth used was called *Tamis*, therefore it also predates 1812. It still had a black fur caterpillar over the top and a black free-hanging horse hair mane, but the caterpillar was now longer at the front and also posed upon a metal/silvered crest. The peak was still pointed but was now flat, no longer uplifted and the funnel for the plume was further back. This model was supposed to have lasted for eight years (until 1818), when new model helmets were delivered.

All these details comes from the research of Jørgen Koefoed Larsen and are based on a surviving helmet in the museum of Bornholm, long erroneously thought of as a night watchman's hat.

The Livgarden til Hest had a short, straw-yellow cloth coatee which was fastened with hooks and eyelets down the front and the coat was trimmed in livery lace (white/silver piped red with a fine red zigzag) on all leading edges. The coat had upturned front corners showing the red lining and it was also trimmed with the livery lace. This had a clothing term of four years.

The coat had a scarlet collar trimmed with livery lace and scarlet shoulder straps edged with livery lace. The collar was quite low in 1804, by 1808 it had become a little higher and finally in 1812 it became quite high (see illustrations). The scarlet cuffs were originally round, but an order for pointed cuffs was issued in 1801 for the officers, with no mention of the men. This can be interpreted three ways, the most logical was that as guardsmen had a senior rank to ordinary cavalrymen this order covered them as well without being specific; or, there was a specific order for them, but it has been lost over time, or they waited for the next clothing issue, the least likely as it would looked strange for this regiment to have a uniforms which were not the same on service around the King. The cuffs were red and piped white and had a loop on the point of the cuff, with two buttons, and they were also trimmed with livery lace. The buttons were silvered. Under the collar was worn a black neck stock over their shirt. The uniform issued in 1810 appeared to be duller in shade than the previous issue.

Full dress included a pair of fall front pale yellow leather breeches and high-cuffed black boots. For service dress there was a pair of dark blue overalls with leather inserts and a fall down flap front with a button on each side. It had a red welt down the side and was closed with silver buttons. These blue overalls were replaced with grey ones *c.*1810–1812, they also had leather inserts and red welts. For foul weather dress there was a long red riding cloak laced white.

The basic clothing issues were:

A new yellow coatee (*Collet*) with a red collar, cuffs and white/silver lace as well as a pair of yellow buff leather trousers which were generally delivered every third year.

In 1798, blue riding overalls with red lace down the seam were received. They had a term of four years. In January 1810 the colour was changed to grey.

The general service shabraque in red with white lace was termed to last for four years.

In 1798 the new 'casque' (leather helmet) was issued, to last for 12 years (a new term of eight years was introduced in1813, for the new M1810 helmet).

All waist and cross belts, and the new sabretache (*Sabeltaske*) introduced 1798, had a term of 12 years. In 1808 the men were to receive new sabretaches, with the monogram of the new king, Frederik VI. But it is possible that they first changed clothing terms instead of normal terms in 1810, together with new waist and cross belts.

Other 'extras' included a Guards' red, full dress shabraque (*Valdrap*) with silver lace, and a Guards' red cape (*Kappe*) with white lace also was received, again with a term of 12 years.

Some repairs and maintenance was carried out in between, to keep the uniform and accoutrements as good looking as they could. Helmets, as an example, received a new plume and new red turban cloth (*Tamis*) every second year, and the helmets and sabretache 'were lacquered' too. Even under the economic pressure of 1813 this was still maintained. A renewal of horsehair tails and crests was carried out probably every fourth year, but this is not completely clear.

Arms and Equipment

Arms equipment consisted of a wide black carbine belt which had a metal shield with the crowned royal arms and a thinner black leather bandolier over the other shoulder for the black leather cartridge pouch. In the new issue of 1808 the carbine belt was now not so wide and the bandolier for the cartridge pouch was larger. The carbine model is not clear, but as late as 1808–10, according to pictures apparently it was an unmodified M1755 *Rytter* (long) carbine. Although it was mentioned, there is no known issue of rifled carbines.

Note: the Horse Guards still had individual ramrods inserted into the stocks, for both carbines and pistols. They carried two M1748/98 *Garde* pistols, to be primarily used in close combat, therefore rarely for this unit. They had a calibre of 17.5mm and were 44.5cm in length. Their weight is unknown. They were carried in holsters, one to each side of the saddle, covered by the shabraque.

It was probably for this reason that the regiment saw no need to totally upgrade their arms, but preferred rather to concentrate on the men who lacked them.

The uniform included a black leather waist belt which had a white metal buckle plate stamped with the royal arms which were gilded, and suspended from the belt was a black leather scabbard with steel fittings.

Only the officers received the famous M1772 *Solvpallaske* (silver *Pallask*) sword, of which only 12 were officially made, together with a couple or more made and bought privately, and they were all 'owned by the regiment', not by the officers. The shell was decorated with the crowned greater arms of Denmark. This sword was carried

Danish Livgarden til Hest *c.*1804–1814 (I)

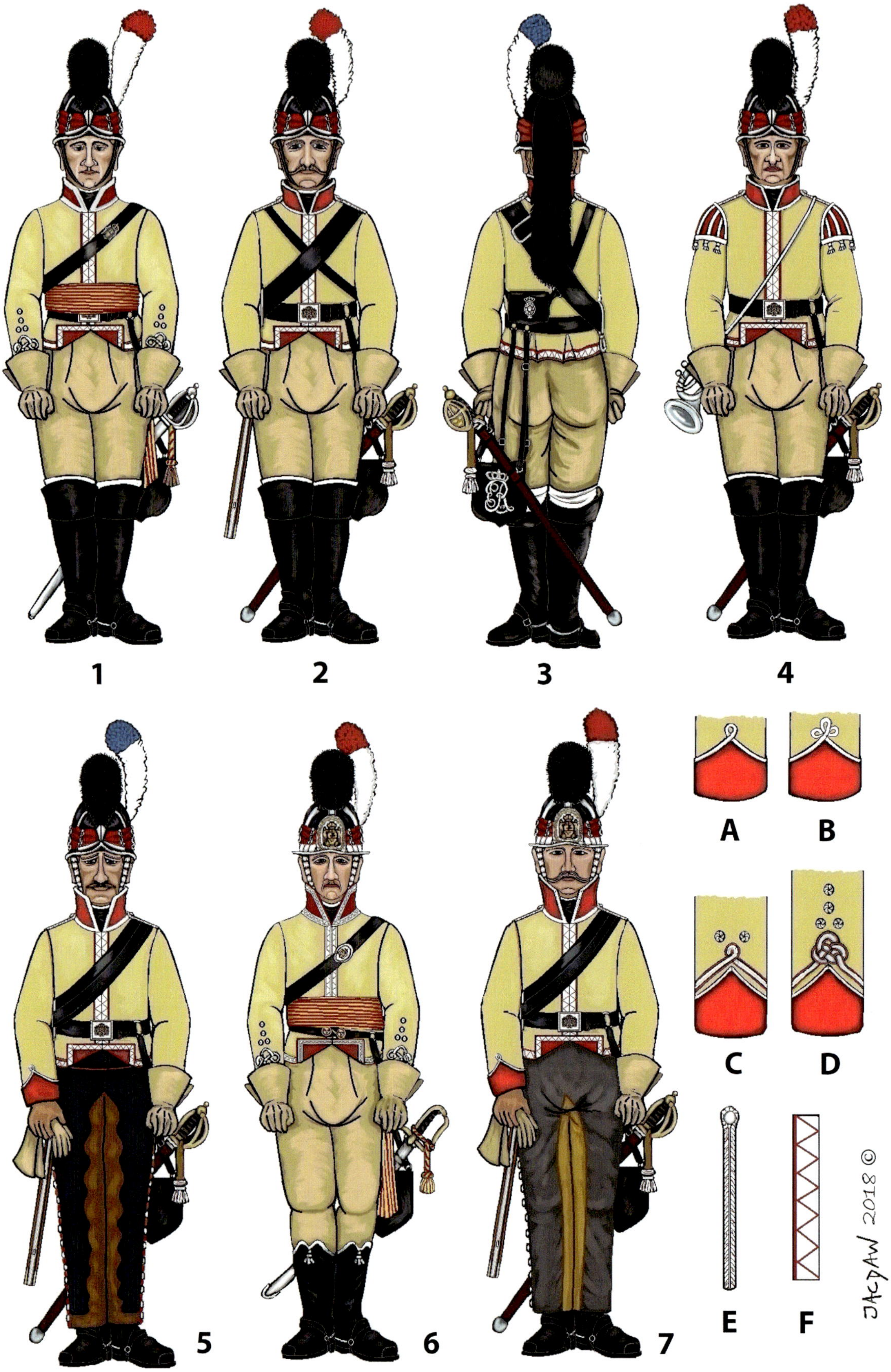

Plate 2. Danish Livgarden til Hest *c.*1804–1814 (I)

1. Officer, 1st Squadron, full dress *c.*1804.
2. Trooper, 1st Squadron, full dress *c.*1804.
3. Trooper, 2nd Squadron, full dress, rear view *c.*1806 showing new long tail.
4. Trumpeter, 1st Squadron, full dress *c.*1806.
5 Trooper, 2nd Squadron, service dress *c.*1808 wearing the 1801 model blue service overalls with red welts.
6. Officer, 1st Squadron, ordinary service dress *c.*1810. Note this dress had been worn since 1801, with the previous model of the helmet. The shoulder belt plate shown is the ordinary service model. Also note the new officers lace introduced after 1808.
7. Trooper, 1st Squadron, wearing service dress *c.*1810–1814 with the new grey service overalls now with black welts introduced in 1810/1811.

Normally the officer's waist sash would hide the sword belt, but it is left visible here to show its position and the different buckles.

A. Trooper's cuff.
B. NCO's cuff.
C. Second lieutenant's cuff.
D. *Rittmeister*'s (captain's) cuff.
E. Trooper's shoulder strap or 'dragon'.
F. Detail of jacket lace.

until *c.*1828 when a new model was made. It was never popular, as although the hilt was quite splendid it was very difficult to get one's hand around the grip, but it was always to be carried 'on parade and on formal and guard duties'. Drawn after a model in the Tøjhusmuseet collection in Copenhagen and preserved under the reference C.2843.

The troopers were issued with the *Dragonpallask* M1785 (dragoon straight sword) model for the Livgarden til Hest. The few pictures *c.*1785–1807 appear to show it being carried in a model 1778 scabbard, not in the official M1785 scabbard.

In 1798 the barracks of the Livgarden til Hest burned down and a large amount of equipment was lost, which had to be replaced. A bill made in 1801 stipulates that 12 'long leather scabbards' and one 'officer's silver scabbard' had been made as replacements for those lost, and were delivered. So if it is a 'leather' scabbard, this no doubt was still the original M1785 brown leather scabbard.

This is further underlined when the Guard was considering making a new sidearm in 1808, the commander inspected other possible scabbard models in the arsenal, and wrote, 'They are all much heavier than the standard scabbard' (for the M1785 *Pallask*), so these leather scabbards were indeed used until 1808 at least.

Around 1808 the Livgarden til Hest were issued with a new sidearm the M1808 *Hestegarde Pallask* (horse guards straight sword) which replaced the *Dragonpallask* (dragoon straight sword) M1785.The new straight sword had the original M1785 hilt mounted with a single-edged blade from the M1789 straight sword, slightly ground into a more pointed form; it was carried in a newly produced scabbard, made with the M1772 officers' scabbard as a model, and a much lighter scabbard, than used before.

These details are from new research by Jørgen K. Larsen regarding their scabbards: 'We know from different letters that when changing their M1785 swords for the new M1808 sword, they also wanted a new model scabbard made at Frederiksværk.' We also know they wrote that a 'Proof model made by the Guards [armourer] had been sent', and they were waiting for this new scabbard. It can be recognised by the three distinctive leather 'windows' along the scabbard.

This is clearly the scabbard shown in 1820–1837 in several contemporary pictures, so everything points to this being the scabbard model they used *c.*1809–*c.*1837 with the Model 1808 sword. It had a brown leather sword knot and tassel. There may have been company colours, but this is not confirmed with contemporary evidence.

The guards had a black leather sabretache bearing the crowned royal cypher 'C7' in silvered metal which hung from black leather straps attached to the waist belt. From 1808 they were changed for a new black leather sabretache, the form of which differed slightly from the precedent model, bearing the crowned royal cypher of the new king 'FR VI' in silvered metal.

For horse furniture there was a black leather light cavalry harness with gilt fittings. For service dress there was a scarlet Hungarian-style shabraque with white lace border and embroidery, and silver lace for the officers. Parade dress had the same shabraques, but apparently in crimson cloth (see illustrations).

Danish Livgarden til Hest c.1806–1814 (II)

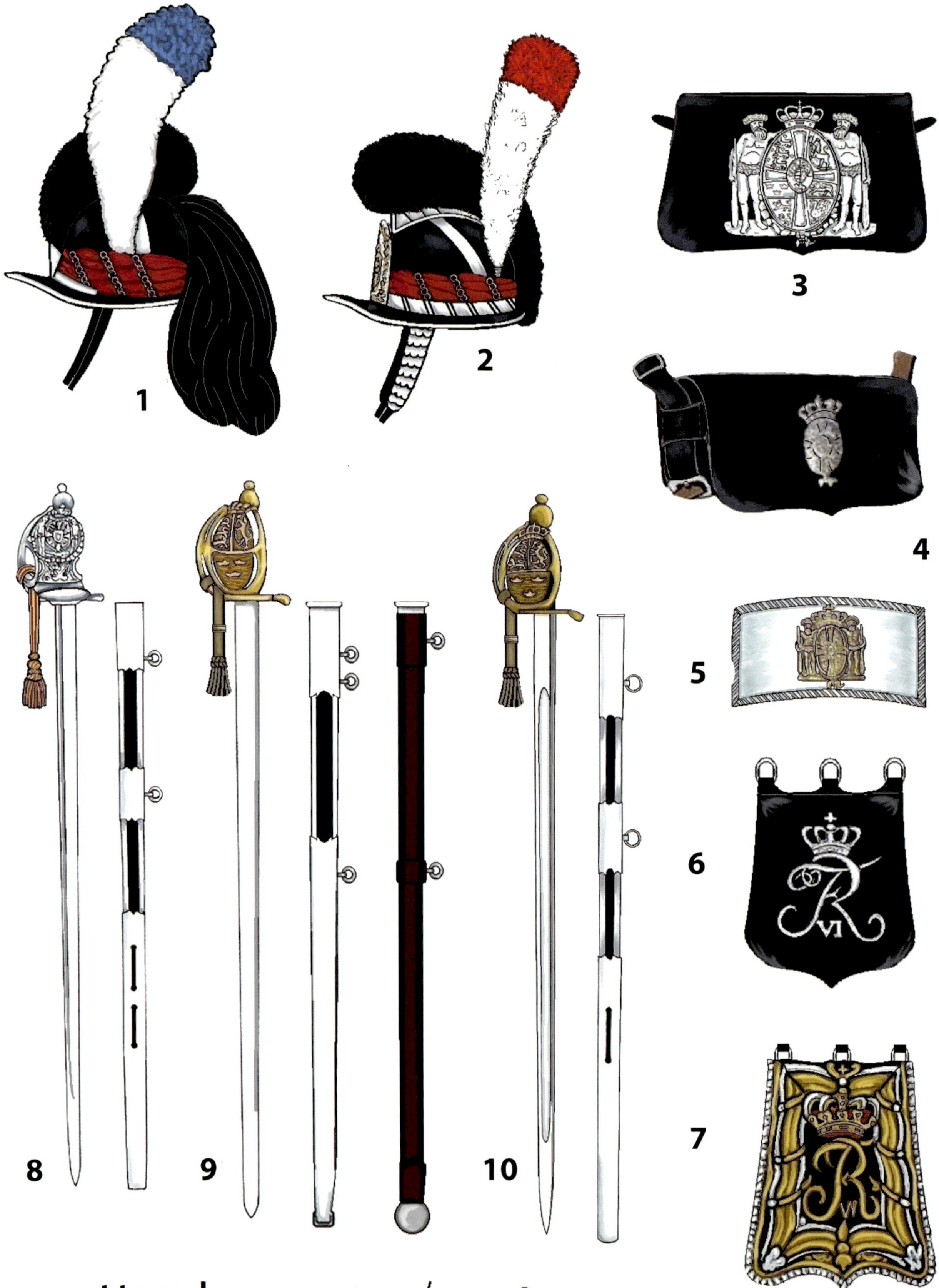

not to scale

JACDAW 2018 ©

Plate 3. Danish Livgarden til Hest *c.*1806–1814 (II)

1. Helmet M1798 with the new longer tail added in 1806. From 1808 it had white metal chin scales attached with a steel rosette. These were worn for parades and as they were to protect the head in combat they were worn for field service as well. But for ordinary daily duty they would not be worn as they were not so comfortable, and also to spare them for too much wear.
2. Helmet M1810, a reconstruction by Jørgen Koefoed Larsen after a helmet preserved in the Museum of the Island of Bornholm.
3. Officer's full dress cartridge pouch.
4. Officer's and trooper's cartridge pouch.
5. Belt buckle for all ranks, except for officers carrying a sabre in which case they used the lion's head buckle, which appears to have been silvered. There appear to have been a number of minor variations during the period, probably new ones.
6. Sabretache all ranks post 1808, the trumpeter's version appears to have been slightly smaller
7. Officer's full dress sabretache *c.*1810.
8. The famous officer's *Solvpallask* (silver *pallask*) model 1772. Note the early model scabbard (four windows).
9. Trooper's *Dragonpallask* M1785 model for the Livgarden til Hest. The few pictures dated *c.*1785–1807 (Møller) appear to show it being carried in a model 1773 scabbard, not in the M1785 scabbard. Drawn after two swords in the Tøjhusmuseet collection in Copenhagen, they are preserved under the references C.2844 and C.2845. Also shown is the M1785 model brown leather scabbard, probably the most common service model until the arrival of the M1808 *Pallask.*
10. The M1808 *Pallask*. I have added a drawing of M1808 sword with the new M1808 scabbard which was received much later. One is also conserved in the Tøjhusmuseet collection.

NCOs' Uniforms

The NCOs wore the troop dress but with wider silver lace on their collar, but on their cuffs they had triple loops of lace clover style to denote their rank, like the hussar NCOs. They also had silver lace at the edges of the 'dragon'/ shoulder strap. One could only identify their rank by the wider lace on their collars and 'dragons'/shoulder straps, as their cuffs were hidden by the gauntlets and the fact that they did not carry a carbine. The NCOs did not carry the carbine or the carbine belt, but according to contemporary illustrations they appear to have a thinner shoulder belt with a small cartridge pouch. They were armed with a *Pallask*, the same model as the troop, and a pair of pistols. The separate ramrod for the pistols was carried on the belt or on the bandolier of the cartridge pouch.

Officers' Uniforms

With the exception of a few details the officers wore the same helmet and uniform as the troop, but without the shoulder straps, but their uniform was made from a better quality cloth, which would suggest that their uniform was very slightly lighter in colour. Their lace was similar to the men's until around 1808 when they started to receive a new all-silver lace made specifically for officers. This is confirmed by a portrait dated 1809–1810, and the preserved uniform of Frederik VI. The officers had Hungarian-style lace and rank insignias on the cuffs (see hussar officers). They wore the usual yellow and red silk sash woven in stripes, and tassels around their waist. On occasion the senior officers could also be found wearing a bicorn with heavily silver-laced border and a white plume and silver loop, button and tassels.

Further research clearly shows that the 12 *Solvpallaske* M1772 also received new scabbards of the 1808 model. This scabbard is sometimes referred to as the 'officers' scabbard model of private issue'. The old M1772 scabbards had by then been used for 36 years, so they must have been worn thin, also the only original scabbard in existence today looks rather battered. So this confirms that they also received a new model scabbard, also shown by Senn in his paintings as early as 1809.

All the officers could and frequently did buy privately an officers' sabre (M1789 or similar), with a silvered brass hilt or a steel hilt and scabbard, which they could use for field service and everyday duties. This was carried on a hussar-style belt with a silvered lion-head clasp. The sword had a gold and crimson red sword knot and tassel.

The bandolier of the cartridge pouch was decorated with the crowned royal arms with supporters. There were two versions: the plate for ordinary service was a silvered oval with the gilded crowned royal arms with supporters, whereas the full dress version was a slightly larger version

Plate 4. Danish Livgarden til Hest *c.*1806–1814 (III)

A. Officer's general service shabraque with silver lace.
B. Trooper's general service shabraque with white wool galloon.
C. Officer's full dress shabraque, note the three hanging tassels on the rear points.
Details of the trooper's version of the full dress shabraque are unknown.

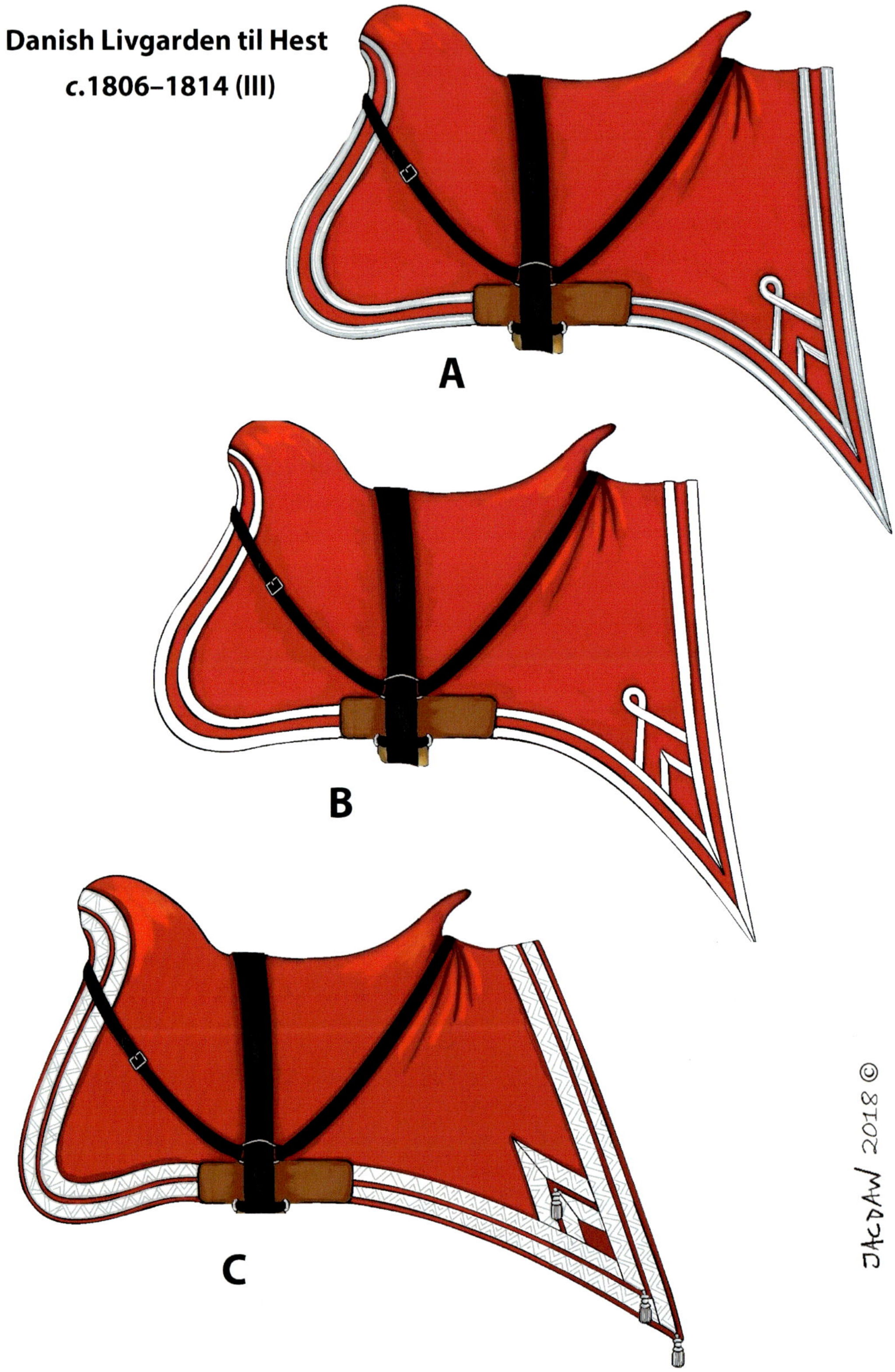

of the arms without the oval plate and probably of real silver. The interior of the bandolier was lined to protect the coat.

The officers also had a M1772, M1806 or M1807 pistol carried on the saddle. Note the model used by the officers were different to the model carried by the troop, as their model could accommodate the ramrod beneath the barrel.

The officers had two different models of sabretache, one similar to the troop model for everyday use and a dress sabretache embroidered with gold and silver lace and the crowned cypher embroidered in gold, all set on a black field.

A contemporary illustration *c*.1801 shows an officer with a square sabretache similar to the hussar's model, this only appears once and is not mentioned in any contemporary descriptions. Perhaps it is a private fantasy by one officer, or perhaps the artist had things mixed up, as the officer is shown with a group of hussars in a tavern.

For general service they used a scarlet Hungarian-style shabraque with silver laced border and embroidery. For full dress the officers had another model with more silver lace and tassels.

Trumpeters' Uniforms

The trumpeters wore the NCOs' dress, but with scarlet swallow nests with silver lace trim and four silver tassels. The swallow nests had lace all around the edges and three vertical lace stripes.

The trumpeters had the same model of sabretache as the men, but if one looks carefully at contemporary illustrations they appear to be smaller than those of the men. Their horsetails also appear to be shorter than the troop, probably so as not to get in the way of the trumpet.

The trumpet was made of silvered brass with silver cords and four or five ball tassels were hung from the lower bar.

A note in the archives tells us that in 1806: 'The Royal Horse Guards have received six new trumpets of a new and modern model with vibration piece and loose mouth piece, so as to better stand the rigours of daily use and field service, from the royal instrument maker J. Fasting.'

They were now the only cavalry unit who still had a kettledrummer in 1802. His dress was the same as the trumpeters. The kettledrum banners were described as red or more likely originally crimson red banners embroidered with the crowned full Danish royal arms, chains of the orders and supporters in natural colours, with silver fringes all around and the hanging cords and tassels were also silver. In fact according to the accounts they appear to have had two sets of banners, one set with crimson red fields and a second set with silver/white fields. The only logical explanation is that the red set was for ordinary service and the silver, and probably more fragile, set was for state occasions.

At least one of these banners was still in existence in its original form in the 1970s, as it was photographed for C.C. von Krogh's *Meddelelser om Den Kongelige Livgarde til Hest* (History of the Royal Horse Guards). Two standards and two kettledrum banners were presented to the regiment in 1758, and heavily restored between 1801–1828 and visible at Christiansborg Castle until quite recently, when they were taken down for storage and preservation; two standards and two kettledrum banners, in their original form, have been stored for a long time in the Tøjhusmuseet in Copenhagen.

Horses

The first squadron rode brown or chestnut horses and the second squadron rode black horses. The trumpeters and kettledrummer had grey horses, probably Frederiksborgers and horses of the Holstein breed.

3

The Heavy Cavalry, the Rytterregimenter

There were officially four heavy cavalry regiments in the Danish army. In battle the heavy cavalry was primarily intended to fight on horseback, and its classic form of combat was the massive cavalry charge in a close-ordered line: starting at a trot, turning into a canter and then ending at a gallop delivering a shock attack to break the enemy lines.

The anonymously-written instruction manual *Exerceer-Regler for hesteryg Copenhagen 1806* (Exercise Regulations on Horseback) instructed the Danish cavalry how they should operate when on service in the field. It gave the prescribed unit breakdowns within the regiment, squadrons, divisions and brigades, how one rank changed into two ranks and into columns of four.

This manual also contained detailed instructions for forming up for special revues, deployments, the tactics to use when attacking the enemy as well as saluting with sabre and *Pallask*.

A regiment was commanded by a colonel (*Oberst*), a lieutenant colonel (*Oberstløjtnant*) and a major. Each regiment was composed of four squadrons each of which had five officers, 11 NCOs, two trumpeters and 144 cavalrymen and a headquarters staff (*mellemstab*) which had a quartermaster (*Kvartermester*), a juridical officer (*Auditor*), and a surgeon (*Feltskærer*), together with the squadron staff of five squadron surgeons (*Eskadronskirurger*), four master medical orderlies (*Sygehusvagtmestre*), a blacksmith (*Fanesmed*), a saddler (*Sadelmager*), a gunsmith (*Bøssesmed*) a provost, a kettledrummer (*Pauker*), up to 1799, and a staff trumpeter (*Stabstrompetere*), which probably corresponded to a trumpet major.

Within each squadron 10 cavalrymen and two NCOs were selected to act as skirmishers or flankers (*Flankører*). This gave each regiment a theoretical strength of 670 officers and men.

In 1809, when the squadron strength was increased to 160 cavalrymen, this brought the regimental strength up to 729 officers and men, at least in theory.

Ryttere Uniforms

These included a black felt round hat bearing a diamond-shaped brass plate stamped with the letters RR, which stood for 'Rytter Regiment', under a crown and with a palm leaf each side. The Livegiment originally had a brass plate like the other regiments, but in 1808 the Livregiment Ryttere was allowed a silver plate, as a sign of 'Their position as the first cavalry regiment of the army'. On left side it had a white plume over a black cockade with a white loop. It had red and yellow cords and tassels and a black leather chinstrap. The officers looped their cords and tassels over the top button and the men over the second button because of their shoulder belts.

From 1808 the hats were replaced with a black felt shako with black leather top and lower bands and side 'Vs', with a black leather peak and chin strap, it had the same plate as before (except for in the Livregiment who now had white metal plates, and a white plume over black cockade with white loop). The cockade and plate was now placed on the front. The officers appear to have kept their longer yellow and red cords and tassels.

The cavalrymen wore a short *Kraprød*/ordinary red cloth tunic in with upturned front corners showing the straw-yellow lining. The collar, the lapels, the shoulder straps and the cuffs were all in the regimental facing colour. The cuffs had a red cuff flap (rectangular with three buttons) piped in the facing colour for the regiments which had piping. The lapels were closed to the waist with seven buttons on each side, one at the point and six shown grouped in pairs from 1808. The coat had two buttons in the small of the back with piped pleats. The buttons were made of white metal. Originally the buttons were a little larger than those used by the infantry, but then they changed to the same-sized buttons as those of the infantry.

At this time as there were no straps to hold the belt in place and as the sword was rather heavy, the troopers would rest their sabre belt on the two lowest buttons on the front of the lapels and the two buttons at pleat at the back of the coat. Eventually a strap was added to the left side of the uniform coat, but this was only introduced after 1817.

Under their collar they had a black neck stock.

From 1808 the inside linings of their coatee became white, but turnbacks but the outer lining remained buff. From 1812 the coats of officers and NCOs changed to pointed cuffs and no cuff flap. The 1812 regulations only concerned the officers and NCOs at first, as the men were allowed to let their existing uniforms wear out, according to the normal terms of exchange of uniforms, so they probably did not start wearing the M1812 uniforms before 1814.

Full dress included fall front buff leather breeches with black leather Hungarian boots edged with black lace and a tassel. These breeches were replaced with white cloth breeches for full dress from 1809. From 1797/1800 for service dress they had a pair of dark blue overalls with a fall down flap front with a button on each side. It had brown leather inserts and a red welt on each side with white metal buttons. From 1810, they were gradually replaced with grey overalls with a black welt, again with the flap front.

The men were issued voluminous cloaks/greatcoats, first in red, and then from 1810 onwards they were made of grey cloth. These red cloaks seem to have been more hardwearing and longer lasting than those used by the infantry, possibly due to the easier service of the cavalry, so red cloaks were still being worn until quite late in the period.

As for the infantry, all the different articles of winter dress appear to have been issued in the autumn, and then they were collected and returned to regimental storage again in the spring as both an economy measure and to lighten the load carried by the horse, both in Denmark and in Norway. So anything strapped on top of the saddle or rolled over their shoulders in summertime (although somewhat brief) would be rather unusual.

Arms and Equipment

The troopers were armed with an M1797 *Pallask* (broadsword), the Danish heavy cavalry sword. This *Rytterpallask* was a shortened and simplified version of the previous models, the M1773, M1778 and the M1789 of which some 6,000 were modified. This was the main straight sword for the heavy cavalry *Ryttere* for 1803–14.

The guard resembled an open basket-style. These swords were issued to the Ryttere regiments from between 1797 and 1804. The *Rytterpallask* was 112cm long with a blade of 94cm. It had a brass hilt which had a leather bound grip and a brown leather sword knot and strap.

The Danish expert Erik Troldhuus (a member of Danish Våbenhistoriske Selskab) and the historian Jørgen Koefoed Larsen have both found evidence that, although several models of straight swords have been suggested as having been used between 1803 to 1814, they have now come to the conclusion that just one main model was actually carried, and in a version not previously recognised. Until now, all had agreed that the most likely model carried during this period was a sword known as the Model 1797.

During 1773–89 a number of different models of the so-called Pallasker were carried, but nearly all were found lacking in some respect. Therefore it was decided to combine two of these models into one. This was called the Model 1797, which combined the blade of the model 1789, which was found to be the best, and the hilt of the *Dragonpallask* Model 1785 as a surplus stock of these could now found in the arsenals as the (light) dragoons had now been issued hussar sabres.

This combination was duly tested at the new school of cavalry. It has been widely accepted that this 'combination' was then duly issued to the regiments without further modifications.

The previously 'accepted' look of this M1797 sword has until now been a straight sword which resembled the *Pallaske for Den Kongelige Livgarde til Hest Model 1808*. The experts were suspicious, as all the photographs taken of the few existing swords showed another weapon, and none of the (very few) swords found today had any regimental cavalry markings, only those from their previous owners, the dragoon regiments and the school of cavalry! For many years another sword model had been recorded, found in rather large numbers and known as Horse Guard Pallask M1828. All of them had active service markings from all the four *Ryttere* regiments as well as some from the two *kyrasser regimenter* who were formed in 1817. So something was clearly wrong, the M1828 is in effect a M1797 with, from the start, a heavily cut-down hilt!

So the research has been going on for a number of years, led by Erik Troldhuus, who also saw that there was something wrong there as well. First he found written evidence confirming that the model 1828 was in active service in 1817 and at that time it was noted that they had already been in use for some time. A compromise was then made to rename the M1828 as the M1813.

Further research carried out by Larsen led to the conclusion that the so-called M1813/28 sword was probably already in use from at least 1803, from all the pictorial evidence. He was also able to claim, according to the markings, that very few of these swords, except those of the Royal Horse Guards and those of the cavalry school were the only ones ever used, in the previously conceived version of the M1797, but that all the M1797, when they were issued to the regiments in 1799–1804 had already had their hilts and guards cut down.

We know that the M1785 hilt had been criticised several times for being 'too narrow' for drawing and handling when wearing gloves and that the large decorative shield was rather heavy and was 'kicking' the riders' legs, and also that it wore holes in the uniform (though it did look rather impressive). These swords were carried in a dark brown or black leather scabbard with brass furniture. So cutting the hilt down to just three small 'bars' resolved most of these problems (see illustrations).

Danish Ryttere Regiments (I)

Plate 5. Danish Ryttere Regiments (I)

Top row, left to right:
Officer of the Livregiment Rytter *c.*1805, wearing full dress. He is carrying the M1798 officer's *Pallaske.*
Trooper, Sjællandske Rytter Regiment *c.*1805 wearing field service dress with the blue overalls with red piping first issued in 1797/1800. He is carrying the M1785 dragoon *Pallaske.*
Trumpeter Holstenske Rytter Regiment *c.*1805, wearing full dress. He is carrying the M1797 Rytter *Pallaske.*
Officer, Slesvigske Rytter Regiment *c.*1808 wearing field service dress with the officer's version of the blue overalls with red piping first issued in 1797/1800.
Trooper, Livregiment Rytter *c.*1808 wearing summer training dress, note that here the bandolier for the cartridge pouch is carried over the carbine belt were as in full dress the shoulder belts would be crossed.

Bottom row, left to right:
Trooper, Sjællandske Rytter Regiment *c.*1810 wearing field service dress with the blue overalls first issued in 1797/1800. He is now carrying the M1797 Rytter *Pallaske.* He still has the musket, but this will shortly be replaced with a carbine.
Officer, Holstenske Rytter Regiment *c.*1812 who is wearing full dress showing the new white dress breeches. Note the officer is carrying a light cavalry sabre, which was preferred by the officers for ordinary service and service in the field.
NCO of the Slesvigske Rytter Regiment *c.*1812 wearing field service dress with the new grey overalls with black tape piping first issued in 1810, the men being allowed to wear out the blue overalls first.
Trooper, Livregiment Rytter Regiment *c.*1813 wearing field service dress with the grey overalls. Note that although new cuffs are are shown it is more than likely that the men did not change them until 1814 as the change for the men was at the regiment's expense.
Trumpeter, Sjællandske Rytter Regiment *c.*1813 wearing field service dress with the grey overalls.

Only about 1,000 M1797 swords used cut down old M1785 hilts, as no more could be found in the arsenals. The next 2,000 hilts were made by recasting 2,000 old M1773 hilts found in the arsenal. We believe that all these newly cast hilts were cast in the 'cut down' or so-called M1828 version/M1797–1803, not in the old M1785 version, confirmed by the fact that all were cast without a mounting hole for the large shield in the pommel!

For most collectors the M1828 Royal Horse Guard Pallask is considered 'ugly' and the previous idea of how the M1797 should have looked (in theory), has been considered as more elegant, so collectors have kept on ignoring the facts in favour of what is no more than a collectors' myth!

So from at least 1803 (or probably more correctly 1797) all *Pallasker* swords which were previously labelled the M1828, (which also for a short time was also named the 'model 1813') were in fact the authentic M1797 *Pallask.*

So this has narrowed down the number of models of straight swords (*Pallasker*) that were carried between 1803 and 1814. In fact three models were in use (M1797, M1808 and *Dragonpallask* M1785), including the officers' version.

The few contemporary images show that they were carried in a black or brown leather scabbard with brass fittings and a round steel chape.

Around their waist they wore a white leather waist belt from which their heavy cavalry sword was slung. The formal buckle was a rectangular brass plate with a badge of the crowned lesser royal arms and supporters in the centre similar to the model used by the Livgarde til Hest. The service buckle was an ordinary brass, open square type.

Firearms

At first they carried mainly the short 1755/98 modified dragoon carbines of which about 1,798 had been modified along with large numbers of older pistols, being shortened, the ramrod was removed and new locks added to some of them. From 1807, the M1807 cavalry carbine (*Rytterkarabin*) was slowly introduced to replace this previous model, but most of the Ryttere regiments probably carried the earlier model of carbine until after the 1814 campaign. It was 90cm long overall with a barrel length of 52cm; it had a calibre of 17.5mm and weighed 2.48kg. The carbine was carried slung from a white leather shoulder

Danish Ryttere Regiments (II)

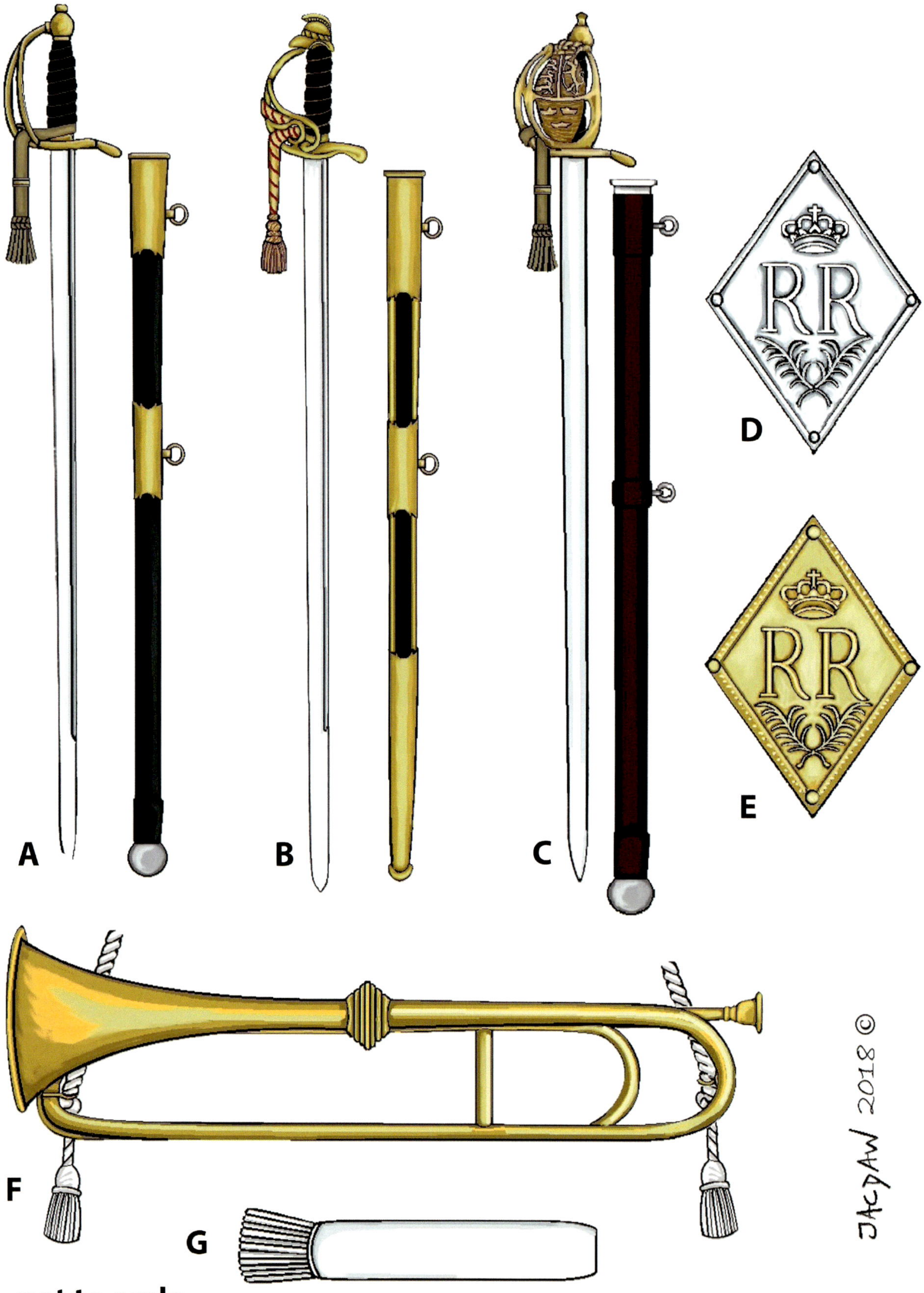

not to scale

Plate 6. Danish Ryttere Regiments (II)

A. Trooper's sword, the M1797 *Pallask*, the standard straight sword carried from 1797 until *c.*1814. This sword was a combination of the cut-down hilt from model 1785, the shield was removed and just one bar was conserved, and the superior blade from the model 1789. This gave a light, simple sword, with a fine blade. This was issued starting in 1799 to the *rytter* regiments except the Sjællandske Rytter Regiment. It was later issued to the new *kyrraser* regiments (after 1815). This was the main straight sword for the heavy cavalry *rytterne* for the period 1803–14.

B. Officer's sword, officer's *Pallask* (straight sword) model 1798, the official sidearm of officers of a *rytter* regiment from 1798 till 1814. It was a modified officer's model 1780 (*Landskabspallask*) with the hilt and shield cut down in the same way as trooper's M1797 sword, but with a different scabbard. Although this scabbard is drawn after an existing model, a plate from the ex-von Brockendorff collection* shows the officers using the same model as the troop. Another surviving model has the spirals of the hilt placed differently (Kays Nielsen, *Danske Blankvåben*) On active service in the field the officers preferred to carry a light cavalry sabre M1789 used *c.*1796–14. They had hilts from M1762 officers' hussar sabres. This was probably the most common model used. Note that the frog and belt were black, unlike those of the men who had white belting.

C. The *Dragonpallask* (dragoon straight sword) M1785, a straight sword with an elaborate (but heavy) handle with a beautiful shield, and a blade which was prone to break in battle. These were used by the Sjællandske Rytter Regiment as well as the Livgarden til Hest from 1798–1808/10, as they were used as dragoons when patrolling the coast of Zealand. Only in 1808–10 did they change them for the M1797 Rytter *Pallask* (straight sword). The sword is shown with the M1785 model brown leather scabbard, probably the most common service model.

D. Silvered brass or white metal plate as worn on both hats and shakos of the Livregiment.

E. Brass plate as worn on both hats and shakos of the Sjællandske, Holstenske and Slesvigske *rytter* regiments.

F. The standard brass trumpet used by all mounted units. Only the colour of the cords would change. Possibly they were a mix of silver/white and the facing colour threads.

G. NCO's epaulette

* see note in main body of the text.

Plate 7 (overleaf). Danish Ryttere (III) Shabraques

1. Officer's shabraque, Livregiment Rytter 1801–1814. Broad silver lace edged with straw yellow.
2. Officer's shabraque, Sjællandske Rytter Regiment 1801–1814. Broad silver lace edged with dark blue lace.
3. Officer's shabraque, Holstenske Rytter Regiment 1801–1814. Broad silver lace edged with green lace.
4. Officer's shabraque, Slesvigske Rytter Regiment 1801–1814. Broad silver lace edged with light blue lace.
5. Trooper's shabraque, with a blue grey valise with (*Mantelsæk*), this shabraque was identical for all regiments 1801–1814.
6. Trooper's shabraque, Livregiment Rytter *c.*1811 with blue grey valise with red ends (*Mantelsæk*) is the exception. In fact this is the shabraque for the Livregiment cuirassiers in 1817, but it is believed to have originally been issued *c.*1810–1811.

The officer's shabraques are based on a series of prints from the von Brockdorff collection dated 1804, the only complete reference in existence. The Livregiment Ryttere and Slesvigske Rytter regiments were converted to cuirassiers and the Holstenske Ryttere and Sjællandske Rytter regiments were converted to lancers after 1816.

Danish Ryttere Regiments (III)

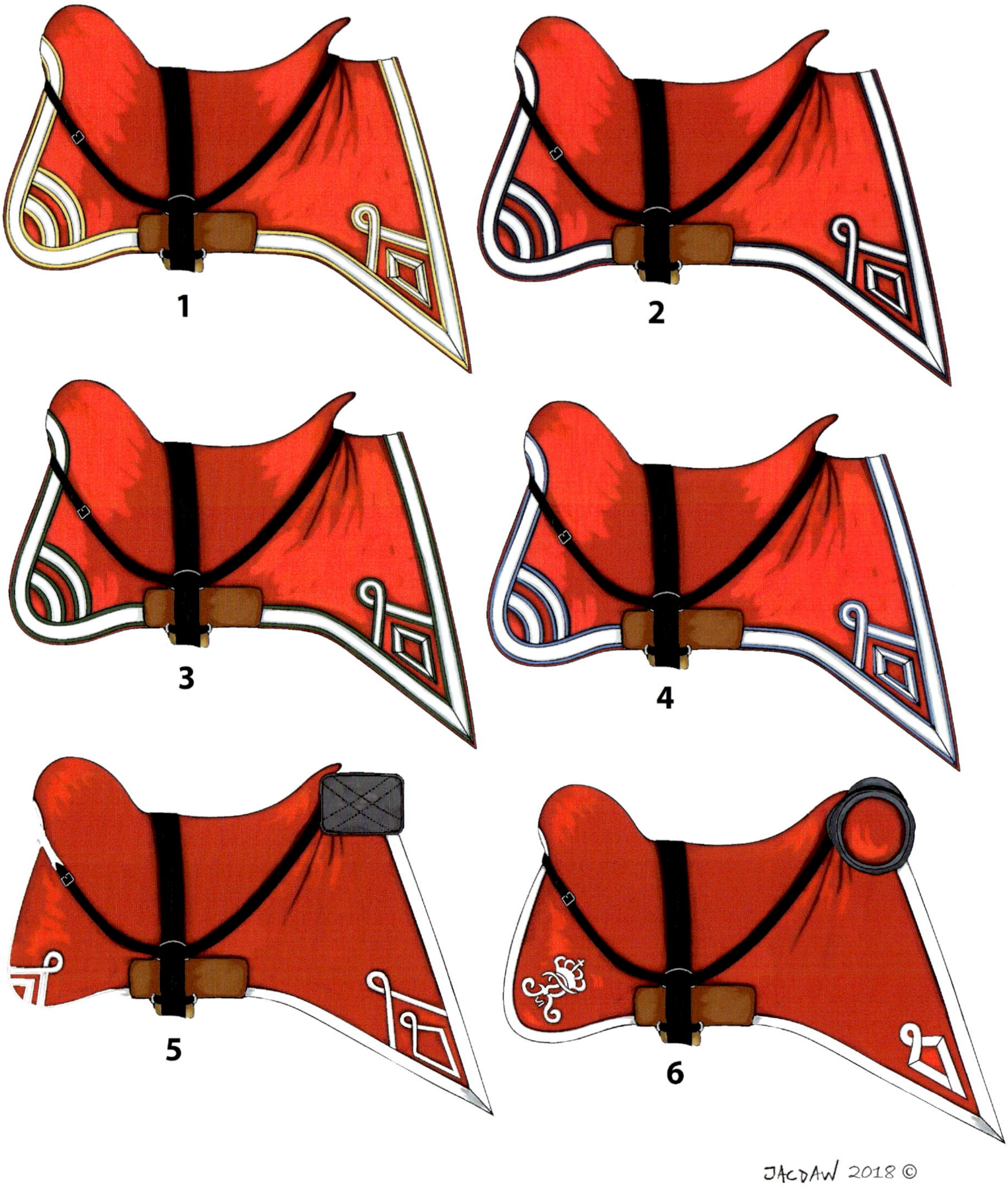

Table I. Line Cavalry Regiments *c.*1808

Regimental Name	Facings & Piping	Button Colour	Shoulder Straps & Shako Plate
Livregiment Rytter	Straw-yellow	White Metal	Brass hat/shako plate, white metal hat/ shako plate from 1808
Sjællandske Rytter Regiment	Dark blue with straw piping	White Metal	Brass hat/shako plate
Slesvigske Rytter Regiment	Light blue	White Metal	Brass hat/shako plate
Holstenske Rytter Regiment	Light green with straw piping	White Metal	Brass hat/shako plate

belt. The carbine was designed for use both on horseback and while skirmishing on foot. The 'flankers' received the M1798 model rifled carbine.

Note: the ramrod for the carbine and pistols was carried suspended from the waist belt; it was not inserted into the stock as in most other countries.

They were equipped with a white leather bandolier with a black leather cartridge pouch.

On parade the cartridge pouch was carried over the right shoulder and the bandolier for the carbine over the left shoulder, giving the crossed belt appearance, but on campaign both items were carried over the left shoulder. A new model was issued in 1808.

To start with they were armed mainly with the M1751 and the M1772 pistols (which like the carbines, in 1798 they were shortened, received new stock without a place for the ramrod and some received new locks), they were now referred to as the M1751/1798 pistol. The M1772/85 received the same upgrade (M1772/85/98). From 1808–1810 they began to be rearmed as a supplement, with first the M1806 pistol and maybe also with the M1807 pistol with the Kyhl's lock.

The M1807 was very similar with the exception that this model was fitted with the new Khyl's lock already described; it had a calibre of 17.5mm and it had an overall length of 45cm.

Another pistol, the M1806, was 45cm overall with a barrel length of 27cm, it had a calibre of 18mm and weighed 1.33kg. It has not been possible to ascertain how many of this model existed.

A separate long ramrod was required, which was used for both the pistol and the carbine and was suspended from the belt.

The pistol had a very limited range, but its butt could also be used as a club in a moment of necessity.
This was the official version, but below is a list of arms which were finally issued.

The Livregiment Ryttere

Sword: *Rytterpallask* M1797.

Pistol: Mix of pistol Model 1751/48 and Rytter pistol 1772/98, after 1810, the regiment began receiving the Rytter pistol Model 1806, and later maybe the Model 1807.

Carbine: In 1797 they were to receive the *Dragongevær* M1769 with bayonet, but they were replaced in 1798 by the modified M1755/98 *Rytterkarabin*. At a later date, around 1810 they began receiving the 'Cavalry Carbine Model 1807'. The rifled carbine, the M1798, was only for the flankers.

The Sjællandske Rytter Regiment

As this regiment had as its main field of operations, the guarding and watching of the coast and interior of Zealand, they were armed and trained as dragoons and only officially operated as a Rytter regiment from 1809–1810. This is reflected by the choice of arms.

Sidearm: *Dragonpallask* M1785, but from 1809 rearmed with *Rytterpallask* M1797/1803.

Pistol: Rytter pistol 1772 with individual ramrod, after 1810 they began receiving the Rytter pistol 1772/98 and probably the 'Rytter pistol Model 1806'.

Carbine/Musket: In 1797/1798 they were supposed to receive the *Dragongevær* M1769 (dragoon musket), but these were probably never delivered, as instead they were issued with the dragoon musket M1767 (with a bayonet carried in a scabbard on top of the left pistol holster, underneath the saddle cloth). At a later date, around 1810, they began receiving carbines, possibly including the 'Cavalry Carbine Model 1807'.

Rifled Carbine: Until 1808 they had no trained flankers, so consequently they had not been issued with rifled carbines. But from 1808 they had also flankers and so received either the M1798 'cavalry rifle' or the Model 1807 cavalry rifle, intended for the flankers only.

Nearly 15,000 *Dragongevær* 1767/69/89 were made, but very few were ever used (many were converted into

Skarpskyttegevær M1789). A number of different cavalry regiments were ordered to use this weapon, but in the end only Sjællandske Rytter Regiment (1797–1809), and Prins Frederik Ferdinands Dragoner also used them for a short while (1807–12). But in Norway and on the island of Bornholm all the cavalry used them until the end of the war.

The Slesvigske Regiment Ryttere

Sidearm: *Rytterpallask* M1797 (issued around 1803).

Pistol: A mix of Pistols, Model 1751/48 and the Rytter pistol 1772/98, after 1810, they began receiving the 'Rytter pistol Model 1806', and later maybe the 'Rytter pistol Model 1807'.

Carbine: The M1750/98 *Rytterkarabin* was issued. At a later date, around 1810, they began receiving a few examples of the 'Cavalry Carbine Model 1807'.

Rifled Carbine: The M1798 was issued only to the 40 flankers.

The Holstenske Regiment Ryttere

Sidearm: *Rytterpallask* M1797 (issued from 1802).

Pistol: A mix of pistols, Model 1751/48 and the Rytter pistol 1772/98, and after 1810 they began receiving the 'Rytter pistol Model 1807'.

Carbine: The M1750/98 *Rytterkarabin* was issued. At a later date, around 1810 they were issued with the 'Cavalry Carbine Model 1807'.

Rifled Carbine: The M1798 was issued only to the flankers.

Horse Furniture

The harness was made of black leather and they had a red Hungarian-style shabraque with white lace border and knot. There were some regimental variations, but they have not all been clearly identified.

At the rear of the saddle the troopers had a cloth valise called a *Mantelsæk*, literally a cloak bag. At first they were probably red for the *Ryttere* but later (*c.*1808) they became dark grey, maybe with red ends for some (probably this was only for Livregiment Ryttere, which received a special permit to 'make new valises with red cloth'. This was because of their status 'as first cavalry regiment of the army' and because they took part in royal corteges in Copenhagen – it is this regiment Lorentzen portrays in his painting *c.*1811).

In this *Mantelsæk* they carried all their extra kit, and NCOs had strict orders to inspect them often, to make sure that nothing prohibited was carried. Under this valise they kept a fodder bag and cord with a spike, to tether the horse. On top of all this the troopers were instructed to carry a little bale of hay which they were taught to braid in a special way, so they always had fodder ready for their horse.

At the front of the saddle, on both sides, under the saddle cloth, they carried their pistols in leather holsters. On left side the troopers' carried their bread bag and the canteen was strapped on the front of the saddle.

It was only after 1816 that they carried them slung across their shoulder ('but only when on foot').

Note that the cavalry troopers first received a shoulder strap on the right shoulder after 1816, and the was the consequence that they now had to festoon themselves with a canteen strap. Over the front of saddle top running from side to side, they attached their cavalry cloak.

Officers would normally not have carried a *Mantelsæk*, but they had all their kit transported in a wagon reserved for their use, under care of their batman, called an *oppasser* in Danish, which literally means a soldier serving as a servant to an officer.

Skirmishers or Flankers

These men were dressed the same as the cavalrymen, but they carried the rifled carbine M1798 which was issued to the 10 flankers or sharpshooters in each squadron in all the heavy cavalry regiments. It was 90cm overall with a barrel length of 52cm, it had a calibre of 16.6mm and weighed 2.71kg. The carbine was carried slung from a white leather shoulder belt. They also carried two pistols and a *Pallask*.

NCOs' Uniforms

The NCOs wore the regimental dress with on their shoulders the following distinctives. The sergeants (*Vagtmester* or *Kvatermester*) had a silver, narrow fringed epaulette on the right shoulder and a shoulder strap in the facing colour piped silver on the left shoulder and a corporal (*Korporal*) had a silver, narrow fringed epaulette on the right shoulder but on the left he had a thin 'dragon' shoulder strap in silver cord. Until 1812 the staff sergeants (*overvagtmester*) were also allowed a silver sword knot and tassel. These distinctives disappeared in 1812 with the new cuff rank regulations.

The other NCO sword strap and tassel was white, it became brown from 1812. They did not carry the carbine, but they did carry the cartridge pouch, over their left shoulder. Their belt buckle was a rectangular brass plate with badge of the crowned royal arms and supporters in the centre. The buckle had a stamped twisted cord-style border. The NCOs were allowed to wear these square belt buckles throughout the period.

From 1812, with the new rank distinctions, the cuffs became pointed. They had a simple facing-coloured shoulder strap with white lace trim on both shoulders, and rank chevrons in white lace on both arms over their cuffs, as for the Line Infantry NCOs.

The NCOs carried a pair of pistols which had a separate pistol ramrod, carried on their belt. This was because NCOs did not carry carbines, only a set of pistols as did the trumpeters who were also classed as NCOs.

They carried the same *Pallask* as the troop and wore their belt the same way as the troopers.

Officers' Uniforms

From 1804 the officers had originally worn black leather hats with a leather strap around the base of the crown, with a diamond-shaped regimental plate mounted on the front and gold. They also had red cords with flounders and tassel, a silver cockade strap holding a black cockade and a white plume. The plumes were originally made of chopped feathers but they were replaced with brushed wool by 1810.

The officers looped their cords and tassels over the top button, but on the second button they starting carrying a cartridge pouch because of the shoulder belt.

The hats were replaced from 1808 by the shako, as for the troopers. Generally their shakos were completely made of leather, but without the 'V' strengtheners on the sides. The shakos conserved the same diamond plates, cords and flounders, the plume and cockade were now placed on the front. The officers appear to have kept their longer yellow and red cords and tassels, at least for a while, but probably not after 1812. They also had chin scales, but in silvered metal.

The officers had a long-tailed coat made of scarlet red or occasionally crimson red cloth with horizontal pockets and the same distinctions as the regimental troop uniform coat. The crimson coats were kept for parades only. The coat originally had straw-yellow turnbacks and lining, but this was changed to white linings in 1808–1810. The turnbacks remained buff. They wore a red and yellow silk or wool waist sash with gold tassels knotted on the left hip until they were abolished in 1812.

From 1810 the coat was allowed to be made from ordinary red *Kraprød* cloth and this was to be their field uniform, and from 1812 the epaulettes and silk sash were abolished when the new rank insignia was issued, of in the button colour, to be worn on both arms over the cuffs. From 1810 onwards the officers were allowed a single-breasted coatee in red cloth with the same facings as their standard uniform jackets to be used when not in service. They followed the 1812 change of cuff style and there were even some made of grey cloth. In 1803 they wore a pair of fall front buff leather breeches for full dress, which were theoretically replaced with a pair of fall front white woollen breeches for full dress from 1810.

From 1801 for campaign dress they had a pair of dark blue overalls with a fall down flap front, piped red with a button on each side and brown leather inserts. They buttoned down the outside leg and the buttons could be metallic, white metal or made of bone. Some of them appeared to have been embroidered with a simplified silver arrow pattern down the front legs. These were replaced by a pair of dark grey overalls piped red around 1810/1811, after the blue ones had been worn out. Generally they had two red stripes.

They had two pairs of Hessian-style boots; the pair reserved for parades had larger and better-quality silver lacing and tassels.

From 1810/1812 the Ryttere officers could wear a grey cloak with a large cape for winter dress, but they were allowed to wear out the older red cloaks with a large cape beforehand, and even then some of the officers continued to wear privately new-made red and blue cloaks.

A new 'undress cap' was allowed to be used from 1812 by the officers to reduce wear on shakoes and helmets, it resembled a peaked cap with a floppy top, unfortunately no models have survived and only one period sketch exists. It was probably made from soft felt or tightly woven grey wool with an embroidered crown, the embroidery appears to have been red. To what extent this was worn is not known.

Arms

Officially the officers carried the officers *Pallask* (straight-sword) model 1798, the official sidearm of officers of a Rytter regiment from 1798 till 1814. It was a modified officer's model M1780 *Landskabspallask* with the hilt cut down and a different scabbard.

The hilt was made of tombak (a brass–copper alloy), which if it had a high copper content would give a yellow metal colour. The officers were supposed to carry this for active service but it tended to be relegated to parades and official duties. It was carried in a tombak and black leather scabbard suspended on a black leather frog. The belt buckle for officers was the fairly standard buckle, of two round silvered or gilded lion-head buckles and an S-hook and black leather belt and suspenders.

As elsewhere, many officers substituted a light cavalry officer's sabre for the *Pallask* when on campaign and for daily service, unofficially of course, but they were popular due to their lightness and efficacy.

All of these arms had a red and gold sword knot and strap, the sign of an officer. From 1808 a bandolier with cartridge pouch were allowed. The interior of the bandolier for the cartridge pouch was of leather with a silver-laced cloth front, and was lined with red cloth to protect the coat on the backside. The cartridge pouch was made of black leather and bore a silver crowned royal cypher of Frederik VI. The bandolier had a silvered brass buckle, slider and plate.

The officers carried a pair of pistols in holsters under the shabraque. The officer's versions of the M1795, M1806 and M1807 pistols or other privately acquired models (even rifled) were made with the ramrods inserted under the barrel in the conventional manner, for the use of both cavalry and infantry officers.

Their scarlet shabraque had a broad silver lace border, piped in the facing colour on both edges (see illustrations).

Trumpeters' Uniforms

In the Danish army trumpeters were generally of NCO rank as they were recruited from the NCOs, unlike the infantry drummers and musicians, and for this reason they generally had an epaulette on their right shoulder over the swallow nest. They wore the regimental dress, but with facing coloured swallow nests on their shoulders with three stripes of vertical lacing and tassels (in the button colour). After 1812 the lacing was white tape and the tassels had disappeared.

As trumpeters were regarded as NCOs they also had a small fringed epaulette over the swallow nests, usually in the button colour. Their hat, later a shako, had the same white plume as the men, the often mentioned red plumes date to the 1820s. The trumpet cords were probably white/silver and the facing colour mixed. The Livregiment Ryttere trumpet cords had silver tassels. Their belt buckle was a rectangular brass plate with badge of the crowned royal arms and supporters in the centre. The buckle had a stamped, twisted cord-style border. The trumpeters were allowed to wear these square belt buckles throughout the period. Their sword strap and tassel was brown like that of the troopers. The trumpeters rode horses with either a grey or white robe.

4

The Dragoons and Light Cavalry Regiments and Their Uniforms, Dragonregimenter and Lette Dragonregimenter

There were originally three light dragoon regiments in the Danish army. The light dragoons fulfilled the usual duties of light cavalry: reconnaissance, outposts and the pursuit of the enemy. The light dragoons were, at least during the first years of the period, still trained to fight dismounted, but with their new role as 'light' dragoons, they very seldom dismounted.

Each regiment was composed of a staff and four squadrons with same establishment as in line cavalry or Ryttere regiments.

In 1807 the number of cavalry regiments was augmented to nine regiments, when the Prins Frederik Ferdinand's Dragonregiment was raised as a kind of 'reserve regiment' formed mainly from former troopers from Jællandske Rytter Regiment (at first named the Sjællandske Dragonregiment) serving in the Landeværn. From the start they shared the schools, training, arsenals and equipment with the Sjællandske Rytter Regiment (not one of the light dragoon regiments).

The regiment was officially renamed the Prins Frederik Ferdinands Dragonregiment in December 1807, and to differentiate them from the light dragoons a number of minor differences were visible in both their uniform and their weapons (see illustrations). In reality this was a real dragoon regiment, not light dragoons. Only in 1816 were they renamed 'Lette Dragoner' (light dragoons).

From 1810 new recruits drawn for the Prins Frederik Ferdinand's Dragon Regiment were to be 'From those not drawn into the hussar regiment on Zealand'. That meant that the height requirement changed from *Rytterhøjde* (minimum 170cm) to hussar height (minimum 160cm) for new recruits.

In 1809, as for the line cavalry, the squadron establishment was augmented to 160 dragoons.

Dragoon Uniforms

Light dragoons were distinguished by their black leather helmet (M1794), which vaguely resembled a Tarleton-style called a *Raupehjelm*, but which had a black leather bowl, a black leather peak and chinstrap and in fact it was closer to the Bavarian Rumford helmet. The most obvious visible difference between the British and Danish helmets was that the latter all had a thin brim all around them; this is not always that obvious as it was partially hidden by the turban and caterpillar, which was not present on the British model; also the Danish helmet had a one-piece bowl, unlike the Tarleton which was made of two separate parts which were stitched together.

The other difference, again not that visible due to the caterpillar crest, was the form of the bowl, the British model was rounded if somewhat elongated whereas the Danish model was more bomb-shaped like Russian helmets, if somewhat lower.

The peak and brim had a white metal or brass bound edging, it had white metal reinforcing bands on the sides and a black fur caterpillar or crest over the top, fore and aft. This crest hung down the back at least 10–12cm to protect the neck from sword cuts (the illustrations of both Köller *c.*1801 and von Prangen *c.*1809 give the impression that they may have been even longer, up to 20cm). The peaks of the early model was pointed and angled downwards. Around the base of the helmet there was a crimson red or facing-coloured turban (crimson red for regiments with black facings) bearing three lengths of white metal or steel chain on each side. On the left side there was a white plume with red tip in a metal holder, originally these were of chopped cock's feathers.

There were what appears to several versions in use during this period, but in reality they were the same helmets which were modified over time; firstly the original model 1794, this one had a white metal plaque around the base of the skull bearing a text, 'LIV.REGIMENT', a diamond in the centre, followed by 'LETTE DRAGONER' for the Livregiment, these early versions were more noticeable by the more pronounced tail to the crest. An early engraving, *c.*1809 shows a trooper of the Livregiment with metal chin scales and not leather chin straps.

Danish Lette Dragoner (Light Dragoons) (I)

Plate 8. Danish Lette Dragoner (Light Dragoons) (I)

Top row, left to right:
An officer of the Livregiment Lette Dragoner wearing the full dress uniform of *c.*1805.
A trooper of the Jydske lette Dragon Regiment shown wearing a pair of the blue M1802 service–campaign overalls of *c.*1805.
A trumpeter of the Fynske Lsette Dragon Regiment shown wearing the blue M1802 service–campaign overalls of *c.*1805. The trooper and trumpeter are both shown carrying the M1791 'hussar' sabre.
A trooper of the Prins Frederik Ferdinand Regiment shown wearing a shako. He is wearing the full dress of *c.*1808–1810.
A trooper of the Livregiment Lette Dragoner who is shown wearing full dress of *c.*1810. Both are shown carrying a M1791 sabre in a new M1808 steel scabbard.

Bottom row, left to right:
A trooper of the Jydske lette Dragon Regiment wearing the new grey M1810 service–campaign overalls *c.*1810/1811. He is shown carrying the M1808 'hussar' sabre.
Officer of the Fynske lette Dragon Regiment in the new grey M1810 service–campaign overalls *c.*1813.
Trooper of the Prins Frederik Ferdinand Regiment in the new M1812 helmet and wearing the grey M1810 service–campaign overalls *c.*1813. I have shown this helmet simply for reference as it is unlikely that these were actually issued before the end of the war. The trooper is shown carrying the M1791/1808 'hussar' sabre.
NCO of the Livregiment Lette Dragoner wearing the grey M1810 service–campaign overalls *c.*1813, carrying the new brass-hilted M1808 dragoon sabre.
Trooper of the Fynske lette Dragon Regiment wearing the coatees purloined from the Fynske Infanteriregiment. I have left the brass buttons on, as it was unlikely that they were changed before the end of hostilities. The trooper is shown carrying the M1791/1808 'hussar' sabre.

A number of modifications are known to have been carried out in 1796, 1812 and 1814. From 1812 some of the new helmets now had a rounded peak, a mode which would slowly generalise after 1815; the Prins Frederik Ferdinand Regiment was probably the first to receive this new model in 1812. It is rather complicated to follow the exact evolution, as some of the new ones still had a pointed visor and some of the older ones were modified, a frequent practice in the Danish army of the time.

As only one has survived we must surmise that the others also had their title stamped on the metal plate around the base the same way, at least for the Jyske and Fynske regiments. This was followed by a more simplified version.

This 1812 version appears to have a much more voluminous caterpillar without a tail and the plume had changed for a 'fatter' brushed wool version, again cheaper and easier to make.

Also all regiments had now only red turbans, not made of the expensive Dutch *Tamis* cloth, but of Danish woven *Chalon* cloth. The officer's chinstraps were always made of steel, or possibly of silvered brass chin scales mounted on a leather strap.

From 1813 (Royal Resolution 5 September 1813) it was ordered that their plumes were not to be worn in the field, only for parades, but according to another ordnance issued in November 1813, the plume 'Is to be carried as it has been up till now'.

The Prince Frederik Ferdinand Dragonregiment was officially considered a standard dragoon regiment and performed as such until 1816 when they became classed as light dragoons. The men wore shakos or possibly hats converted into shakos with diamond-shaped pewter plates, which were originally inscribed or stamped with 'DR' (Dragoon Regiment) under a crown with a palm leaf on each side underneath. In 1812 they received the new 1812 Model helmets.

Again, to differentiate between the dragoons and light dragoons they had white frontal turn-ups and lining on their coatees and not buff as used by the light dragoons. This regiment never actually fought in the war, as it stayed in Denmark, close to Copenhagen, although it was not garrisoned in the town and never heard a shot fired in anger, but several individual officers and some NCOs and troopers 'volunteered' for service in Germany in 1813–14.

The helmet model used by this regiment was the M1812 version. The model had a vague resemblance to the British Lifeguards helmet, as the caterpillar was more voluminous in the front. This helmet had the new red Chalon cloth turban

Danish Lette Dragoner (Light Dragoons) (II) Sabres

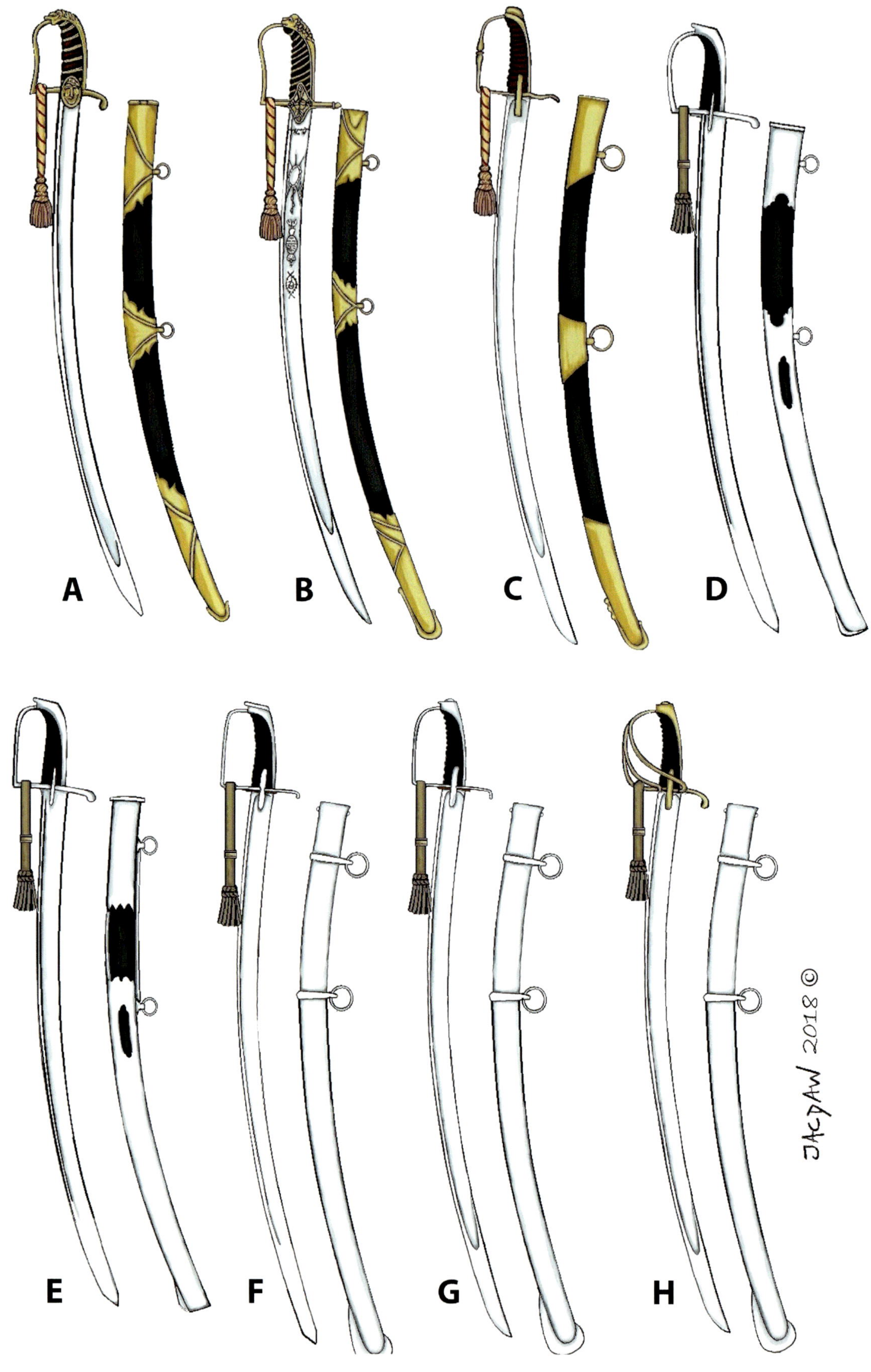

Plate 9. Danish Lette Dragoner (Light Dragoons) (II) Sabres

A. A Lette Dragoner officer's sabre with a lion's-head hilt, 1801–1814, hilt ex-M1762 hussar sabre. This was the standard model used by the Lette Dragoner officers.
B. An elaborately made M1801 officer's sabre with a lion's-head hilt and blade is inscribed with the crowned royal arms and the Order of the Elephant.
C. An elaborate officer's sabre with a hilt from the M1792 hussar sabre.
D. *Husarsabel* M1792, as used by both the Lette Dragoner and the hussars.
E. Hussar/light cavalry sabre M1792 with scabbard M1804, used by both the Lette Dragoner and hussars.
F. Hussar/light cavalry sabre M1792 with M1808 steel scabbard issued to the Prince Frederik Ferdinand Dragoons, Guides and mounted Jaegers.
G. Hussar/light cavalry sabre M1808 with steel scabbard, used by the Prince Frederik Ferdinand Dragoons, Guides and mounted Jaegers.
H. *Dragonsabel*/light cavalry sabre M1808 with brass hilt.
This was apparently a French-inspired brass grip with two sidebars, with the same blade and metal sheath as the 'hussar sabre' model 1808. Because of the brass grip, it was much more expensive to produce and apparently the first were issued the hussars 1809–10. It was issued mainly to the hussars, but a few were issued to the Livregiment Lette Dragoner and a few to the Norwegian mounted jaegers.
These swords cover the hussars also.

and a new smaller type of regimental shield, this shield is in a form of 'band' all around the rim of the helmet, with a brass plate with a pewter centre on the front with the initials 'FD'. The officers' model was larger than the model used by the troopers. The new rounded peak of visor is of the type officially introduced in 1817, but was already in use by this regiment in c.1812. On the troopers' helmet there was one notable detail, that they both had a leather chin strap, but they also had separate 'chin scales' to protect their chins in battle against sabre cuts.

It was specified that the men should wear their helmets for parades only, but would continue to wear their shakos for everyday service dress and campaign dress. They first wore their helmets on service during the occupation of France 1815. The 1817 uniform probably still had many elements of the 1812–14 uniforms.

The light dragoons' red uniform coatee had the same basic cut as the rest of the army cavalry, and they followed the same changes. They were modified again in 1812 with the badges of rank including addition of pointed cuffs, but illustrations show differently and as such it only had an immediate influence on the officers and NCOs as it designated their ranks. The ordinary troopers were allowed to wait until normal terms of uniform change (1814), and most regiments used the old uniforms until at least then although it would appear that changes were made to some units on home service, but that units in the field did not make the changes until later, how much later is still open to debate. They wore their sword belts in the same fashion as the Rytter troopers. Under their collar they had a black neck stock.

In full dress they wore a pair of fall front pale buff breeches and black Hessian-style boots, possibly with button coloured lace borders and tassels for the officers, black for the NCOs and the troopers. These breeches were replaced with white cloth breeches for full dress from 1809. From 1797/1800 for service dress they had a pair of dark blue overalls with a fall down flap front with a button on each side. It had brown leather inserts and a red welt on each side with white metal buttons. From 1810, they were gradually replaced with grey overalls with a black welt, again with the flap front. The buttons could be metallic, white metal or even made of bone.

A new officer's undress uniform was allowed in 1813, this was really the grey uniform, planned for the whole army to be used from 1814 and it was to be made of grey cloth. It did not have facings and just one row of buttons. Few probably were made and used, most officers instead preferring to wear older uniforms out.

The celebrated *Oberst* Høgh-Guldberg of the Fynske Lette Dragoner is shown wearing one such uniform at the Battle of Sehestedt in 1813, but again this was most likely a privately made example as his troop is still shown in red coats and cloaks.

Arms and Equipment

The subject of arms, particularly swords and sabres, is always a little complicated within the Danish army, due to shortages, economy drives and modification of older arms in service which makes it difficult to be exact, but these are the general lines. It was very rare that a totally new sabre or sword was made, normally there just a modification of

Danish Lette Dragoner (Light Dragoons) (III) Helmets

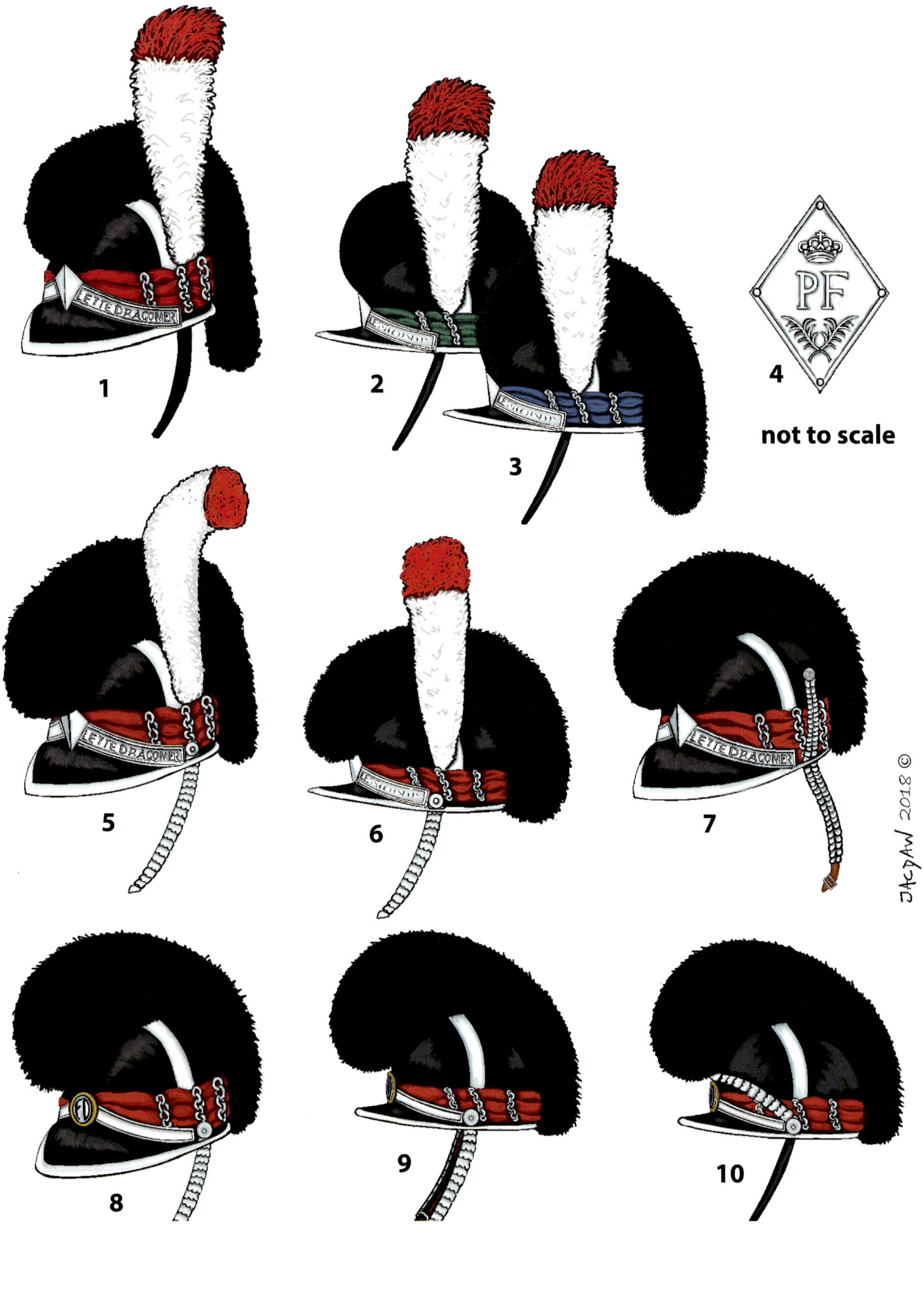

Plate 10. Danish Lette Dragoner (Light Dragoons) (III) Helmets

1. M1796 Helmet Livregiment Lette Dragoner 1796–1810 (after Køller).
2. M1796 Helmet Jydske lette Dragon Regiment 1796–1810 (after Køller).
3. M1796 Helmet Fynske Lette Dragoner 1796–1810 (after Køller).
4. Shako plate, Prins Frederik Ferdinands Dragoon Regiment 1807–1812.
5. Helmet, officer's model, showing first modification or refurbishment. Visor now rounder, the caterpillar has lost its tail and the plume has changed c.1811. White metal chin scales from 1810.
6. Helmet, trooper's model, showing first modification or refurbishment. The caterpillar has lost its tail and the plume has changed c.1811. Note all the regiments now have a red turban (*tamis*) from 1812. White metal chin scales from 1810. Note how the new metal scale chinstrap passes through a slit in the helmet's edging. This would be the M1796 modified 1812. It was worn without the plume after 1812.
7. Helmet, specially made officer's version of the M1796/12 helmet made for Colonel Engelsted, note there is a face on the top stud, probably that of a lion.
8. Modified 1812 helmet for the Prins Frederik Ferdinands Dragoon Regiment with a round badge with FD on it. The visor is now rounder.
9. Helmet M1812 as worn in the field up to the end of the war, showing the new form of the caterpillar. Plumes were no longer worn on campaign. This was probably the standard model by the end of the war, no doubt with various individual modifications, upgrades, repairs etc. in each regiment.
10. Helmet Prins Frederik Ferdinands Dragoon Regiment M1812, trooper's version. The officers had the same helmet as the troop, possibly with more chains on it if we refer to the watercolours of Suhr.

Note, the new model brass-bound helmets were not made until 1816.

the blade, the scabbard or the hilt. In most cases older hilts were reused or recast, with new blades and probably also new scabbards made but seldom all at the same time. To add to the confusion, nineteenth-century collectors also managed to create yet another myth which we shall dispel.

Between 1794 and 1797 a total of 3,000 'Hungarian sabre blades' were received from Solingen in Germany. From between 1794–1800, these blades were mounted in Denmark on old hilts in store in the arsenals; they were made into the following sabres:

The hussar sabre M1792 had an old 1775 hilt and a new blade, and a new steel and leather scabbard from 1804. A small number of the blades were made 'with cabalistic signs engraved on them' a hussar fashion, and the blade was slightly larger, but these were probably intended to be issued to the Bosniaks raised in 1791, though most documents point to that they did not receive them, in the end. The new M1804 scabbard was improved by adding a twisted steel cord between the rings, so the scabbard would not break at the weak point at the middle. This was the model used by all the light dragoons at first. The Jyske and Fynske regiments used it until 1814.

The Livregiment Lette Dragoner were fully rearmed in 1808–10, with the new 'Dragoon Sabre M1808'.

The sabre for light dragoons was the M1792: this is not an official name, as it is just called the *Husarsabel*, and their blades did not have any 'cabalistic signs' (only some of the officers' models had a few, and they were blued); they were different and therefore could be classed as a specific model, for their use only. Of the '3,000' new blades, 1,926 were used to make M1792 sabres for the light dragoons.. From 1804 they received improved scabbards M1804. Some M1792 blades were probably issued to the hussars in Holstein, as they were at the front, but for the rest probably many to repair some of the old M1776 sabres in use.

There were two versions of this sabre. One model had the steel, single bar hussar-type hilt already mentioned, and the other hilt had a bar and two branches and was cast in brass, this is the version erroneously called the *Dragonsabel* by collectors and attributed to the light dragoons, when in fact this brass version was carried by the hussars first.

We know that the King asked why they were more expensive than the M1808 'hussar sabre', and he was informed that it was because they had been mounted with 'brass hilts'. The King accepted this explanation and approved them. But as stated above, the brass version was first issued to the hussars, not to the light dragoons, and then only to the Livregiment Lette Dragoner.

The pistols used were both 1748/98 and hussar Model 1795 pistols.

Danish Lette Dragoner (Light Dragoons) (IV) Shabraques

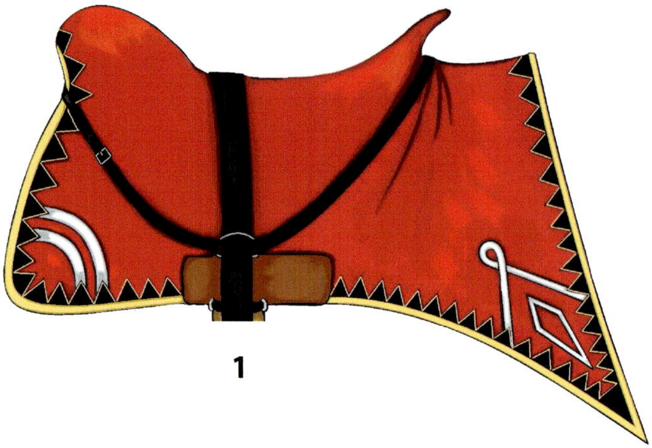

1

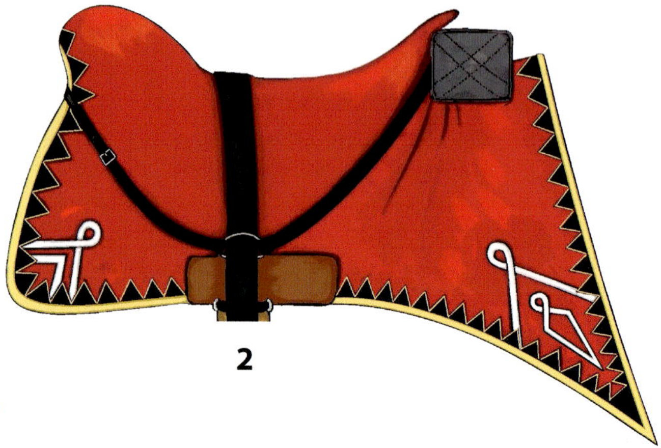

2

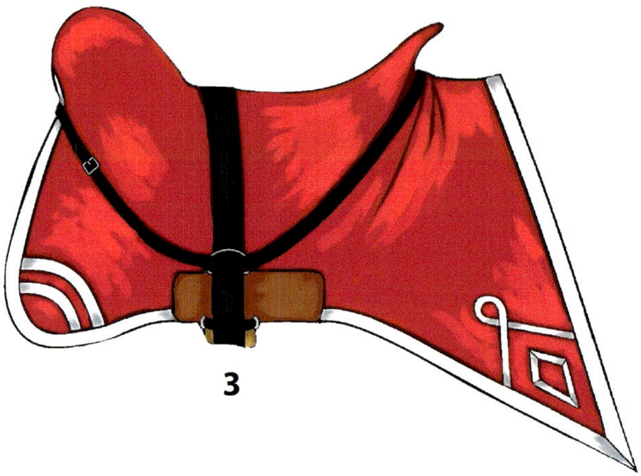

3

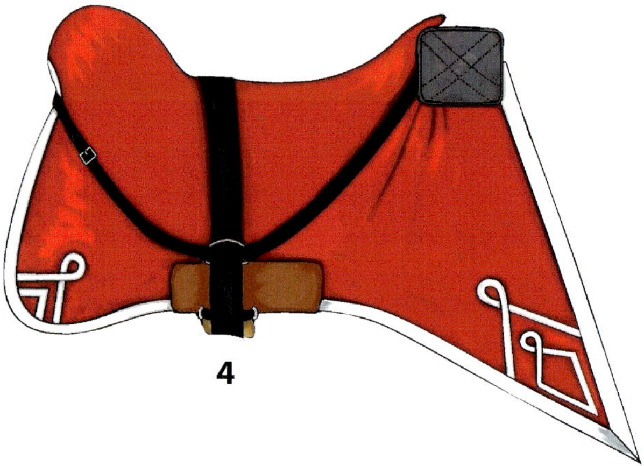

4

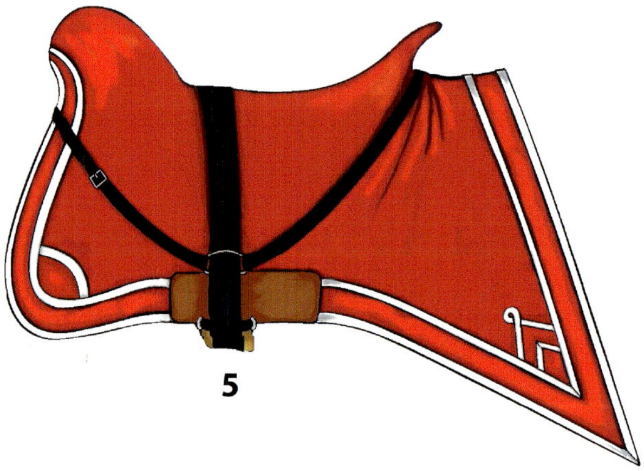

5

6

Plate 11. Danish Lette Dragoner (Light Dragoons) (IV) Shabraques

1. Shabraque as used by the Livregiment Lette Dragoner in 'normal' red and yellow lace. This is a reconstruction of the officers' 'Valdrap' from the drawings found in the Danish Military archives *c.*1817–19.
2. Shabraque as used by troopers.
3. Shabraque for officers *c.*1802–1815. From *c.*1810 it should have been changed to 'normal red', 'But the older ones may be used for the remaining terms'. Jyske and Fynske Lette Dragoner Regiments.
4. Shabraque of a trooper *c.*1802–1815 in ordinary red. Jyske and Fynske Lette Dragoner Regiments.
5. Officer's shabraque for the Prins Frederik Ferdinands Dragonregiment. Apparently different from that of the light dragoons. Only in 1816 did the regiment officially become a light dragoon regiment, until then it was classed as a dragon regiment, so to mark this difference until 1816, they had a slightly different saddle cloth (illustration made after a painting by Senn 1808). Not all the details are clear, but the front of the shabraque probably bore one or two bars which designated an officer.
6. Trooper's model unknown, but would have had the double bands of lace, but in white gallon, not silver like the officers, and the 'V' designating a trooper. They would then correspond with the shabraques used by the Norwegian dragoons.

The Livregiment Lette Dragoner, Fynske and Jydske Lette Dragonregimenter

Sidearm: originally the Livregiment Lette Dragoner had the M1776 sabre. Eventually it was replaced with the *Husarsabel* M1792 in the M1804 scabbard (in fact this was the M1776 blade with a new hilt and scabbard), but probably only reached the depot and they never made it into the field. The Livregiment Lette Dragoner did receive the brass-hilted M1808 dragoon sabres from 1811 at the earliest.

Pistol: A mix of pistols, hussar Model 1748/98 and hussar Model 1795. We know from their markings that the Livregiment Lette Dragoner were at some date issued with M1806 weapons, but we do not have clear dates though it was probably *c.*1810–12.

Carbine: Hussar carbine Model 1748/98 was used by Fynske for sure, and no doubt a few by the other regiments, but most had the hussar carbine Model 1795.

Rifled Carbine: Rifled hussar carbine M1798.

The Prins Frederik Ferdinand Dragonregiment

As they were originally trained as line dragoons their initial armament reflects this.

Sword: When raised from the Landeværn's kavaleriet, they were to receive M1785 or M1797 *Pallasks*, but as there were none readily available in Zealand they were instead issued with the new M1808 'hussar sabres' or more likely the M1792 in the M1808 scabbard (see the painting by Senn).

Pistol: The pistols were at first a mix of probably M1751/98 and M1772/98 models with individual ramrods received from the stores of the Sjællandske Rytter Regiment. Again, at a later date (probably after 1810) they also received the hussar pistol M1748/98 and hussar pistol M1795, both now without ramrods inserted under the barrel, and they also received the M1806 pistol again with a separate ramrod, probably after 1810.

Carbine: As seen on the Approbation plate in January 1808, at first they were intended to be armed as a true dragoon regiment, with the old M1767/69 dragoon muskets together with their bayonets which were carried on a frog on their belts (the 1st Squadron at least received them, although probably only for short period, as a bayonet for a M1767 with the stamp of the regiment still exists today), with a separate ramrod. Probably after 1810 they were issued with the M1750/98 *husarkarabin* and new M1806 carbines to replace the dragoon musket. Apparently this weapon was primarily intended for them as well as the hussars (regimental lettering indicates that both types of carbines were carried simultaneously).

Rifled Carbine: As 'dragoons' at first they did not have rifles, but at least from 1810 they received the rifle *husarkarabin* M1806, and they now had trained flankers to use them.

The carbine was carried slung from a white leather shoulder belt over their left shoulder. The carbine was designed for use both on horseback and while skirmishing on foot.

Note: they had a white leather bandolier with a plain black leather cartridge pouch, which was worn over their

Table II. Light Dragoon Regiments *c.*1808

Regimental Name	Facings & Piping	Button Colour	Helmet Turban	Particularities
Livregiment Lette Dragoner	Black/straw-yellow	White Metal	Red	
Jyske Lette Dragoner Regiment	Dark green/straw yellow	White Metal	Dark green	
Fynske Lette Dragoner Regiment	Light blue/straw yellow	White Metal	Light blue	The officers had gilded chin scales.
Prins Frederik Ferdinand Dragonregiment, ex-Sjællandske Dragonregiment	Black/white	White Metal	Red (from 1812)	Renamed Prins Frederik Ferdinand in 1807. Became light dragoons in 1815/1816

right shoulder. They wore a white leather waist belt with a square brass buckle, from which the steel scabbard was slung on two straps and carrying rings. They carried a separate long ramrod which was used for both the pistol and carbine, suspended from the waist belt; it was not inserted into the stock as in most other countries.

Horse Furniture

The harness was a light cavalry version made of black leather and they had a red Hungarian-style shabraque with a white woollen lace border and a stylised Hungarian knot on the front and rear corners. The light dragoons' version of the standard Hungarian-style shabraque does not appear to be quite as pointed as the cavalry version.

There were some regimental variations, but they have not all been clearly identified, as for the Ryttere. There are clear indications that the Livregiment Lette Dragoners had dog-tooth lacing on the shabraques of the same style as the Guide Corpset, but with their lining colour (yellow) in dog-tooth.

The troopers had a red, round cloth portmanteau piped white *c.*1802, after which they followed the style described in the chapter on the Ryttere. For the rest they carried more or less the same equipment as the Ryttere, although some of the valises appear to have been buttoned up rather than strapped up. For the details see the heavy cavalry.

The dragoon NCOs and trumpeters generally had two pistols; they carried their bread bag at the rear to the left and probably their water bottle on the right side of their (dark grey) valise. The officers would normally not have carried a *Mantelsæk*, but their kit was transported in a wagon reserved for their use, under the care of their batman as in the Ryttere regiments.

NCOs' Distinctions

The NCOs used the same distinctions as the heavy cavalry, using the new regulation style with the pointed cuffs from 1812. Their shoulder straps were of the facing colour piped with the regimental colour. They had white sword knots and tassels until 1812 when they were changed to black. The NCOs carried a pair of pistols which had a loose pistol ramrod, carried separately. This was because NCOs did not carry carbines, just a set of pistols, and as a consequence had a pistol ramrod only, as did the trumpeters who were also classed as NCOs.

Officers' Uniforms

The officers wore coats made of better quality red cloth with the regimental distinction, and used the same rank distinctions as the heavy cavalry and followed the new regulations issued in 1812. The officers of the Fynske regiment helmets had gilded chin scales. The sash was usually worn over the coat, but occasionally it was worn over the waistcoat and pantaloons, but under the coat. After 1812 the sash and epaulettes were abolished and replaced by the new distinctions placed on their pointed cuffs.

In full dress they wore a pair of fall front pale buff breeches and black Hessian-style boots with borders and tassels the same colour as the metallic buttons. From 1809/10 these were replaced by white ones. In service dress they either wore a pair of dark blue breeches with a fall front with two stripes down the outer leg and Hungarian boots or a pair of dark blue fall front trousers also with red stripes. They buttoned down the outside leg, usually with a strip of red lace down the edge. The buttons could be metallic or made of bone. These were replaced by a pair of dark grey overalls piped with two red stripes around 1810/1811, after the blue ones had been worn out.

The officers carried several different types of privately acquired officers' sabres as well as the model issued, generally based on the M1762 hussar sabre and later models. The M1800 had a lion-head hilt carried in a black leather sheath with brass fittings, although some later had privately made fully gilded metal scabbards. They had a red and gold sword knot and strap. Some of the officers' sabres had hilts of another style; these had an antique Minerva helmet on the pommel acquired privately.

The officers had a small black leather cartridge pouch carried on a leather bandolier. The cartridge pouch had a brass or silver badge on it. This badge was probably the king's cypher, a white metal crowned cypher of 'FVIR' from 1808. The bandolier was generally of leather covered with silver lace for reviews, at least until 1812. The back of the cartridge case bandolier was lined with red cloth to protect the coat.

Their cloaks were originally red; the new issue after 1812 officially grey, but again many men continued to wear the old red ones and several acquired blue cloaks in Germany in 1813, probably of French origin. Their scarlet shabraque had a broad silver lace border, piped in the facing colour on both edges. It had a stylised loop in the rear corner, again there were regimental variations.

Trumpeters' Uniforms

The trumpeters were dressed the same as the troop, but with the following distinction, a facing coloured swallow's nest with lace and tassels in the regimental button colour.

As trumpeters were regarded as NCOs they also had a small fringed epaulette over the swallow nests, usually in the button colour. Their helmet probably had a white plume with a red tip. The trumpet cords and tassels were tressed white with the regimental facing colour.

They carried the same sabre as the troopers and two pistols, but no carbine and they carried the separate ramrod on their belt.

From 1812 all regiments changed the colour of their helmet turbans to red. Some known regimental variations.

The Jyske Regiment Lette Dragoner had, according to a picture dated to 1813, a plain grey valise (*Mantelsække*) which was probably the standard model.

Again this was the official view, but in reality things could be quite different. A well-known example is that of the Fynske Infantry Regiment, whose colonel ordered and received new jackets for his regiment just before going on campaign in 1813.However, as he felt the uniforms of the regiment were still not completely worn out, he placed them in the regimental baggage train, where they were carried around without ever being issued. During the retreat after the Battle of Boden in December 1813, the wagons carrying the uniforms became bogged down and were left behind. Here they were found by the passing Fynske Lette Dragoner Regiment and the wagons were opened. The Colonel (Høgh-Guldberg) ordered all his men to pass in line and pick up 'a fine new uniform for all', as their own was 'worn thin and full of holes'. This regiment apparently did not change the uniforms' facings, at least not straight away and it was in this uniform (with white regimental-coloured facings) that the regiment fought at the Battle of Sehestedt on 10 December, only changing the facings for the correct colour at the end of the campaign.

The colonel of the Fynske Infantry Regiment made a formal complaint to the King, wanting his uniforms back. The King turned him down, replying that he should have taken better care of them!

5

The Hussar Regiment, Husar Regiment

The Danish hussars held a distinguished service record in the Napoleonic Wars. They regularly showed their skill and bravery, patrolling the border and participating in the capture of Hamburg 1801, and skirmishing with French cavalry on the frontier in 1806. They fought at the Battle of Stralsund in 1809 where they totally defeated a large detachment of Ferdinand von Schill's *Freikorps*. They fought in several skirmishes and battles in 1813, including the Battle of Gardebush in 1813. Their final battle was the Battle of Sehestedt in December 1813, where they fought both Russo-German and Hanoverian infantry and cavalry. The Danish hussars met both Russian and Prussian hussars blade-to-blade a number of times, generally emerging victorious.

Mention must also be made of the hussar detachment raised from volunteers and commanded by the charismatic Lieutenant Johannes von Ewald, who distinguished themselves during the siege of Glückstadt.

The hussar regiment of the Danish army was a double-strength light cavalry regiment and had the following organisation. It was composed of a staff with same establishment as the other cavalry regiments and they had six squadrons of hussars, each of which had five officers, nine NCOs, two trumpeters who were NCOs with the rank of corporals, and 144 hussars. In 1806 their strength was raised to 10 NCOs (an extra corporal) and 168 troopers. The 2nd and 6th squadrons always served separately in Holstein, and although they were part of the same regiment they were known as the Holstenske Hussar Corps. Until 1807 the regiment also had a small independent detachment in Norway.

During the period 1803–14 the regiment was made up of a large number of Germans (in fact German-speaking Danes from Schleswig Holstein) and some Danes (only 30 percent). Men of shorter stature were preferred for troopers, generally their height was only around 160–170cm (5 feet 3 inches to 5 feet 7 inches).

The cavalry fought in two ranks. Each squadron included 12 sharpshooters (10 troopers and two NCOs armed with rifled carbines), specially trained as skirmishers. But as all cavalry troopers received basic training in skirmish tactics they were more than capable of supporting their skirmishers. As late as 1809 their carried their standards on campaign.

Hussars' Uniforms

From the start the Hussars wore a cylindrical black felt hussar mirliton *Shactelhue* of the Prussian style with a black felt peak and a white lace top, by 1813 with a bottom band over the leather reinforcing and the false wing simulated by white lace, and probably with a red and white rosette on the front. On left side, it had a white plume over a black cockade. The mirliton had red cords and flounders for the troop. Some cockades appear to have been made of wood and painted black.

In 1813 the plume and cockade were moved to the front of the mirliton. This may already have been done unofficially by the detachment in Holstein, as shown on the 2nd and 6th squadrons in the von Prangen plate of *c.*1809. Their mirliton appears to have been rather soft and of crude manufacture. We also know that from 1813 on campaign they could be worn with a waxed cloth cover, and that the plume was worn on the front of the mirliton when on campaign as late as January 1814 (hussar corporal Kloppenborg's memoirs).

Originally the mirliton was slightly tapered towards the base, but had become more or less parallel by 1808. Von Prangen's plate also shows what appears to be a shako rather than a mirliton, so when Friboe speaks of several styles of headdress he was no doubt referring to a mix of mirlitons and shakos, probably for the Holstein contingent.

The hussars wore a light blue cloth dolman, which had five rows of white metal buttons with joined with double white lace braids between them and single white lace braids which joined the horizontal rows; there was white lace on all the borders and on the seams on the back of the dolman, the exact form changing little during the period. It had a red collar with white lace trim and red pointed cuffs piped white, and by 1809 the cuffs had small white loop as well. The trefoils appeared much later on the trooper's cuffs.

They wore a crimson red pelisse had a black fur trim, it had five rows of buttons, three on one side and two on the other with white braiding and loops and a white lace border around the black fur and white trefoils, all the buttons were white metal. They were supposed to be worn slung down the back like a cloak, but in fact they were worn slung over their shoulder like any other hussar in Europe, though not necessarily on the same shoulder as both are shown in contemporary illustrations. In this way it gave a little protection to the bridle arm. Around their waist was worn a barrel sash of red wool with white barrels, cords and tassels.

Originally they had a pair of fall-fronted pale yellow leather breeches, and wore black leather Hungarian boots with black leather tassels or white lace and tassels, probably their best and kept for parades. They had originally had crimson red *scharawaden* (cloth trouser legs worn over their breeches like stockings) until 1801; but these do not seem to have been worn after.

When they were on campaign they had a pair of dark blue fall front overalls which had leather reinforcements down the inside legs and around the seat. They buttoned down the outside leg with white metal buttons and had a red welt; the overalls were worn buttoned over their boots. By 1809–10 they had changed to tight white kersey parade trousers and a pair of dark grey full front overalls which had a black welt for campaign wear. But as in other regiments 'Old stocks have to be worn out first, for daily duty.' In 1813 the hussar commander, Friboe, said:

> Know that at the moment four colours of trousers, are in a way permitted, and used freely –white and grey officially, but yellow and blue as well, but please do not wear any other than white and grey in the presence of the king, also as several styles of headdress are in use, I will form a committee of officers, to decide on one type of headdress common for all officers, (And I will for one state that I personally find the 'mirliton' the perfect headdress for a Hussar), And then we will submit the chosen headdress to his Majesty, for his approval'.

Apparently the headdress that was finally chosen was the shako, officially approved in 1817. Their cloaks were red.

Arms and Equipment

The hussars were originally armed with the *Husarsabel* M1776 which had a single-bar steel hilt. It was carried in a black leather scabbard with iron fittings and two suspension rings from a black waist belt. Probably they also received some M1792 sabres, but the light dragoons were issued with this sabre first, so this is debatable. In 1803 they claimed that 'all our sabres are worn out', and most information confirms this was correct. Probably only the detachment in Holstein received the M1792 sabre. Between 1808 and 1809 these sabres began to be replaced with the M1808 light cavalry sabre (the so-called 'dragoon sabre') which had a brass single bar hilt with two side branches and a leather grip and brown leather sabre strap and knot. It had a curved single-edged 86cm blade and an overall length of 1m 1cm. It was carried in a steel scabbard and fittings and two suspension rings, suspended from a black waist belt.

In turn this was superseded with the 'dragoon' (or 'light cavalry', as they were mainly used by the hussars) sabre M1808, this became their principal sidearm for the rest of the war.

It has not been possible to identify with certainty what style of buckle was used by the troop, and some doubt remains about how many straps were used to suspend the sabretache, the officers certainly had three, but it is less sure for the troop. Personally I feel that three is the right number; the few illustrations show only two, but the prints come from different sources (von Prangen).

They carried a number of different models of carbines, the *Husarkarabin* M1750/98, and the M1777, which was 79cm long and weighed 2kg 2g. In 1798 these were modernised and remounted on new stocks. In 1809–11 they were probably issued with the M1806 *k*, carried from a swivel on a black leather carbine belt. Some hussars were issued with the M1798 rifled carbine. A black leather cartridge pouch on a white leather bandolier, *c.*1809 at the latest, and a pair of pistols completed their equipment. They originally had the hussar pistol M1748/98 together with the M1772/98, later they may have been replaced with the hussar pistol M1806 (issued *c.*1810–1812).

The hussars' pistols were different to the standard cavalry pistol; most noticeable was the incurved butt. Both the cartridge pouch and bandolier were shown as brown leather *c.*1803.

They carried a leather sabretache, the face was covered in red cloth with blue wolf's teeth piped and bordered in white lace. Embroidered in the centre in white thread was the crowned royal cypher 'C7' until 1808, and after 1808 this monogram was replaced with 'FIVR'. The bonnet of the crown was red. They wore buff leather gloves with small gauntlet cuffs, not always shown on contemporary pictures.

They had a black leather Hungarian harness including cowrie shell decoration (meant for use on parades only, not on campaign, but as always some of the dandier officers used them anyway) and the half-moon ornament hanging from the throat strap. They had a red Hungarian-style shabraque with medium blue wolf's teeth piped white and white outer lace border. After 1808 they were to have the King's monogram embroidered on the front of the shabraque, but as they had to wear out the old shabraques first, this would explain why they did not appear in contemporary artwork until after the war. Their valise or portmanteau (*Mantelsæk*) was round and coloured light blue, around 1812 they were supposed to be rectangular and made of iron-grey cloth, but the hussars probably resisted this change.

Note: a shabraque in the cavalry, for the men at least, was expected to last for 16 years, and the more costly officer

Danish Hussars (I) Uniforms

1803 1803 1809 1809 1809

1809 1811 1811 1813 1813

JACDAW 2018 ©

Plate 12. Danish Hussars (I) Uniforms

From left to right:
Top, officer and trooper *c.*1803 in full dress. The contemporary painting shows him with a trooper's sabre. Officer and trumpeter *c.*1809 in service dress with blue overalls. NCO in parade dress *c.*1809, note the crossed belts, the new white leather model and the new M1808 'dragoon sabre'. The belt would normally be worn much higher and was usually hidden by the sash, shown here just so the form of the belt can be seen. Another anomaly, the NCO has a carbine belt, unusual as cavalry NCOs were not armed with carbines (after Senn).

Bottom, trooper *c.*1809, rear view showing traditional way of wearing pelisse, contemporary iconography has a tendency to show a more usual way carrying the pelisse, he has not yet received his new white belting and still has the old natural leather version. Here are an officer and a trooper *c.*1811, wearing full dress uniforms. Officer and trooper *c.*1813, in campaign dress wearing the pelisse. The officer is wearing a shako, and although these were not yet in general use, some officers had adopted them; some even had their mirlitons converted into colpacks with the addition of a fur sleeve and a small red bonnet which was then slipped over the mirliton. The trooper is from one of the Holstein squadrons (2nd and 6th) as is shown by having moved his plume to the front of the mirliton, the other troops adopted this as well towards the end of the war, as it gave a better balance to their mirliton. He is also carrying the older M1792 sabre as it is unlikely they received the new *Dragonsabel*: they were based out in the 'sticks', down in Holstein a long way from the arsenals. From 1808 the hussars (troopers, NCOs and trumpeters) carried the M1808 light cavalry sabre with a two branch brass hilt; in general this sword is erroneously attributed to the light dragoons, and some officers even started to carry them by 1813.

Source: drawing made after an engraving made by C. Eckesberg showing a hussar talking to a Livjæger officer in front of one of the four main gates to the city, the 'Østerport' (east gate) in 1808. The Pelisse is shown draped over the shoulder, which is how they usually wore them, but in fact they were supposed to have them slung over their backs like a cloak.

shabraques would have without doubt been bought and sold among the officers. This rule applied to all the cavalry regiments. All the uniform and equipment parts had a set length of time for how long they should be used before renewal. The details were noted in the printed regulations.

NCOs' Uniforms

NCOs wore the same uniform as the hussar troopers but with elaborate silver lace on the shako and shabraque. Their collar lace was silver, later white, one of normal width and a thinner one on the inside. Their dolman had more elaborate lacing, the lacing on the breast ending in trefoils, with the same on their cuffs. There is some mention *c.*1799 that the NCOs should have an epaulette or 'dragon', without any other precisions. But this was probably only a shoulder-strap to keep the cross belt in place, on the left shoulder, made of two parallel thin silver cords, with a button at the collar.

The NCO's barrel sash was made in three colours, red and blue wool with white barrels, cords and tassels. He carried a leather sabretache, the face was covered in blue cloth piped and bordered in white and silver lace, and embroidered in the centre in silver was the crowned royal cypher, 'C7' until 1808 and 'FIVR' after, and the bonnet of the crown was red.

The men were armed with a pair of pistols with a separate ramrod suspended from their belt and a sabre. They had a crimson red Hungarian-style shabraque with white wolf's teeth and a white outer lace border *c.*1774.

Officers' Uniforms

The officers' mirlitons, which came to resemble the late-model French hussar shakos, had silver scalloped lace around the top, and diagonal silver cords, tassels and flounders. On the front just above visor they had a silver multi-pointed star with a red centre not unlike the order of the Dannebrog. The size of the plumes, which were worn on the side, appears to be in keeping with rank, the taller the plume the higher the rank, in some paintings they are shown impractically high, probably reserved for parades, of which they had a lot. On campaign they were probably more sensible and used smaller plumes. The 2nd and 6th squadrons based in Holstein moved their plumes to the front of the mirliton around 1812.

Danish Hussars (II) Harness & Shabraques

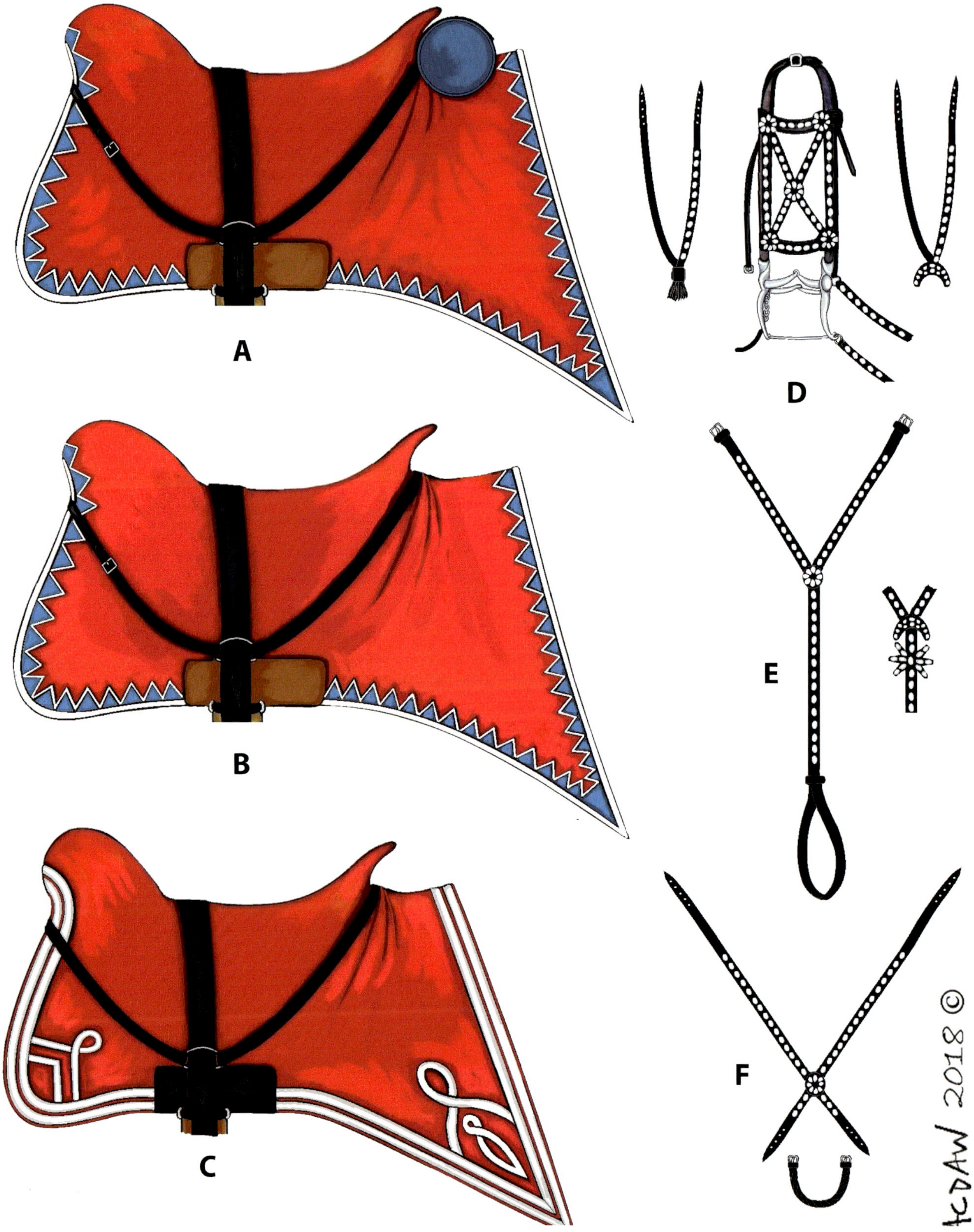

Plate 13. Danish Hussars (II) Harness & Shabraques

A. Hussar trooper's general service shabraque *c.*1810, with the earlier valise (*Mantelsæk*) which was round, but none of these have survived and all we have to go on is a tiny illustration in the corner of a contemporary painting. Originally they were red up to *c.*1802, when they were made in blue cloth, and in theory they were to last 10–12 years, so the new more spacious rectangular model was unlikely to have ever been issued before the end of the war. This shabraque was also used by the uhlans.
B. Hussar trooper's parade shabraque.
C. Hussar officer's shabraque with silver lace. This shabraque was also used by the uhlan officers, and although the lace was supposed to be gold for them, the silver-laced version is more likely.
D. Hussar bridle decorated with cowrie shells, the officer's model probably had more, but as none have survived it is difficult to be more precise. On the left there is a trooper's throat strap with a black leather tassel and on the right an officer's model of which there were probably a number of variations.
E. Hussar breast strap decorated with cowrie shells, on the right an officer's variant.
F. Hussar crupper strap decorated with cowrie shells.
Note, the horse harness is based on the illustrations by the Danish artist Højbjerg-Nielsens.

Some officers started wearing shakos unofficially, generally completely made of leather without the 'V' strengtheners on the sides but with gold lace around the top.

Their uniform was basically the same as the troop, but made from better cloth. It had five rows of silver buttons but no tassels on their dolman, and four rows on their pelisse, two each side, with silver braids and lacing all around. The base of both the dolman and pelisse were heavily embroidered, although this have been for the senior officers. Rank insignias were placed on both arms over their cuffs on both the dolman and pelisse. It was supposed to have been worn slung down the back like a cloak, but in fact they were worn slung over the shoulder like any other hussar in Europe. Around their waist they wore a barrel sash of red wool with silver barrels, cords and tassels.

The officers' belts were of red leather stitched with silver or gold thread with a simple S-clasp, although some men appear to have replaced these with lion-head buckles. The officers had a black leather cartridge pouch and silver laced bandolier; the flap bore the King's crowned monogram in silvered metal, 'C7'until 1808 and 'FIVR' after. In the portrait of Second Lieutenant E. von Ewald *c.*1812, the cartridge pouch appears to be of red leather or velvet and he appears to have exaggerated his lacing as it is more like that of a general rather than a second lieutenant. He even has a French-style colpack, definitely not regimental dress, a few other officers probably acquired these as well.

In fact this state of affairs with hussar officers wearing more and more ostentatious non-regulation dress prompted an official reprimand and the order for them to get back into regimental uniform, which was only very vaguely respected – after all, they were hussars.

They wore the same legwear as the troop. From 1800 yellow buff leather breeches for full dress and blue riding overalls with dark leather reinforcing, but their blue overalls had silver or white and red Hungarian knots embroidered on them for campaign dress from 1802, which had a red welt on the outside leg. They were supposed to be grey from 1812. These grey overalls had a large red welt with a thinner band of grey material down the centre which gave the appearance of two stripes. These overalls had three buttons on the inside leg to enable the officers to put their boots on. They wore hussar or Hessian boots with a silver or white lace border and tassel.

The sabretache was made of leather and the flap was covered in light blue cloth with a wolf's tooth border in silver lace, piped red on the exterior with the crowned royal cypher embroidered in the centre, the 'C7' until 1808 and 'FIVR' after, under a crown, all in silver thread. The crown had a red bonnet. By 1805 the wolf's teeth had been replaced by a large silver lace embroidered border which appears to have been more or less elaborate depending on the officer's rank. It was suspended on red straps stitched with silver thread. All of the officer's sabretaches had a red backing cloth, but strangely they never had oilskin covers with which to protect them on campaign. There were a few odd versions, one had a red cloth-covered flap with a wide gold lace border and crowned cypher, this was probably a privately made fantasy of a senior officer and not at all representative of all the others, and is mentioned only for completeness.

The sabre had a red and gold strap and knot, more gold than red for senior officers. The shabraque had silver lace border, embroidery and piping. They had buff leather gloves with small cuffs.

The officers had a black leather Hungarian harness including cowrie shell decoration and the half-moon ornament hanging from the throat strap. They had a

Danish Hussars (III) Rank Distinctions

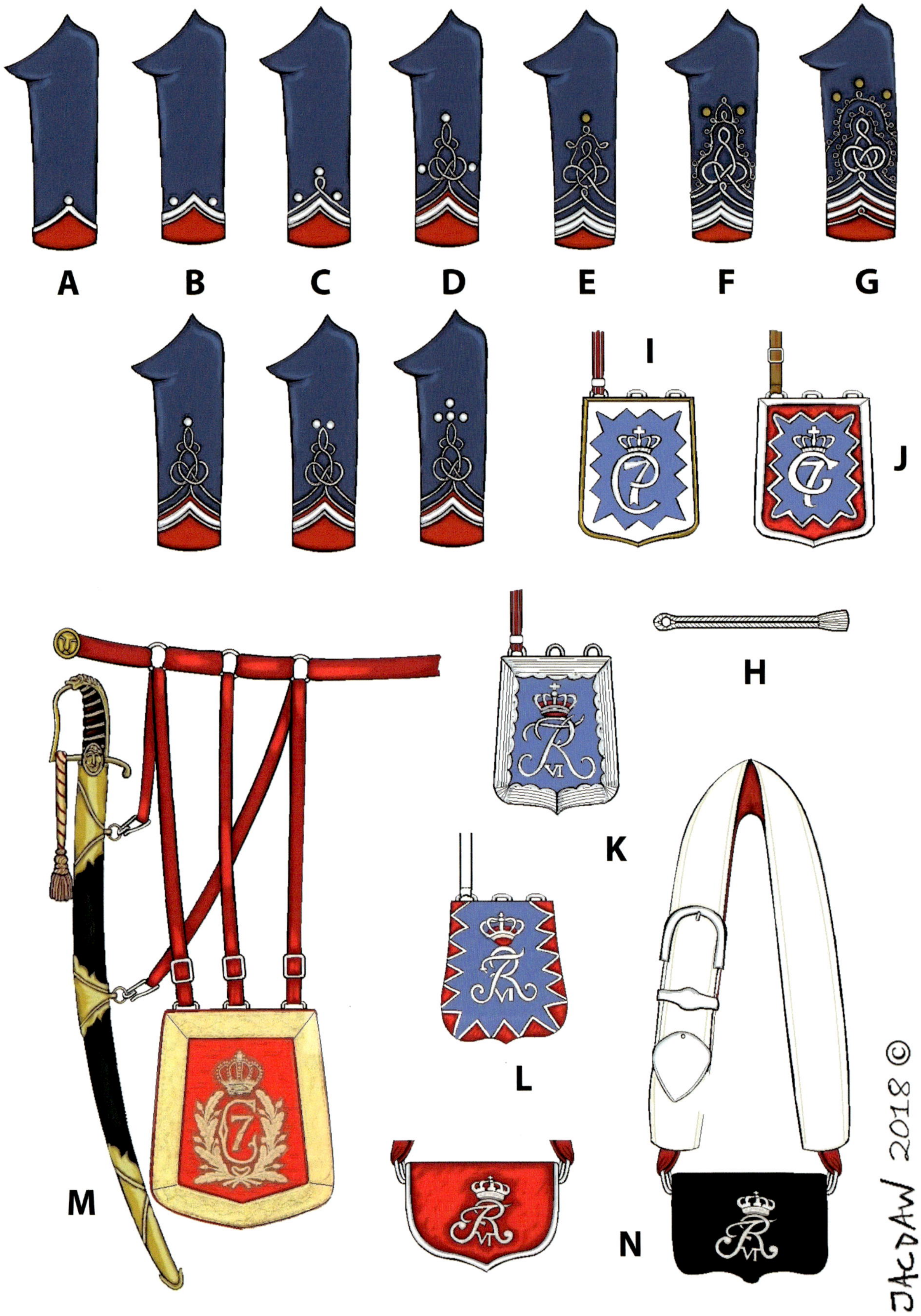

Plate 14. Danish Hussars (III) Rank Distinctions

A. Cornet/ensign. This rank was no longer used after 1809.
B. Top, second lieutenant (*sekondløjtnant*) to 1809, bottom new distinctions post 1809.
C. Top, first lieutenant (*premierløjtnant*) to 1809, bottom new distinctions post 1809.
D. Top, captain (*Ridtmester*) to 1809, bottom new distinctions post 1809.
E. Major 1803-1815
F. Lieutenant colonel (*Oberstløjtnant*) 1803–1815
G. Colonel (*Obrist/Oberst*) 1803–1815
H. Silver NCO's epaulette, same as for the Livgarde til Hest.
I. Officer's sabretache pre 1808.
J. Trooper's sabretache pre 1808.
K. Officer's sabretache post 1808.
L. Trooper's sabretache post 1808.
M. Belt and straps for sabre and sabretache (both privately bought, non-regulation)
N. Officer's cartridge pouch post 1808, left full dress model, right service model. The belt was always silvered for the officers, the troopers' model was similar, both used by the uhlans. The buckle was made either in steel or brass and then silvered.

crimson red Hungarian-style shabraque with silver wolf's teeth and a silver outer lace border *c.*1774. Torstein Snorrason has suggested that their shabraques were the same model as other cavalry officers; this is substantiated by a watercolour showing an uhlan officer *c.*1808 with this note, '(shabraque) same as hussars, but in gold'. I believe that the model changed little from 1774. After 1808 they were to have the King's monogram embroidered on the front of the shabraque, but as they had to wear out the old shabraques first, this would explain why these monograms did not appear in contemporary artwork until after the war. Another detail is that some officers started to put a white sheepskin over the saddle like the French and Prussians.

The officers were issued with red overcoats *c.*1813. Their walking out or undress uniform *c.*1811 consisted of a crimson red-lapelled coat with silver piping on all leading edges, cuffs, collar and pockets, a blue collar and waistcoat. They wore buff breeches with either their boots or with white stockings and shoes, and a plumed bicorn was worn with this dress.

Trumpeters' Uniforms

Each squadron had two trumpeters. According to the regulations of 1774 they had the same uniform as the rank and file. Additionally, they were granted something extra 'for distinction'. What this was is not known for certain, but it was probably extra braids on their dolman. In the uniform regulations of 1799 and 1803 the trumpeters were now issued with the same uniform as non-commissioned officers as they were now classed as NCOs.

Furthermore they received some dress distinctions, but again these are not clearly specified. The trumpeters did not carry carbines, but they did carry cartridge pouches on bandoliers and they carried the ramrod for their pistols on their belt.

These were their distinctions along with 'extra lace', probably a loop on their cuffs and a cord-style epaulette (*dragon*).

The staff trumpeter (trumpet major would be the closest rank equivalent) had additional silver lace on his uniform and he carried a decorative cartridge pouch on a bandolier.

Up until 1799 at least they had a kettledrummer, but after 1799 these were officially discontinued in all the cavalry regiments. The trumpeters rode white horses, not greys.

The Uhlan Squadron, Bosniak Eskadron

A 'Bosniak squadron' (Bosniak eskadron) of Prussian-style lancers was raised in 1791 by transferring 20 men from each of the six hussar squadrons. In 1793 their strength was increased to 144 men. The lancers were administratively attached to the Hussar Regiment as their 7th squadron and they had the same establishment as the Hussar squadrons. The Uhlan Squadron (Bosniaks) is not known to have taken part in any of the Danish campaigns but remained in Copenhagen, basically a decorative guard unit. From 1807 it was commanded by *Major* Frederik Vilhelm Carl Ludvig, Prins of Hessen-Philippsthal-Barchfeld. All of the men were of purely Danish extraction; there were no 'exotic' imports within this unit. The majority of the men appear to have been over 30 years old and a number were even in their 40s. They once had a Polish cavalryman assigned to the squadron to train them in lance drill.

They served with the hussars in Holstein in 1806–1807, and a small detachment of recruits served during the siege of Copenhagen. Although their depot was based in the town of Næstved, they were garrisoned for a while at Køge

Danish Bosniaks & Uhlans
JACDAW 2018 ©

Plate 15. Danish Bosniaks and Uhlans

Top row, from left to right:
A Bosniak trooper *c.*1801 in summer dress. A Bosniak trooper 1802–1808 in both summer dress and in winter dress. A Bosniak officer *c.*1802–1808 in summer and in winter dress.

Bottom row, from left to right:
A uhlan trooper wearing the new 'Polish' dress, front and back view, this was supposed to have been adopted *c.*1808.
My reconstruction of an uhlan officer in 'Polish' dress *c.*1809 with the 'Rally Pennon', showing silver white lacing, hussar belt and scarlet and gold officers cords on the czapska. A uhlan officer in service/field dress *c.*1810–1814 after a contemporary painting by C.A. Lorenzen, wearing what appears to be a hussar pelisse, probably over the new uniform. An uhlan in service/field dress *c.*1810–1814 after a contemporary painting, they are shown wearing a short red uniform coat with light blue cuffs and collar, both piped white. This is an indication that the rather fancy Polish troopers' 1808 uniform were probably never made or issued to the uhlans before 1814, but instead they wore these jackets, possibly made out of the old Bosniak winter coat, instead. Note, the officers' lace was silver.

before the British attack. From 1808 until 1814 they were part of the coastal defence of Zealand.

In 1807 their surplus uniforms in their main clothing depot at Køge, mainly winter dress, were given to the Landeværn Kavaleriet who used it to dress some of their men, and they wore this rather colourful if strange dress at the Battle of Køge in 1807.

In 1808 the unit was renamed the 'Uhlan Squadron' (*Uhlaneskadron*). It was disbanded in 1814.

A certain amount of confusion has arisen around this unit due to the approbation watercolour concerning the officers, which shows the metal as gold when all else shows silver/white for the officers. Firstly this was the project only and apparently the gold was finally replaced by the silver which was much more logical: it harmonised their uniforms with the men and it conformed with the hussar dress as they were theoretically the 7th Squadron, which simplified the confection of the uniforms and avoided confusion in the ranks, and no doubt more economical.

Bosniak Uhlan Uniform

The original headwear in 1791 was a scarlet felt fez-style cap with white cloth turban around it. On left side it had a blue plume over a black cockade. By 1801, the fez had become slightly taller.

In 1808 the soldiers were renamed uhlans, and a Polish style of dress was adopted. They received red shakos/czapskas which had a black peak and a black band, possibly a woollen turban, around the base of the shakos, piped white along the upper part, officially worn until 1811. The shako/czapska had a light blue plume at the front with a white metal sickle moon and probably a black cockade; it does not appear to have had cords. The few images which exist give the impression that the shako was rather soft model without a very rigid form, probably made of felt. It has also been suggested, and not without reason, that these czapskas were made from the old fezzes which were pushed out. The Danish had a habit of recycling materials.

These 'Danish' czapskas were supposed to be octagonal, but they appear to be more hexagonal crowns, not at all square, in scarlet or red felt with a black leather skull, peak and chinstrap. They had a light blue plume over a black cockade with a white loop. They were supposed to have cords and tasselled flounders, which hung down and were looped over a button on the lapels, but none are shown or have survived to bear this out. Although we have this detailed description there is a great deal of doubt as to whether these rigid czapskas were ever actually made and issued to the troop, as pictures dated as late as 1813 still show the softer shako/czapska in use.

When originally raised as Bosniaks, these men they wore a Turkish-style costume which included a short blue cloth jacket which had the front laced white. It had a scarlet collar and pointed cuffs, both trimmed with white lace. The blue is sometimes shown as a light blue and sometimes as a medium blue. Around their waist they had a scarlet sash with white lace trim and stripes. Their trousers or overalls were blue with a red lace along the outer seam which continued across the seat of the pants and re-joined the other leg.

By 1802 the dress was slightly changed and the jacket lost its red collar and now had a very low blue collar piped white. The new trousers now had a white lace welt down the outer seam which did not continue around the seat, but the leg now had a white lace cuff around the ankle. They had three buttons on the lower inside leg.

Danish Cavalry Breeches and Overalls

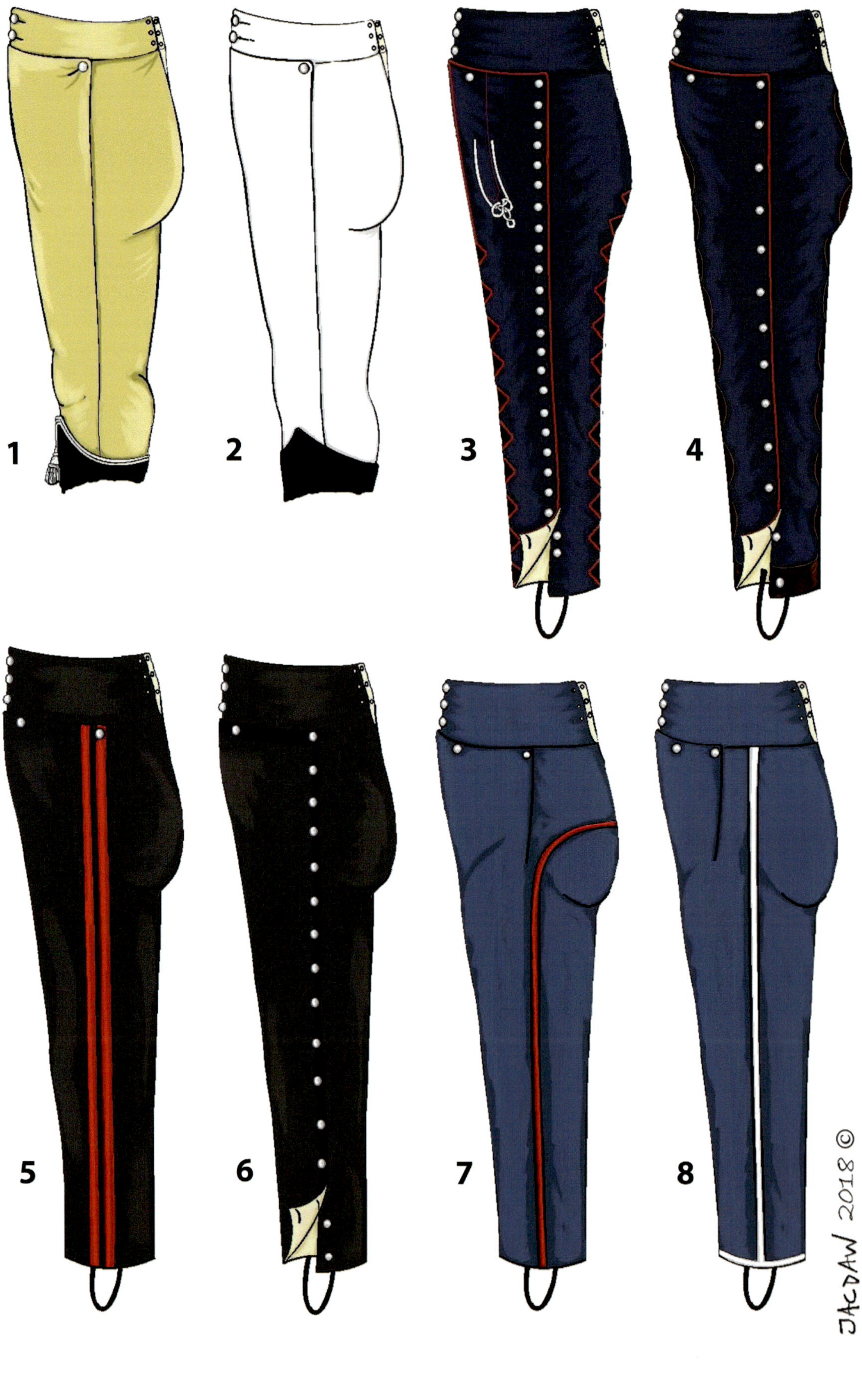

Plate 16. Danish Cavalry Breeches and Overalls

Soft buff leather cavalry breeches worn as full dress for officers and men of all mounted units, 1802–1809. It is possible that some units only had woollen 'kersey' breeches dyed buff yellow due to shortages of leather. They had wooden buttons covered with buff leather for the men and tin buttons for NCOs, and the crotch and flap were lined with white cloth (no underpants were worn at this time). Note eyes at the back for tightening laces.
White kersey cavalry breeches which replaced the buff breeches from 1809, were worn as full dress for officers and men of all regular mounted units.
The officers' version of blue woollen service and campaign overalls with dyed calfskin reinforcing to protect the breeches, ordered in 1797 delivered from 1802/1803. There were different versions with more or less lace; this is probably that of a junior officer. These were obviously made privately due to the non-regulation number of buttons.
Troopers' version of blue woollen service and campaign overalls with dyed calfskin reinforcing to protect the breeches, ordered in 1797 and delivered from 1802/1803. They had 13 tin buttons on the seams either side.
Officers' version of M1808/1810 grey woollen service and campaign overalls (called *Pantelons* or *Pantalons*) with undyed calfskin reinforcing to protect the breeches, they buttoned on the inside leg (three buttons) and the buttons were wood covered with leather. The wide red tape down the outside leg had a thinner stripe of grey cloth down the centre to give the illusion of two stripes. The waistline was much higher on these overalls, 'just below the heart', as the new coatees were much shorter. These breeches replaced the blue ones.
Trooper's version of M1810 grey woollen service and campaign overalls with undyed calfskin reinforcing to protect the breeches, they buttoned down the outside leg, but with 15 tin buttons because of the new higher waistline. They had black tape down the outside leg and over the flap. These breeches replaced the blue ones.
Trooper's version of the M1801 Bosniak overalls with red tape. The 1802 model now had white tape for the troopers and silver for the officers. They buttoned on the inside leg (three buttons).
M1808 uhlan overalls, the tape was white for the troopers and silver for the officers. They buttoned on the inside leg (three buttons).

In winter dress, they wore a scarlet red short sleeved cassock with white lace trim down the front and on the sleeves over the blue jacket.

When they took the Polish-style dress from1808 they had a light/ medium blue cloth kurtka; it had a scarlet collar with two white trefoil buttonhole laces. The kurtka had scarlet lapels closed to the waist with seven white trefoil buttonhole lacing on each side, and scarlet rounded cuffs bearing two white trefoil buttonhole laces and white metal buttons. The kurtka had short tails with scarlet turnbacks and blue shoulder straps.

They continued to wear the tight-fitting fall front trousers in light blue cloth with a white lace down the outer seam and on the cuffs of the trousers. Under their trousers they wore light black leather boots.

From 1808 they had the same trousers, but with white lace again. In service dress they had blue overalls with red piping down the outside seam and white metal buttons.

At least this is the theory; however a contemporary painting dated to 1813 shows them wearing a variety of dress, including the pre-1808 'Turkish' coat, items of hussar dress (pelisse) and a few items of the new uniform, post-1808 uhlan shako. Another interesting point is that, although they officially never went on campaign, the painting shows what appears to be a campaign bivouac. This was probably because they still used old uniform items of 'old stocks' for daily duty, reserving the new uniform for active service.

Arms and Equipment

The uhlans' principal arm was a varnished natural wood Bosniak lance M1791, with a steel lance blade and ferrule, and a red over white pennon.

The triangular spearhead had a length of 50cm ending in a hollow point, lengthened by two bars 59cm in length festooned to the shaft with three rivets. The total length of lance was *c.*2.5m, the same type used from 1791 until 1815 when a new (longer model with different spear point) was made for the new lancer regiments in 1816. The lance had a large leather loop at the middle and a smaller one on the bottom over the ferrule.

They carried a *Husarsabel* M1776/92, frequently referred to as the Bosniak/uhlan lancer's model sabre as a number were engraved with cabbalistic signs on the blade.

Danish Cavalry in Cloaks 1802–1814

Plate 17. Danish Cavalry in Cloaks 1802–1814

Top row, from left to right:
A Livgarden til Hest trooper *c.*1808. Rear view of a Rytter trooper showing the cut of the cloak, *c.*1802–1808. A Rytter officer wearing a privately made cloak worn over campaign dress *c.*1810. A Rytter trooper *c.*1814 in the new grey cloak.

Bottom row, from left to right:
A light dragoon trooper wearing a blue cloak made from 'French' cloth *c.*1814. A light dragoon trooper wearing the old regulation red cloak, which continued to be worn alongside the new grey model. A light dragoon officer wearing another variation of a privately made cloak. A Rytter officer wearing a privately made cloak which has a collar. Note; he is wearing the new undress Rytter officer's cap, said to be *c.*1812, but the contemporary illustration shows a waist sash so this must date to 1811 or very early 1812.

In fact the uhlans were issued with the old hussar sabres with new blades, when the hussars received new ones. The sabre had a single-bar iron hilt and black leather scabbard with iron fittings, carried on a light brown narrow leather sabre belt. When the men became uhlans they received some hussar M1791/1808 sabres.

They carried a pair of M1748/98 hussar pistols, one on the wide buff leather or light brown carbine belt from which a pistol was suspended from the carbine swivel, Polish-style, the other pistol was carried in the normal holster. As they were never issued with carbines they had a cartridge pouch on a thinner shoulder belt and carried a pistol ramrod suspended from their belt. They kept these brown leather belts until 1816. From 1808 they had a black leather cartridge pouch.

Horse Furniture

They used black leather harness and had red Hungarian-style shabraques with a white lace trim, and from 1808 they had exactly the same shabraques as the hussars.

The NCO insignias are unknown. We can assume that on the Turkish dress the laces were, as in the hussar squadrons, silver on the jacket and cloak and when in Polish dress all the buttonhole lacing and the NCOs' epaulettes were certainly silver.

Officers' Uniforms

In 1791 the officers wore the regimental Turkish-style dress in a similar style to the troop, with the white lace replaced with silver lace on jacket and the trouser seams. The rounded white turban was held in place with silvered chains around a red fez which had a blue plume. They wore a red cassock over this uniform in winter, with two bands of lace around the sleeve.

In 1808 when they were renamed, and their uniform was changed to the Polish-style uniform, they wore the regimental dress, but with gold buttonhole trefoils, buttons, laces and gold rank epaulettes according to the approbation drawings, but this is not borne out by the little other evidence we have, as Senn only shows silver/white lace and the czapskas do not show the gold embroidery lace. The plume on the approbation watercolour shows a blue, short but wide plume with a red base and gold and red cords and tassels, and Senn shows a tall, thin red over blue plume. The trousers had silver lace. Around their waist they wore a hussar sash, which was supposed to be red and gold, but in fact they appear to have worn a hussar model in silver and red. Rank was to be shown with epaulettes and they did not adopt the new rank system in 1812.

They had a white belt and bandolier, both edged in silver lace, and a red cartridge pouch laced silver. On campaign they had a black leather cartridge pouch with a crowned monogram in silver. The sabre strap and knot were red and gold.

The officers carried brass-mounted sabres of the same model as the hussars. They did not carry lances, but the troop leader carried an unofficial lance with an extra-large pennon, this is probably the so-called *Ralimentsfane*, a kind of unofficial troop pennon carried by troop leaders, so that the men could rally around them if necessary. The shaft was painted with red and blue bands and it had a large red over blue pennon.

The harness was virtually the same as the hussars and was made of black leather and decorated with cowries hells and they had a red Hungarian-style shabraque, theoretically with gold lace border and knot, but more likely to have been in silver like the hussars'.

NCOs' Distinctions

Their distinctions were a figure of eight epaulette with white fringes on right shoulder/each shoulder in silver on a blue base, and possibly an extra loop or a trefoil of lace on the cuffs.

Danish Cavalry Pistols

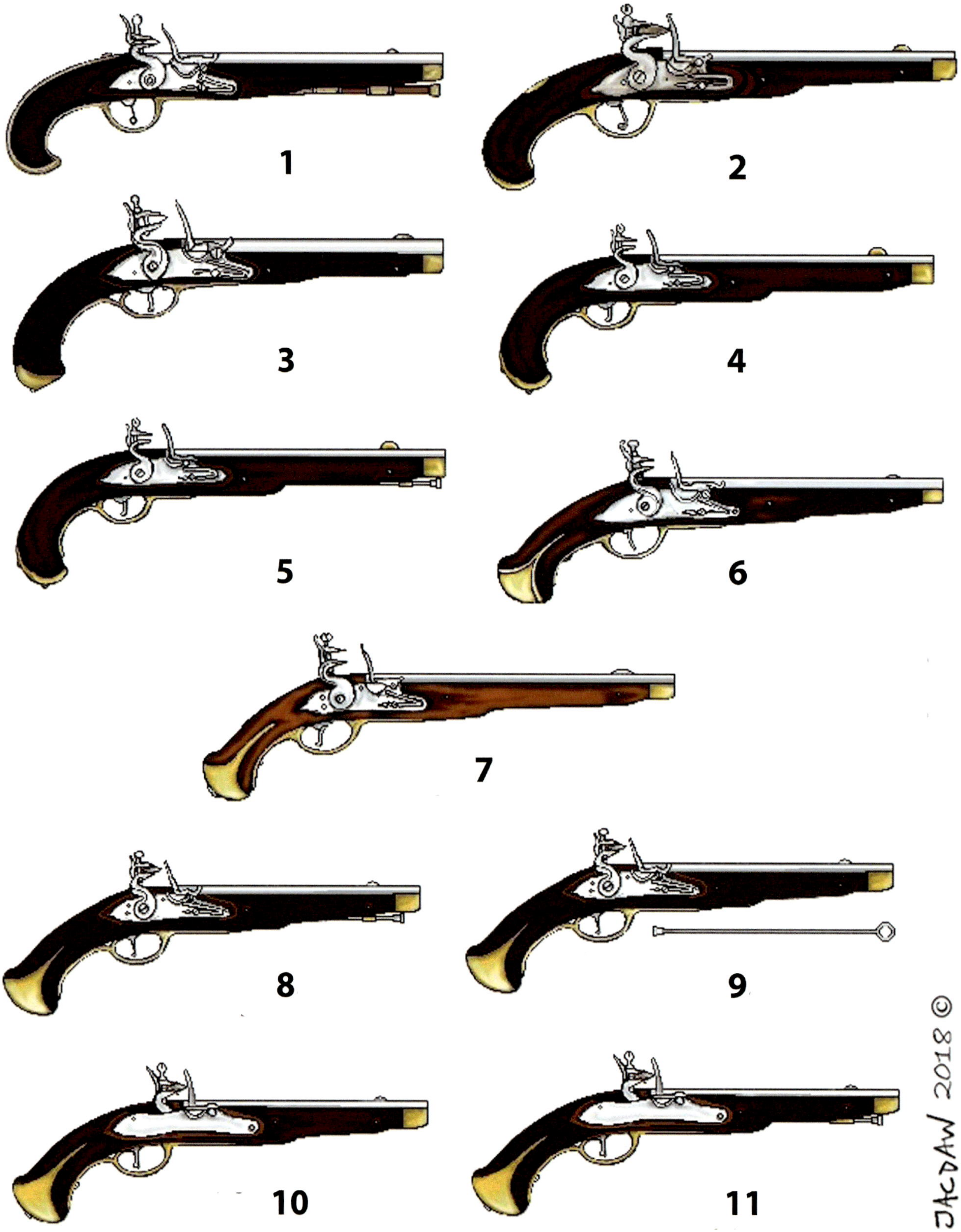

Plate 18. Danish Cavalry Pistols

Garderpistol M1748/1798, for the Livgarde til Hest. The length was 44cm, weight 1.34kg, calibre 17.5mm. This pistol had the ramrod inserted into the stock. Three hundred were made. The first of the parrot-beaked butts were modified a number of times as the 'beak' had a tendency to break.
Husarpistol M1751/1795. The length was 44.4cm, weight was 1.27kg, calibre was 17.5 mm. 1,400 of these were made.
Husarpistol M1777/1795. The length was 44.4cm, weight was 1.27kg, calibre was 17.5 mm. 1,400 of these were made.
Husarpistol M1777/1798. The length was 44cm, the weight was 1.20kg, calibre was 17.5mm. 2,400 of these were made. Converted in 1798 by filling in the ramrod canal.
Husarpistol M1795, officer's version, it is not known how many of these pistols were made.
Rytterpistol M1772/1798. The length was 46cm, weight was 1.53kg, calibre was 17.5mm. 2,500 of these were made.
Rytterpistol M1751/1798. The length was 45cm, weight was 1.60kg, calibre was 17.5mm. 2,080 of these were made.
Rytterpistol M1806. The length was 45cm, weight was 1.33kg, calibre was 17.5mm and the barrel was 27cm long. The number of these pistols made is not known, probably around 2,000. It is shown with the special ramrod which was only used for a pistol.
Rytterpistol M1806, officer's version. It is not known how many of these pistols were made.
Rytterpistol M1807. First model with the new 'inside' lock. The length was 44.7cm, weight was 1.30kg, calibre was 17. 5mm. 3,000 of these were made.
Rytterpistol M1807, officer's version. The number of these pistols made is not known.
Sources: collection and archives of the Tøjhusmuseet, Copenhagen, now called the Krigsmuseet.

Note, the firearms carried by the troopers, NCOs and trumpeters had separate ramrods, no provision was made for the ramrods to be inserted into the stocks of cavalry weapons and the ramrods had to be carried separately, usually suspended from the waist belt. There were two sizes of ramrods, a long trooper's version for use with both the carbine and the pistol, and a shorter version for pistols only, carried by NCOs and trumpeters. The officers' pistols had the ramrods inserted into the stocks. The calibre noted by the Danes always refers to the ball and not the bore as they were variable, and as they became worn this obviously had a negative effect on accuracy.

Trumpeters' Uniforms

The trumpeters' wore the same uniform as the NCOs. Their distinctions were an epaulette on each shoulder in the button colour on a blue base and an extra loop of lace on the cuffs. His trumpet was silvered as for the hussars. It was carried on a silver/ white cord.

The Sjællandske Hussar Corps

In 1813 a special detachment of 225 hussars (five officers 16 NCOs, five trumpeters, and 200 hussars) was to be raised, following a French request, under the name of the Sjællandske Hussar Corps.

This short-lived unit was created by raising volunteers from all six cavalry regiments and the mounted Sjællanske Ridende Jæger Corps which was stationed on Zealand with a cadre of six NCOs and 100 troopers. The rest were to be found from hussar recruits in Holstein and former cavalrymen from the *annekterede* battalions. Also 225 horses were found in Holstein and collected in the horse depot of Itzehoe.

They were promised uniforms, to be made by the French authorities in Hamburg in the same style as the other hussars, but with yellow cords and probably a shako. The promised uniforms were to be collected from Hamburg, but no one appears to have ever received them, and the troopers apparently served in the uniforms from their parent regiments. The five officers destined to lead the corps, who had travelled ahead to organise it, were nearly all transferred back into existing formations as due to sickness there was a general lack of cavalry officers. So in the end few served with the corps as intended before or after 11 December (the exact number is unknown, but probably only one or two).

On 6 December the cadre of six NCOs and 106 troopers (all mounted) arrived at the fortress of Rensburg which had no cavalry at the time, and was in danger of

Danish Cavalry Longarms

Plate 19. Danish Cavalry Longarms

1. *Rytterkarabin* (carbine) M1755, this carbine was only carried by the Livarde til Hest (Royal Horse Guards).
2. *Dragongevær* M1767 with its bayonet. The calibre was 17.6 mm, weight was 4.6kg, length was 140.7 cm. There were some 10,000 examples of this musket made, including the Model 1767 and 1769. Another 3,000 were made of the later model, the M1785/88. This was absolutely the most numerous firearm ever made for the cavalry. But also it was the least used of any by the cavalry: most were converted into *Skarpskyttegevær* Model 1789 muskets. They were only used generally by the cavalry in Norway until *c.*1808–11, when they were re-equipped with carbines, and on the dragoons of the island of Bornholm (who continued to use them until 1855). Both the left and right sides are shown, including ring and slider. This model still had its ramrod stowed under the barrel.
3. *Husarkarabin* M1795. The length was 90cm, weight was 2.60kg, calibre was 17.7mm. Number made, 1,800. Although this was called a *husarkarabin* (hussar carbine), in fact the hussars were never issued with them. Each of the light dragoon regiments received 600 of them. The Model 1777/98 was similar in appearance, some 10cm shorter with a slightly larger bore. Calibre 18.1mm, weight 2.63kg, total length 79.2cm.
4. *Rytterkarabin* M1750/ 55/1798. The calibre was 17.6mm, weight was 2.85kg, length was 89.3cm. The number made is unknown, but probably around 3,000; as all were converted from different types of older cavalry carbines there are some minor variations. Both the left and right sides are shown, including ring and slider.
5. *Riflet* [rifled] *Dragonkarabin* M1798. The length was 89.5cm, weight was 2.71kg, calibre was 16.5mm. Number made, 400. These carbines were used by the 'flankers', hence low quantity produced.
6. *Rytterkarabin* M1807. The length was 89.6cm, weight was 2.48kg, calibre was 17.5mm. Number made, unknown. This model had a hinged slider. The *Riflet* [rifled] *Rytterkarabin* Model 1807 looked the same, except for the rifling of the barrel and the rear sight. The calibre was 16.5mm, weight unknown, length was 89.6cm. Between 300 to 400 examples of this rifle were made.
7. *Jægerkarabin* for Ridende Jæger M1791. Length 91cm, weight 3.36kg, calibre was 15.7mm. One hundred of these arms were made, but only 24 had the slider for mounted use by the 'Feltjæger Corpset'. This carbine had a ramrod carried in the stock. This arm was never used by the cavalry, with the exception of the Guides.
8. *Husarkarabin* Model 1806 (with new type of 'hinged' carbine bar) with a view of the slider from the underside. The calibre was 17.5mm, weight unknown, length was 92.8cm.
9. Universal cavalry ramrod for carbine and pistols, carried suspended from the waist belt.

Sources: collection and archives of the Tøjhusmuseet, Copenhagen, now called the Krigsmuseet.

being attacked by superior forces. *Løjtnant* Edvard von Ewald, the brother of Johannes von Ewald who was on sick leave in Rensburg at the time, took command of the corps and started active patrols, keeping enemy forces at bay until his force was relieved on 9 December by the Jyske Lette Dragoner Regiment, and on 10 December by the complete 'Auxiliair Corps'.

On 11 December the corps was incorporated in to the cavalry brigade of the auxiliary corps, until disbanded on 18 January 1814.

There was another hussar detachment that was also, in a way, part of the Sjællandske Hussar Corps, but it was generally known as 'Ewald's Hussar Corps' and also served with distinctions. The story was as follows. In the depot of Itzehoe an officer, five NCOs, a trumpeter and 27 hussar recruits had been gathered for the Sjællandske Hussar Corps, together with an officer and 94 dragoon recruits also partly intended for the same unit. There were 230 horses in the stables for their use. The depot at Itzehoe also contained large stores, archives, a remount depot, training school horses and a hospital. The officers in charge were old and not inclined to engage any active operations, which meant that on 5 and 6 December, when they were informed of the retreat of the Danish forces to the north and given orders to follow or to move to the nearest fortified position, nothing was done.

Table III. Hussar Officers' Distinctions	
Second Lieutenant (*Sekondløjtnant*)	Silver Lace
First lieutenant (Premierløjtnant)	Silver lace and one silver button
Captain (*Ritmester*)	Silver Hungarian knot and three silver buttons
Major (*Major*)	Silver Hungarian knot and one gold rosette
Lieutenant Colonel (*Oberstløjtnant*)	Silver Hungarian knot and two gold rosettes
Colonel (*Oberst*)	Silver Hungarian knot and three gold rosettes

Instead, on 7 December the place was raided by 200 Cossacks, and as no ammunition had been issued to the soldiers, after a short fight the place was taken with 34 prisoners, all of the training school horses, the stores and some of the horses intended for the Sjællandske Hussar Corps.

However the hussar recruits and their NCOs, together with a couple of their officers and some of the dragoon recruits, managed to escape, together with a large number of their horses, and they marched to the fortress of Glückstadt, arriving on 10 December. They did not receive much of a welcome from the old fortress commander, *Generalmajor* Czernickow, however, as he felt he had no need of cavalry within his command.

The older brother of Edvard von Ewald, Johannes von Ewald, was considered probably one of the best officers of the hussar regiment: he had distinguished himself on numerous occasions for example at Stralsund in 1809 (where he received the Order of Dannebrog), and also during several other combats during the campaign of 1813, notably at Gadebush. During the above-described events at Itzehoe he was on sick leave in Glückstadt, and as always had his younger brother at his side. He at once took the command of the hussar and dragoon recruits, and together with former cavalrymen and others on sick leave, he formed a 'hussar corps' of four officers, one trumpeter and 92 'hussars'. Few had uniforms, as they had travelled partly in civilian dress to escape capture. Von Ewald at once took care of this by collecting the uniforms of all the cavalrymen in the hospitals, and demanding all the tailors to sew him uniforms of a 'hussar style', but also 'black lancers' uniforms and green uniforms' (they are all described as 'fantasy uniforms', but they were probably 'Litewka'-style coats). Later, captured enemy uniforms were also used.

All the depots were scoured for cavalry weapons, surplus uniforms and headgear. As soon as 11 December he went on his first raid, capturing a postmaster working as spy for the enemy. Over the next few days active patrolling forced the enemy cavalry back, and several prisoners were taken, bringing in vital information. During this patrolling, von Ewald had his hussars dressed in different uniforms, totally confusing the enemy of his true strength, and convincing them that there was also a large force of French cavalry in the fortress (so presumably at least a couple of men were dressed in a uniform resembling a French uniform, although we do not know which one!) On 17 December von Ewald led a major foraging raid, bringing in much needed supplies for the fortress, although the next day it was closely invested, and he was no longer able to raid and patrol.

From 22 December the following detachments were also part of the corps: around 60 mounted Jaegers of the volunteer Jyske Jaeger Corps (in their green uniforms) and 22 heavy cavalry troopers from the Holstenske Rytter Regiment. In the end they had a complement of around 150 mounted soldiers. Instead he took a active part in the defence of the fortress, and later in the talks about terms of surrender, as *Generalmajor* Czernickow – seeing the situation as hopeless – managed on 6 January 1814 to negotiate an honourable treaty of surrender 'to leave the fortress with their arms, and standards flying'. During the march out of the fortress, one of the *annekterede* battalions of Dronningens Livregiment became disorderly (apparently drunk), and began deserting. Von Ewald took one of their standards and brought it safely with his unit, but maintained strict control of his disciplined 'hussar corps', who trotted out in their best uniforms, with their standard and von Ewald in the front. The enemy detachment did not show his corps the respect they were due and with swords drawn they were called to attention by von Ewald, to let him pass at attention. Two enemy officers insulted him, at which he responded immediately by challenging them to a duel, and severely wounded both of them. Forthwith everybody now showed him and his corps the respect they deserved, and without anymore hindrances they rode north to join the main army. A true hussar!

6

The Cavalry Standards

Generalities

In 1785, when the infantry had received a completely new stand of colours, the cavalry regiments were not issued with new standards; they had to continue using their old ones, sometimes very old ones.

Here the older standards were carried much longer. However, in 1795, because of a specific case:

> As the standards and pauke [kettle drum banners] standards of the 'Slesvigske Rytter Regiment', are now in total tatters, a new standard will be given to this regiment. They shall [now] be painted [not embroidered]. The Dannebrog at topmost corner, royal cyphers in remaining corners, the shield of its province [Or the royal shield of arms in case of 'a royal regiment'] and the main colour the regimental one. This will also be the design on any further standards, and Kettledrum [pauke] banners given to the other regiments.

The 1785 reform of standards and colours did not just concern their decoration but also a reform of how they were made. Until then they had all been embroidered, often with lots of fringes etc., but from 1785 all infantry colours were to be painted on silk cloth. Also the white 'life colour' was no longer allowed. The same was to be applied to the cavalry standards, but while the infantry changed at once (because their old colours were needed to equip the newly organised Norwegian infantry regiments), the cavalry were allowed to keep all their pre-1785 standards and continue to use them for now.

However in 1795 the standards of the Slesvigske Rytter Regiment were totally worn out, and as a consequence this regiment was the very first allowed to change its standards into the new painted model (so all painted standards must then be the Model 1795). The new cavalry standards were to lose their fringes as well.

This was not a general issue, but only 'when in tatters'. Shortly afterwards the *Paukes* (kettledrums) and their banners, as an economy measure were 'Not to be used anymore as too costly for the regiments.' The money saved would be better used in the future to form cavalry and NCO schools. In 1799 the hussars were ordered not to use kettledrums any more.

Most cavalry regiments seem to have clung on to their old standards anyway, often because of regimental veneration. The Livgarde til Hest, the Livregiment Lette Dragoner and the Fynske Regiment Lette Dragoner are known examples.

In 1808 a new standard with the new king's monogram and a new finial was introduced (the first one was issued to Prins Frederik Ferdinands Dragoner), but no others are known to have been issued before 1815 at the earliest.

The cavalry regiments each consisted of four squadrons, except for the Horse Guards who only had two small squadrons, each of which, according to the 1795 regulations, carried an identical squadron standard; the cavalry does not appear to have been officially issued with the King's colours, white standards, but they do appear to have kept those which had been issued previously. The standards were made of silk, and were around 64cm long x 55cm high, generally they appear to have been in the regiments facing colour and were decorated in the same style as the infantry regiments and with some regimental variations.

The finials varied from regiment to regiment, but the basic model was a brass-gilded triangular pointed pike head with the crowned monogram of Christian VII chiselled out in the centre, and had rather long red and gold or silver cords with tassels.

In 1808 a new model of standard with the new king's monogram and a new finial were designed (the first and the only one issued before 1815,was issued to the Prins Frederik Ferdinands Dragoner). In a royal resolution of 23 August 1808 (with a drawing not yet found), a standard for the regiment was approved to be made (four examples). The following description can be made out from the text: it was to be black, with the Prince's arms shield, and with 'F.VI' cypher under a crown in the three corners. It would have cords in gold and red. The standards were so issued after this date.

The colours were nailed to the staves with gilt tacks and over a strip of white cloth, which served to reinforce the colour and avoid tearing, so most of the colours would have this white strip of cloth on the staff; sometimes the strip was nailed over the colour.

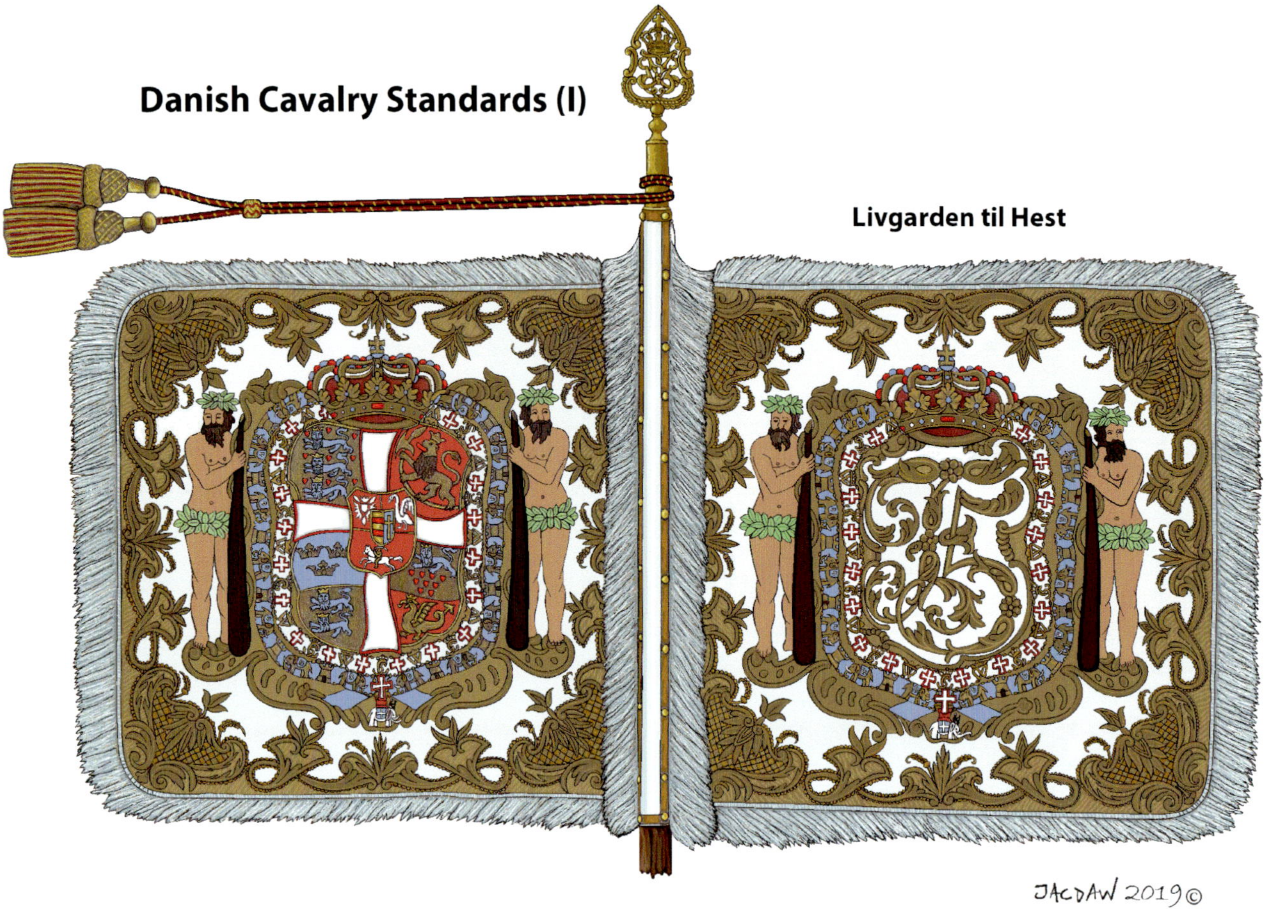

Cavalry standards were mounted on a staff 2m 60cm in length and had a slider-type handle for clipping to the carabiner of the bandolier.

The bandoliers were of leather covered with red or crimson cloth, possibly velvet; they were generally heavily embroidered and fringed in the button colour, according to a surviving example and a period print, and they had a brass ring to attach the carabiner.

The Life Guards, Livgarden til Hest

In 1758 they had originally received four new identical standards, but because of their reduction to only two squadrons in 1763 they carried only two, one for each squadron, of silk damask with silver fringes. Both standards had a white damask field. On the obverse there was a gold embroidered floral border all around the edge, in the centre there was the gold embroidered crowned (crown with red bonnet and red and blue stones) monogram of Frederik V within two collars, the outer collar being the Order of the Elephant and inner collar that of the Order of the Dannebrog.[1]

The obverse had the same gold embroidered floral border with in the centre a gold crown with a red bonnet over the full arms of the kingdom within two collars, the outer collar being the Order of the elephant and inner collar that of the Order of the Dannebrog, held by two supporters, wild men in natural colours. The reverse bore the crowned monogram Frederick Vin silver on a red shield, surrounded with silver embroidery and fringes. The standard of the 2nd squadron was identical with the same embroidered motifs in gold and silver fringes.

The fringes are generally shown as gold, but this is may be an error, as the silver has probably discoloured with age and they now appear to be brown: even an artist who painted them *c.*1800 added yellow brown fringes, so they must have already become discoloured due to nearly 50 years' service. Both the approbation design and clothing

1 The two 'Order chains' found on Royal standards and colours are the two highest Orders of the Danish monarchy. The outer most chain is that of the 'Order of the Elephant': The chain has alternate elephants (with a blue cloth bearing a silver embroidered 'D' for Dacia = Denmark), and crenellated gold towers (the doors are only placed on one tower in two). It was created in *c.*1457, and was formalised in 1693. The inner 'order chain' belongs to the Order of the Dannebrog. According to the myth, Denmark received the first 'Dannebrog' from the sky during a battle in Estonia in 1219 (800 years ago, it was commemorated in 2019). This happened during the reign of Waldemar II, so his crowned 'W' is the first symbol between the crosses. Then comes the 'Cross of the Dannebrog'. As King Christian V created the Order in 1693, his crowned monogram 'C5' is placed alternately between the crosses and the Ws. At the bottom there is a white 'Dannebrog' cross.

bill confirm the silver fringes, in fact it was traditional for all cavalry regiments in Denmark to have silver-fringed standards. However until a though examination and restoration is carried out and the fringes are analysed there will always be a doubt.

The stave was 2m 50cm long with a long slider. The gilt finials have the double reversed monogram of Frederik V which were cast and cut out. The cords and tassels were gold and crimson mixed.

The standards were carried on shoulder belts. These were silver, piped red and embroidered with floral motifs, the belt had a silver fringe.

Apparently two other 'restored' standards and two 'restored' kettledrum banners were on display for several years at Christiansborg Castle; they had been in use until the disbandment of the Royal Horse Guards. They were, as far as we can ascertain, restored somewhere between 1800 and 1828 and were used as ordinary everyday service standards. The earlier M1720 standards are also preserved in the Tøjhusmuseet. See Appendix I for a complete history.

Livregiment of Heavy Cavalry, Livregiment Ryttere

They had had four standards, one of white silk *Livfane* (ref. no. 236) and three of pale yellow or buff silk squadron standards (two are preserved under ref. nos.237 and 238). The obverse motif is unknown; on the reverse; in the centre is the crowned arms of Denmark with two wild men as supporters, it is possible that it had the same design on the obverse. The standards had silver fringes and cords. There is no exact dating of these standards but they are noted as 'M1785', which may be misleading because if they are embroidered and bear the 'C7' monogram, we can only really date them as 1766–1785. If embroidered but with no royal monogram, they must be older than 1766. The Livregiment Ryttere had a number of names and organisational changes between 1763 and 1772, so may have received new standards in one of those years, but nothing is recorded so it is difficult to know what happened.

The model 1785 was definitely white and the arms and supporters in natural colours were larger than normal, taking up most of the surface of the standard. The standard of the 2nd Squadron does not appear to have had the Dannebrog on it. The yellow stave was 2m 60cm long. The obverse and reverse were identical.

The Schleswig Heavy Cavalry Regiment, Slesvigske Rytter Regiment

The regiment had four standards M1795. Theoretically they were of medium blue silk with, painted in the centre, a gold crown with a red bonnet over the arms of Schleswig, on a shield, which were Or, two lions Azure within a gold frame. When on display in the arsenal of Rensburg *c.*1820, they were described as 'light blue' in colour which would correspond more or less with the regiment's facing colours, which were medium blue. I say they were medium blue 'theoretically' because a contemporary illustration shows them as green but without explanation, perhaps due to an error by the colourist, or more likely due to fading and or discolouration. Today they are faded to a very greyish/bluish colour, and were probably already beginning to fade in 1820.

There was a canton with a Dannebrog in the top hoist and a yellow flame on each side. In the other three corners there was a gold crown and the monogram 'C7' within green laurel wreaths. There were no fringes, but silver cords and tassels. The obverse and reverse were identical. The red stave was two metres 51cm long and it was shaped as a slim, stylised jousting lance.

The Holstein Heavy Cavalry Regiment, Holstenske Ryttere Regiment

The regiment had four M1795 regimental standards of grass green silk. Painted in the centre was a gold crown with a red bonnet over the arms of Holstein, which were Gules a nettle leaf Argent charged with an escutcheon, per fess Argent and Gules, within a golden frame.

There was a canton with a Dannebrog in the top hoist and a yellow flame on each side. In the other three corners there was a gold crown and the monogram 'C7' within green laurel wreaths. There were no fringes, but gold cords and tassels. The obverse and reverse were identical.

Note: on 4 September 1813 the 4th Squadron lost its standard to the Swedish cavalry. The standard was kept as a trophy in Sweden and is still preserved in the Swedish Army Museum, reference ST5:143. It is now pale yellow in colour, having completely faded.

In 1851 all the remaining standards hanging in Rensburg Arsenal (including the new 4th Squadron standard) were described as light green. The red stave was 1m 83cm long.

The Zealand Heavy Cavalry Regiment, Sjællandske Rytter Regiment

The regiment had four M1783 standards of silk, the standard of the Life Squadron had a white field, and the other three had blue fields. The obverse bore the arms of Or, three lions passant Azure crowned Or, armed Gules within a gold frame, surrounded with a trophy of standards and kettle drums. The Order of the Elephant was beneath. In each corner there was a flame burst.

The reverse had a scroll with the motto 'LYKKEN FØYER DEN DRISTIGE', 'Fortune Favours the Brave', under a crowned double 'C7' cypher. In each corner there was a flame burst. The embroidery, fringes and cords were silver. The obverse and reverse were identical. The red stave was 2m 20cm long.

Danish Cavalry Standards (II)

Liv Regiment Rytter M1785 Liv Standard

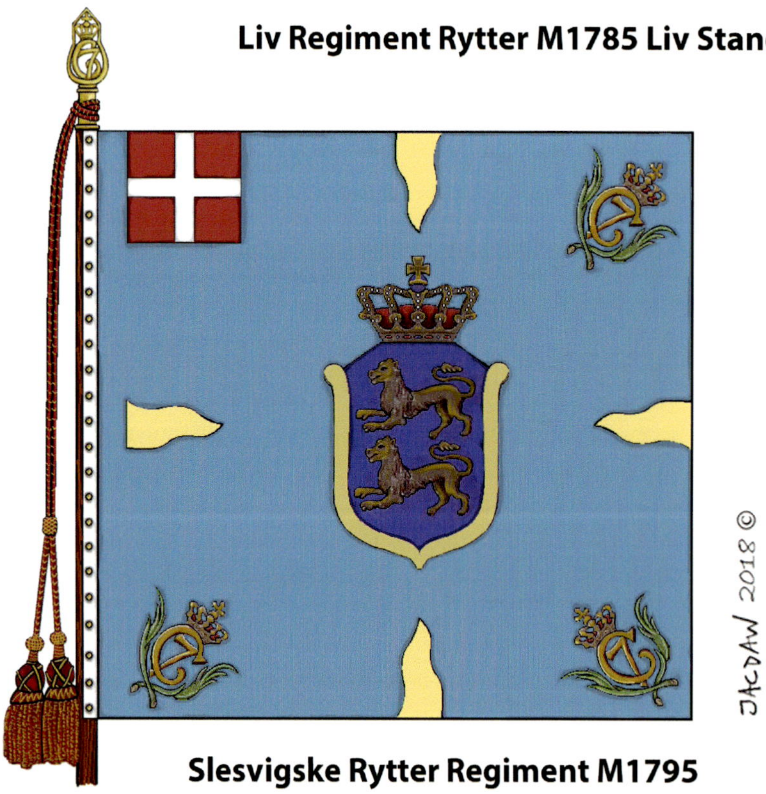

Slesvigske Rytter Regiment M1795

Danish Cavalry Standards (III)

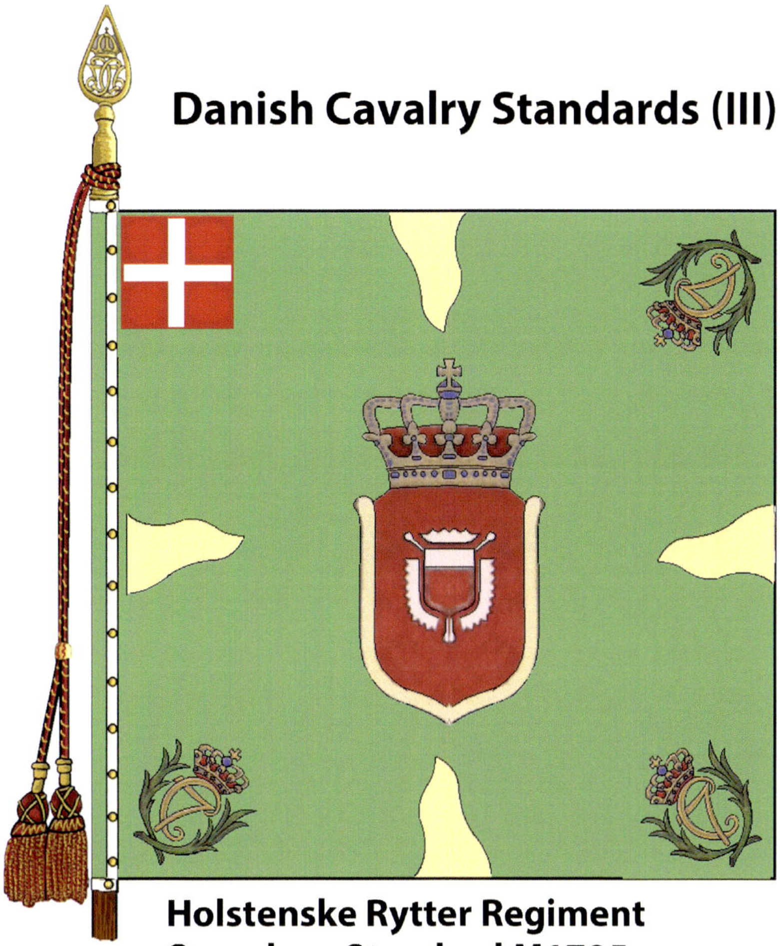

Holstenske Rytter Regiment
Squadron Standard M1795

Holstenske Rytter Regiment
Squadron Standard M1814
*** only one made, to replace standard lost to the Swedish**

Danish Cavalry Standards (IV)

A

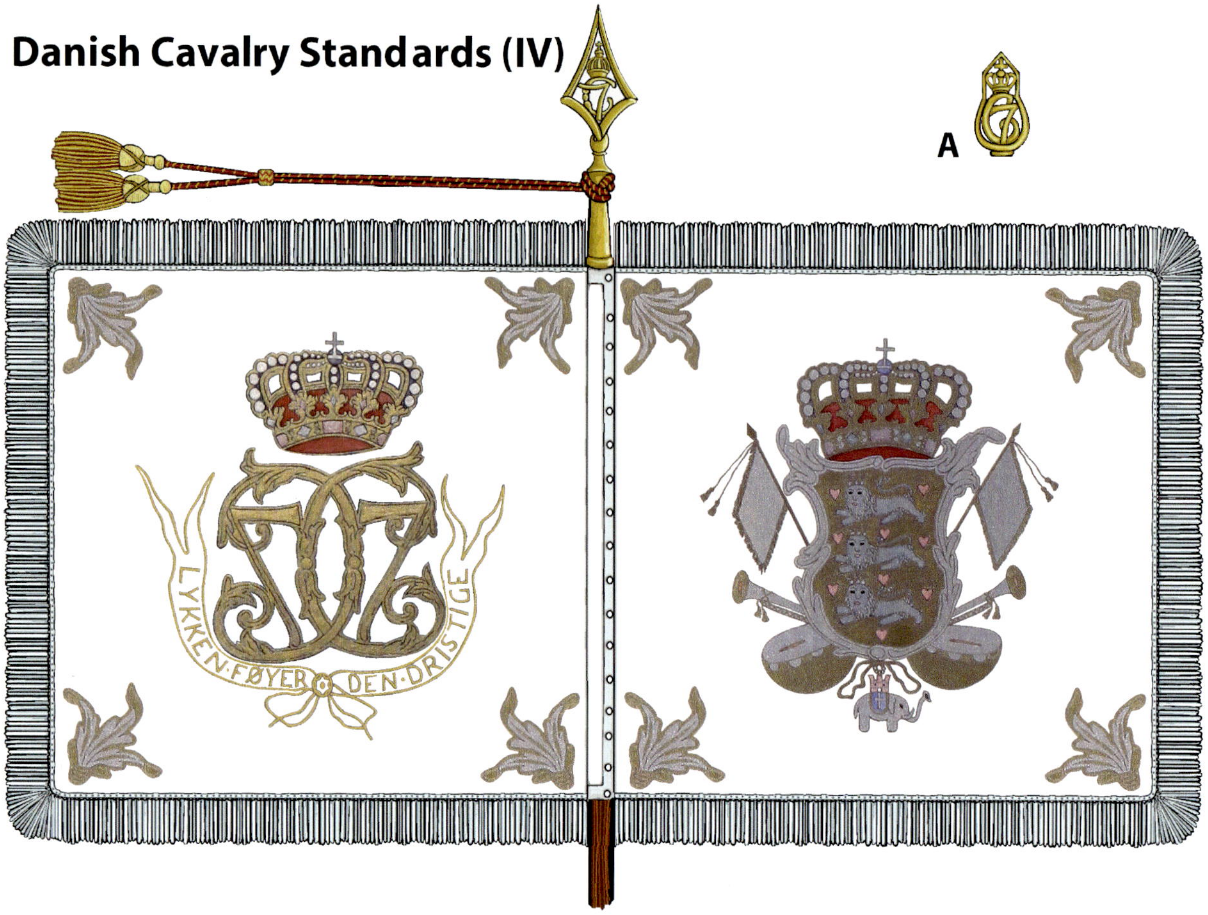

Sjaellandske Rytter Regiment, Liv Standard 1783–1808

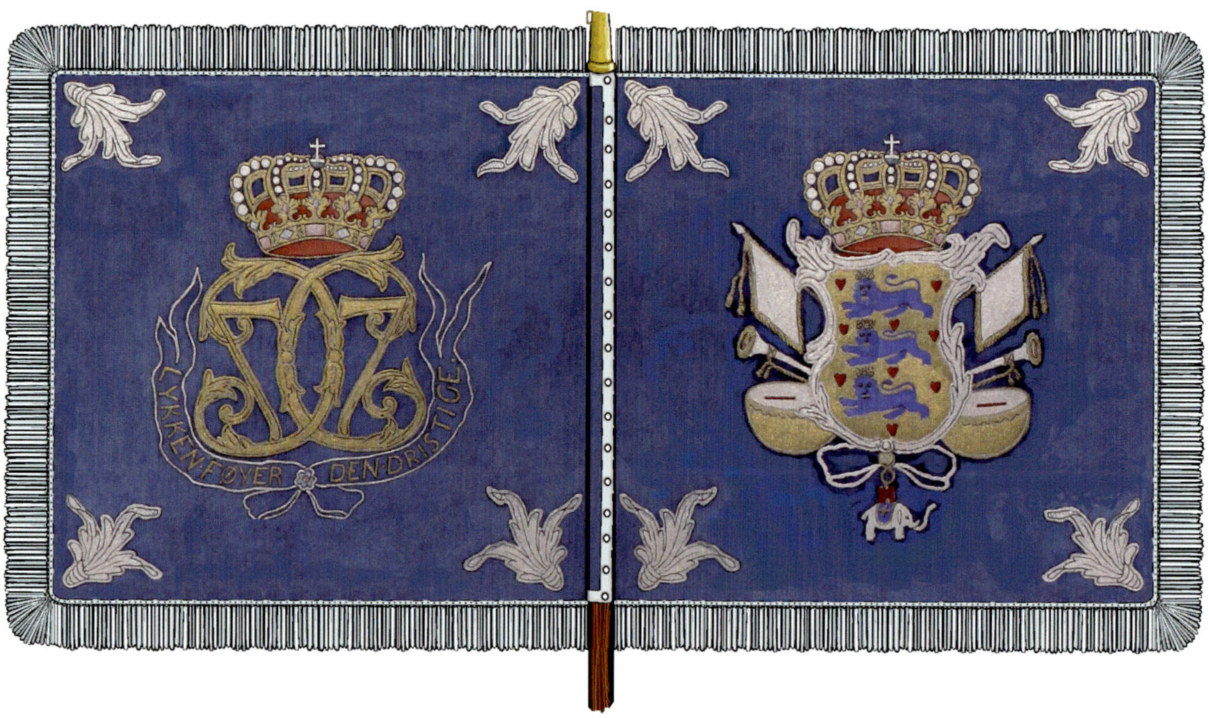

Sjaellandske Rytter Regiment, Squadron Standard 1783–1808

Danish Cavalry Standards (V)

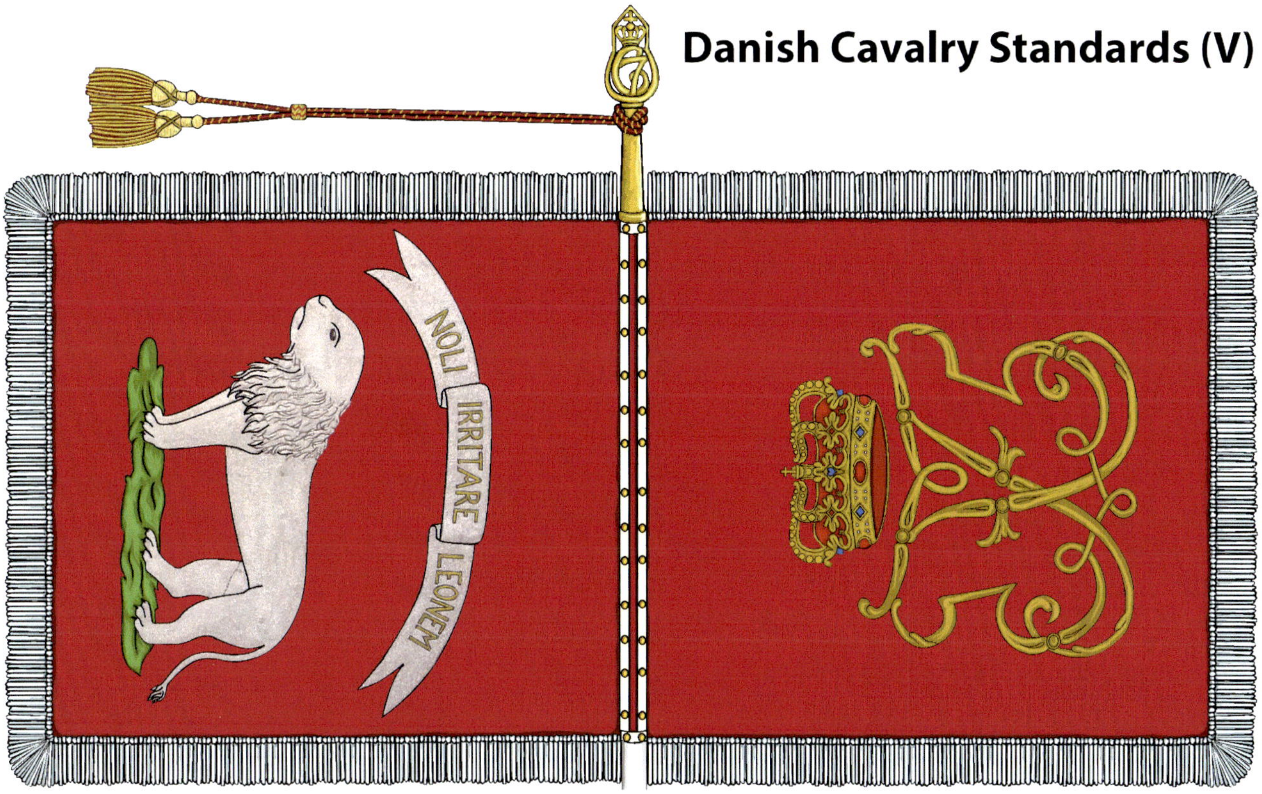

Liv Regiment Lette Dragoner *c.*1750–1814

JACDAW 2018 ©

Jyske Regiment Lette Dragoner M1804

Danish Cavalry Standards (VI)

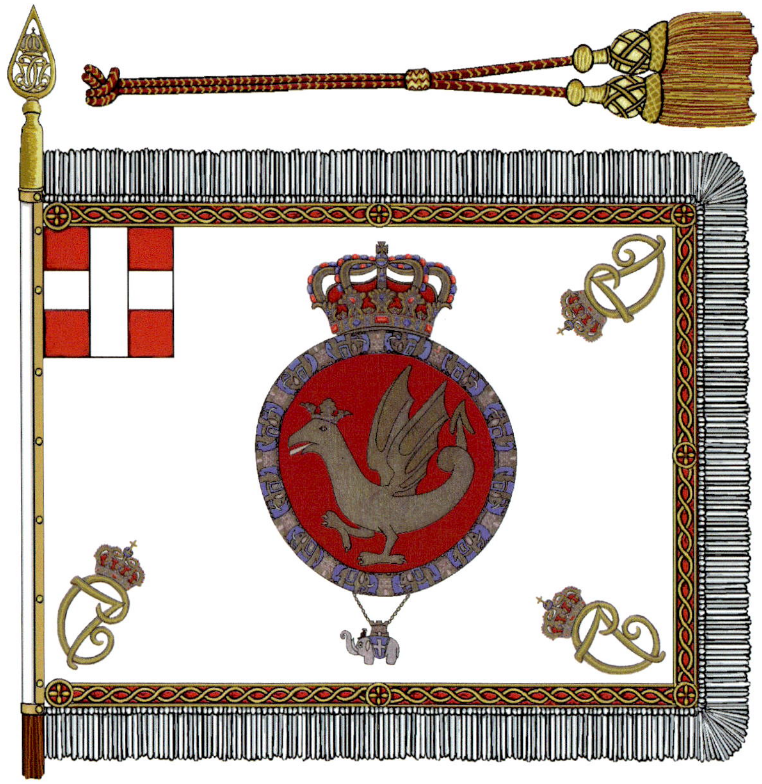

Fynske Lette Dragoner, Liv Standard *c*.1782

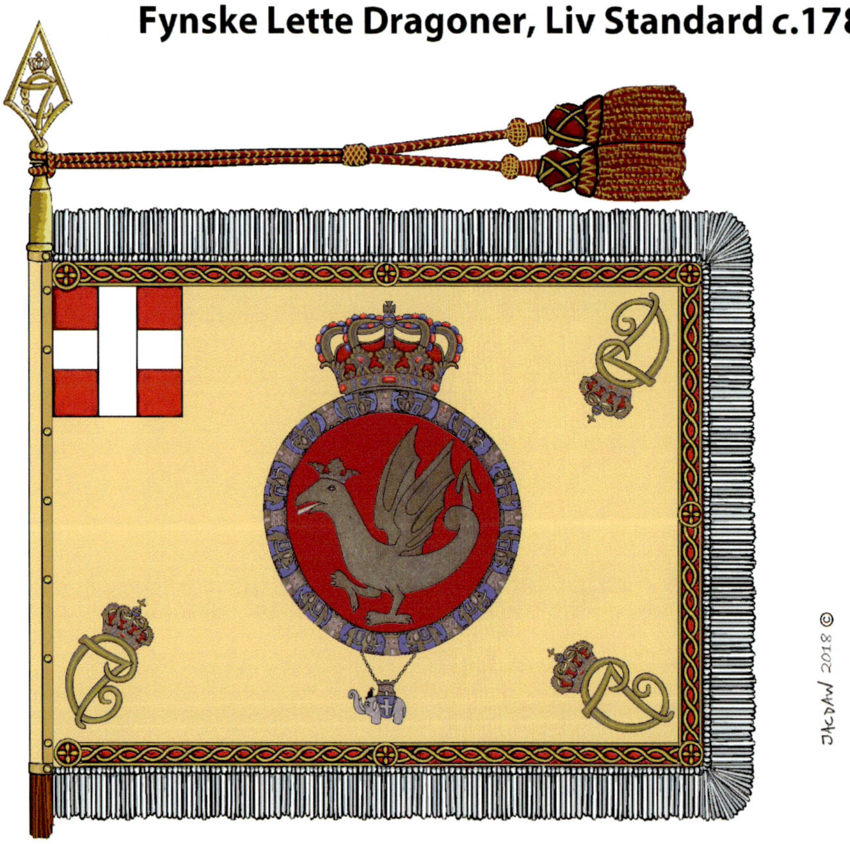

Fynske Lette Dragoner, Squadron Standard, *c*.1782

Danish Cavalry Standards (VII)

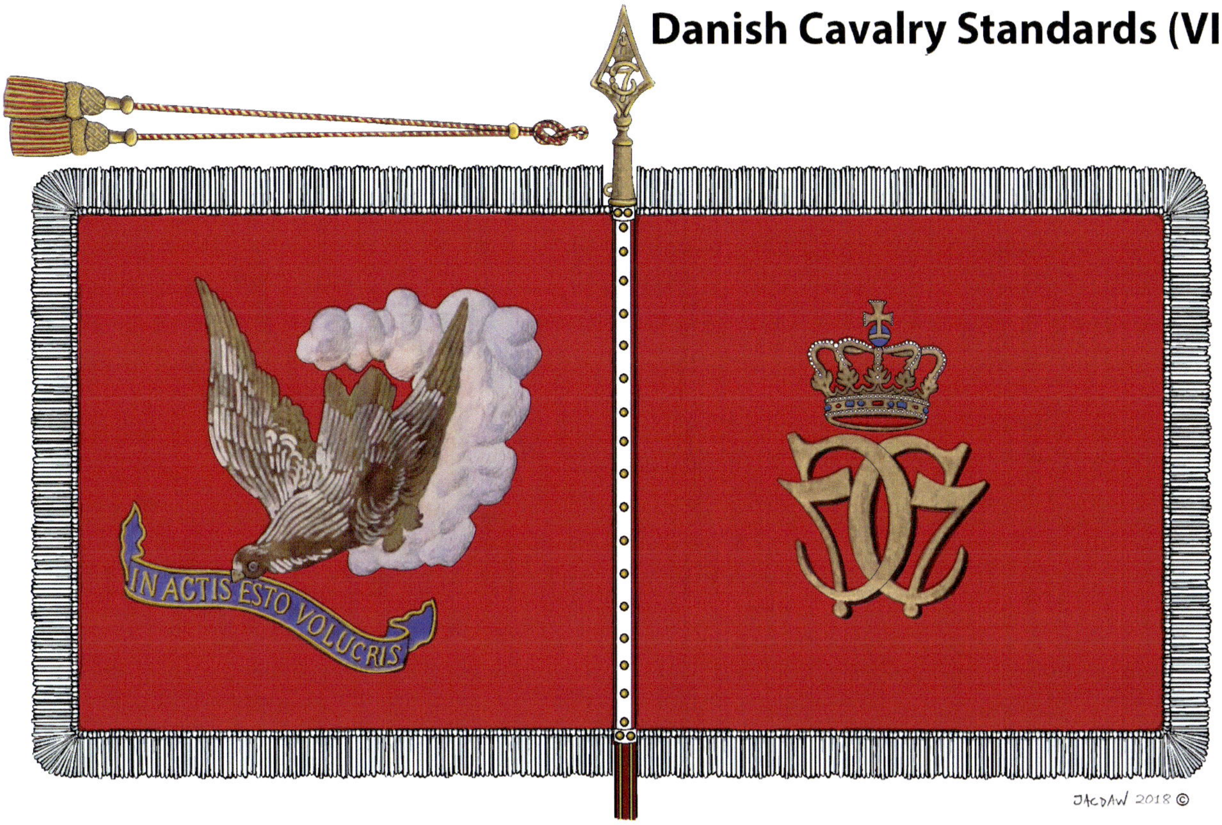

Hussar Regiment, Squadron Standard
Model C7. Carried until 1816 at least

Danish Cavalry Fanion
Fanion Sjaellandske Ryter Regiment *c*.1778

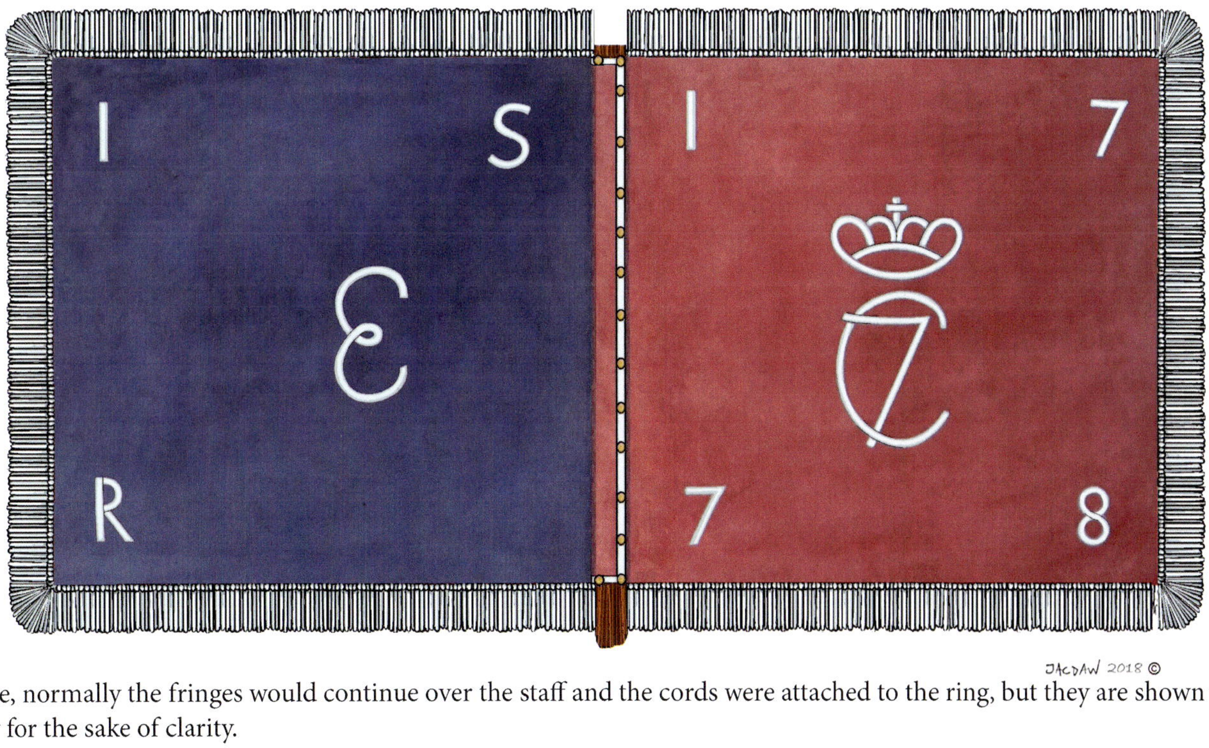

Note, normally the fringes would continue over the staff and the cords were attached to the ring, but they are shown this way for the sake of clarity.

The regiment also had a number of fanions, the model we know dates to 1778. The obverse was crimson red, in the centre was a crowned cypher of Christian VII outlined in silver tape. In each angle there was: top shaft a number 1, top fly a number 7, bottom shaft a number 7, bottom fly a number 8, all in silver tape. The reverse was deep blue with, in the centre, a reversed number 3 outlined in silver tape, and in each angle, top shaft an S, top fly an I, bottom fly an R, all in silver tape. The fanion had a thin silver fringe all around.

The Lette Dragoner (Light Dragoons)

In the light dragoon regiments, each squadron was issued with a standard also made of silk, they were 64cm long x 55cm high, the same size as the cavalry, in the regiment's facing colour and were decorated in the same style as the infantry regiments and with some regimental variations. These standards did not have any fringes.

Prins Frederic Ferdinand Dragoner Regiment

Originally raised as the Sjællandske Dragoner Regiment (Zealand Dragoon Regiment) in 1807, they were renamed the Prins Frederic Ferdinand Dragoner Regiment in December 1808, and Prins Frederic Ferdinand Lette Dragoner Regiment in 1816.

In a royal resolution on 23 August 1808 (with a drawing since lost), a standard for the regiment is approved to be made (four standards, one for each squadron). The following description can be made out from the text: they were to be black, with the Prince's arms shield, with a crowned 'F.VI' cypher in the three corners; it would have red and gold cords. So the standards were obviously issued after this date.

The standards attributed earlier to the regiment were first issued after 1819, so there is some doubt as to their exact appearance. However we do know for two very clear reasons that that the standards earlier attributed the regiment were first issued after 1819: firstly the wreath finial is dated to *c.*1819–1820 and these finials were only issued to a very few units (Bornholm Militia dragoons and hussars) in the same time frame. Secondly, the colour shows the new Danish Royal armorials, minus the Lion of Norway, again only officially instituted in 1819, but forcibly after 1815 when Norway had been invaded and occupied by Sweden.

The Livregiment Lette Dragoner

This regiment had four very old standards which have erroneously been described by some sources as being in use since 1693. They were made of red silk with silver fringes, on the obverse there was a gold crown over the silver monogram of 'F5', (Frederick V) and this clearly dates them to between 1746–1766, probably from the earlier part of his reign. On the reverse there was a lion with a collar standing on under a silver scroll with the motto 'NOLI IRRITARE LEONEM' (do not annoy the lion).

As all regiments had been allowed one white 'life standard' until 1785 it is more than probable that one of the four which are preserved at the Tøjhusmuseet under the reference numbers 124–127) is a white 'life standard'. The dimensions were approximately 56cm long x 48cm high. The standards had crimson and gold cords and tassels. Apparently it was carried until after the end of the war, when a standard was issued of the same style as that made for Prins Frederik Ferdinands Dragoner.

The Jutland Light Dragoons, or the Jyske Lette Dragoner Regiment

These colours had a dark green field, with a gold crown in the centre with a red bonnet, over a shield bearing the arms of Jutland within a wreath under a red scroll bearing the device 'FORTES FORTUNA JUNTA (JUVAT)', (fortune favours the brave), and the date in Roman numerals of M DCCXC IV (1794) underneath the central shield in gold lettering.

There was a canton with a Dannebrog in the top hoist and a red flame on each side. In the other three corners there was a gold crown and the monogram 'C7' within green laurel wreaths. The standards had silver fringes, cords and tassels. The obverse and reverse were identical.

A picture of a squadron marker flag/fanion of this regiment exists, it follows the standard pattern, pale yellow or green with a Dannebrog, the crowned Danish arms in the centre surrounded by a collar of the Order of the elephant and the text 'J R : l : D' above the arms and '1st Squadron' below. The natural wooden stave was 1m 82cm long.

The Fünen Light Dragoons or the Fynske Lette Dragoner Regiment

In 1795 the regiment had a kept an old white life standard from before 1785/1795 and three buff yellow coloured standards. They all bore the same motifs, which were a gold Nordic chain painted around the edges of the fly, in the centre of which were the crowned arms of the province which were, Gules, a dragon Or, all within a gold chain of the Order of the Elephant. The finials are of an older model on the *Livfane* and a later 'C7' for the squadron standards.

There was a canton with a Dannebrog in the top hoist and in the other three corners there was a gold-crowned monogram 'C7'. The cypher did not have a wreath around it. They had gold fringes, and red and gold cords and tassels. The obverse and reverse were identical. The red stave was 2m 35cm long. The stave was painted white for the Livfane.

They are often erroneously shown as light blue in modern illustrations and there is no confirmation as to whether a black version was ever made.

The Hussar Regiment, Husar Regimentet

This regiment theoretically had six M1785 standards (one per squadron) of crimson or carmine silk with a gold fringe and decorated on the obverse with, a silver hawk emerging from a cloud with a blue ribbon in its beak with gold inscription 'INACTIS ESTO VOLUCRIS' (Be swift in action) upon it. On the reverse there was a gold crowned monogram of 'C7'. The finial was the spear-shaped C7 model. These were the models carried throughout the Napoleonic wars. There is no confirmation of a *Livfane*.

The regiment later received the M1808 models, exactly when is not clear, but the model of finial shown dates to at least 1817 if not later, 1820 being a strong possibility, which makes it highly unlikely they were made and issued before this date.

7

The Artillery, Det Kongelige Artillerikorps, Including the Engineers

The Danish Artillery Corps was a small, fairly professional, well-trained unit. In 1800 it was divided into the Field Artillery, the Garrison/Fortress Artillery and the Siege Artillery, the latter was only embodied in periods of conflict. The Danish Field Artillery (*Den Danske Artilleribrigade*) was made up of seven foot batteries and a horse battery with another eight batteries in Holstein (*Den Holstenske Artilleribrigade*), with a total of 164 guns.

In 1808, following the abolition of the previous artillery organisation, mobile batteries were 3-pdrs and 10-pdr light howitzers, and each brigade being allotted a 3-pdr mobile battery, but a number of 6-pdr gun batteries were deployed as well.

During these wars, the mobility of the artillery proved to be vital on the battlefield, particularly in the Scandinavian theatre.

The Foot Artillery, Artilleri til Fods

Basic Tactical Use

In battle the artillery was deployed in batteries to fire solid shot and canister at the enemy formations. The howitzers would fire shells instead of solid shot or canister. The heavy artillery would cover friendly formations while trying to delay and harass enemy movements and deployments. The lighter batteries would be deployed between the friendly infantry brigades and shell the enemy positions. Officially a well-trained light battery was reckoned to be able to fire up to 24 shots per minute, obviously not from a couple of guns, but a full battery of eight guns, but this still seems rather high as three shots in a minute from one gun would be an exploit, closer to wishful thinking. This often resulted in the devastation of enemy units. These 3-pdr batteries became the mobile or Kørende artillery.

During the restructuring of 1808 the territorial militia, the Landværnet, was disbanded as were the artillery companies of old regular gunners, and the 'regimental' artillery companies.

These men were used to form 16 artillery companies divided into two new battalions, 10 in the Danske Artilleribataljon (eight companies formed around Zealand and two in Jutland) and six in the Holstenske Artilleribataljon.

Each company was to be composed of 160 gunners and a 'ready reserve' of 40 men to be used as 'replacements when needed'. They were intended for local defence along mainly along the long coastline. The companies had varied organisations and strengths, due to local influences, but normally they were formed into two divisions. One was classed as 'stationary' (Fast in Danish, so obviously this word can easily be misinterpreted and has been in some European works) and this division helped man the fortress, town and coastal defences, normally aided by local militia artillery units. The other division was called 'mobile' (Bevægelig in Danish) and would normally man a four- to six-gun 3-pdr battery (both M1687 and M1762/22 calibre pieces were employed). They were to aid wherever they were needed, often in collaboration with other local defence forces. There were two small, land-based rocket batteries which were formed in 1813, but they never saw any real combat.

The typical composition of a foot battery was eight officers, 18 NCOs, 14 master gunners (*Overkonstabel*), eight gunners (*Konstable*), 140 junior gunners (*Underkonstable*) and two hornists, giving a total of 190 officers and men per battery. This was raised to eight officers, 18 NCOs, two musicians and 214 gunners and other ranks (254 in the Holstenske Artilleribrigade).

Theoretically these batteries should have had the following equipment:

A 3-pdr battery, consisting of 8 x 3-pdr pieces and 2 x 10-pdr howitzers
A 6-pdr battery, consisting of 8 x 6-pdr pieces and 2 x 20-pdr howitzers
A heavy battery, consisting of 8 x 12-pdr pieces and 4 x 36-pdr howitzers.

The heavy batteries were rarely deployed in the field during this conflict as they do not appear in the order of battle for any of the principal actions. They appear to have been consigned to coastal defence and fortress batteries.

The Foot Artillery Uniforms, Including the Danske Artilleribataljon and Holstenske Artilleribataljon

In 1803 the uniform of the regular foot artillery was a red a short red coatee with a dark blue collar, dark blue lapels with flat brass buttons, cuffs with a red cuff flap, three flat brass buttons and dark blue turn ups at the front. Their dress was completed with a pair of long, close-fitting dark blue trousers for use in the field and a pair of white trousers of the same cut to be worn for parades and summer wear. The headwear was a black round hat with a yellow band around the base, with a white side plume held in place with a yellow lace loop and a brass button. The men were equipped with a white leather belt, open brass buckle with a short sword, a black leather pouch on a white leather shoulder belt.

The NCOs' dress was similar, but the higher-ranking NCOs received coats and trousers made of better quality cloth, and they also had NCO epaulettes to show rank on right shoulder only.

A note on service and ranks. All those gunners who 'served the guns' had the rank of either a *Konstabel* or *Overkonstabel*, while those only doing the pushing, pulling, running for ammunition or being a driver were only ranked as *Underkonstabel*. Being a gunner was a special 'technical trade' so the artillery was divided up into more 'classes' than any other part of the army, An artillery gunner served a much shorter term of service than a cavalryman or an infantryman. Artillery service was for four years of 'constant service', two years of 'part-time service' and then transfer straight to the General Reserve (an ordinary soldier had to serve two years of 'constant or full-time' service, six years of 'part-time service', eight years in the Direct Reserve and eight years in the General Reserve).

Danish artillery non-commissioned ranks were a little different to the British (see Table III).

It is difficult to give an exact idea of how artillery distinctions looked before 1812. We know that originally (1789) an NCO 'distinction' was approved, and also before that there were two NCO 'epaulettes' which had been approved in 1769, and it is possible that the older ones may have continued to be used until 1812.

In 1806 there is a clothing list given for all the artillery which gives the different prices for each NCO distinction, which is the best indication we have (see Table IV).

It may be that from 1808 the *Overkonstabel*/Bombardier had two NCO M1789 distinctions, while the *Konstabel*/ lance corporal had only one NCO M1789 distinction.

This is probably how the infantry wore them from this date, so they may also have been changed accordingly in the artillery as well.

The officers wore a long-tailed coat which was deep crimson in colour with flat gilt buttons. The shade was fairly dark, but a number of the earlier iconographic sources show in a very light colour, but the explanation is that the crimson colours in the source, used by different artists, faded very quickly, and were not the colours of the real uniform. At first the officers wore a bicorn with a plume on the front over a black cockade held in place with a gold lace loop and button, and a gold tassel at each point. The bicorn had been replaced in 1804 by an officer's version of the hat including a gold hat band and long gold and red hat cords with flounders (or rackets) and tassels looped over a button of their coat from 1805.

A black leather belt with a rectangular brass plate and a pair of medium dark blue trousers and short black leather boots completed their uniform. From 1806 they carried the same type of sword belt as all other officers, with lion-head buckles.

The new uniform from 1808 followed the same style as the preceding uniform. But it now had a much higher-set waist, and a higher collar, also now the trousers had a higher waist, resembling modern 'overalls', but with shorter legs. The gunners also received short black gaiters. From 1810 onwards grey trousers for service use were also issued, and the blue models were retained for parade dress, together with new white ones (although in reality most men clung to the old blue ones for as long as they could). In winter dress there was a grey greatcoat with a dark blue collar and cuffs.

At first the old-style round hats continued to be worn 'until stocks of shakos are available', and by 1809–10 all line artillery had received them. But there were not enough shakos in stock to equip the newly formed (1808) National Artillery as well. So in 1810 the King decided that the Danske Artilleribataljon and Holstenske Artilleribataljon should receive M1810 'shako-hats' which were converted from the old hats, instead. The first modification made in 1808 was to move the cockade and white plume to the front, and the officers kept their cords, although less elaborate than before; the soldiers' model M1810 shako-hat had a white plume at the front (of the old hats) over a black cockade with a yellow loop, brass button and a yellow and red cord and tassel. This was ordered by the Royal Resolution of 6 May 1810, which simply specified that a heavy coat of laquer was to be painted over the old felt hats M1789 and the M1803 models found in the arsenals. This gave them a better durability and a shiny look. Added to them was a new model plume placed on the front of the hat, and on most, new model cords (from the 1808 shako). The brim was apparently turned up very slightly on both sides.

In 1815 the remaining M1810 shako-hats (M1803 version), were shipped out to the Danish West Indies to re-equip the Danish forces stationed in these colonies after the British occupation.

At first the National Artillery officers' 'shakos' kept their old cords and the white plume on the left hand side

Danish Rank Distinctions *c.* pre-1812

Cavalry NCOs

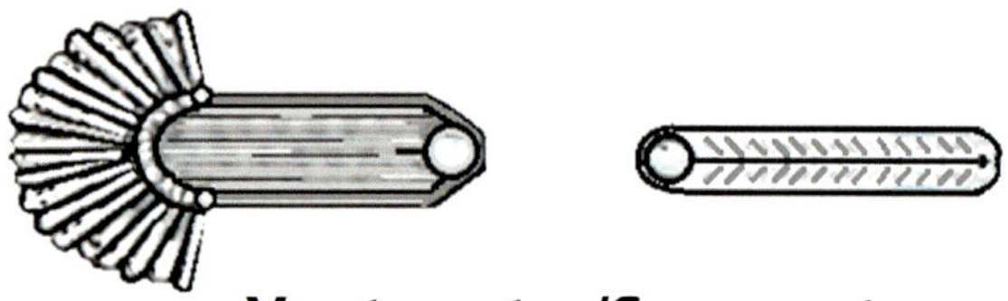

Vagtmestre/Sergeant

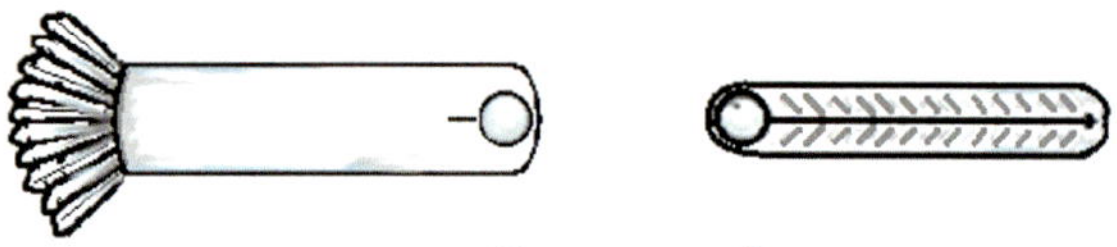

Corporal

Artillery NCOs

Sergeant

Overkonstabel/Bombardier/Corporal

Konstabel/Lance Corporal

JACDAW 2019©

Table III. Danish Artillery Non-Commissioned Ranks		
Danish Rank	**British Rank**	**Extra Role**
Underkonstabel(Stykkusk)	Gunner	(and driver – see above)
Konstabel (served the gun)	Lance corporal/gunner first class	
Overkonstabel (and *Hornblæser*)	Bombardier	(Horn blower of artillery)
Bombader (and trumpeter)	Corporal	(Trumpeter of the 'horse' artillery)
Sergant/Fourer	Sergeant	
Kommandersergant	Staff sergeant	

Table IV. Costs of NCO Distinctions		
Rank	**Distinction**	**Cost**
Kommandersergant	'Epaulette' – (right shoulder)	1 RDL and 16 SK[1]
	from December 1806 also allowed to have a golden *Porteepee* (sword knot)	
Sergant/fourer	'Epaulette' (right shoulder)	1 RDL and 16 SK
Bombader	'Epaulette' (right shoulder)	1 RDL and 16 SK
Overkonstabel	'Distinction' (right shoulder?)	60 SK (approx half the cost of preceding)
Konstabel	'Distinction' (right shoulder?)	60 SK (rather cheap?)
Underkonstabel	'No distinction'	

* The units of account of the Danish coinage were: 1 krone (crown) which had the value of 1½ *rigsdaler*; 1 *rigsdaler* (rix-dollar / RDL) = 6 *mark* = 96 *skilling (SK)* (263mg fine silver per coin) (Kroneskillinger) = 144 common or current Skillings. This system of accounting was applied to two different coinage systems: the special system and the *kurant* (current) system. A krone in 1804 equals more or less €23, but this does not reflect its period value which would obviously have been much higher.

of their hats. Later all these men bought themselves new officers' shakos M1808.

In the National Artillery the gunner's 'new' coats were to be made out of uniforms originally made for the Landeværn units by just adding new dark blue collars, slightly higher than before, cuffs, turnbacks and lapels in the colour of the Artillery Corps. This coat was cut somewhat shorter, the lapels were also shorter and a little wider and the seven flat brass buttons were set in pairs with one at the point. The cuffs had a blue cuff flap with three large flat brass buttons. Originally they had worn blue breeches now worn with shortened black gaiters. They were supposed to have had a pair of dark blue fall-fronted gaiter trousers, although there are no contemporary illustrations of these, but the blue trousers and breeches were slowly replaced with a pair of fall-fronted breeches which were generally made of grey cloth, worn with calf length black gaiters or less frequently a pair of trousers made of blue cloth.

Officers

In 1808 the officers still wore crimson long-tailed cloth coats with dark blue collar, lapels, cuffs and turnbacks, but the coat had a more modern cut with a higher waist and a taller collar. Although some of the junior officers wore coats made of the same-coloured cloth as the men, higher-ranking and older officers still clung on to their crimson coats until way after this period, probably as late as 1848. Generally the officers wore blue breeches with black Hessian-style boots, but from 1812 they could wear grey trousers and white breeches as either summer or full dress with the black boots.

The shabraques for mounted officers were red edged with two bands of gold lace with a blue lace in between and a Hungarian-style knot on the tail (see illustrations). From 1813 the lace was now silver and the blue lace had gone, this probably reflects shortages, with the officers receiving infantry or light dragoons surplus.

NCOs

The NCO shakos were similar to those of the men, but better made and the chinstrap button would have been brass. The artillery NCOs wore the same epaulettes with gold lace as worn by the line infantry NCOs until 1812, and also carried a white bandolier with the large black leather cartridge pouch. They continued to wear the same distinctions until 1812 when the new regulations were introduced.

From 1812 the uniforms were modified for officers and NCOs, as although the basic details and colours were unchanged, the cuffs were now pointed, and the epaulettes had been abolished and replaced by a new rank distinction system on the cuffs.

Danish Foot Artillery & Mounted Artillery

Plate 28. Danish Foot Artillery & Mounted Artillery

Top row, left to right:
The Artilleri til Fods (foot artillery) in 1805, showing a gunner, officer and hornist wearing service uniforms. The newly formed Kørende (mounted) Artilleri in 1808, gunner and officer in service uniforms.

Bottom row, left to right:
Fodartilleri NCO and gunner 1810 in service uniform, Kørende Artilleri 1812, gunner, officer and hornist in service uniform, if the officers and NCOs had modified their cuffs and distinctions to conform with the new regulations; it is not certain that the troop followed them, if at all. From 1810 officers were supposed to use only *Kraprød*/ordinary red for their field uniforms; the older officers generally continued to wear crimson coats, but some of the younger junior officers started to use coatees made of red cloth similar to the NCOs and gunners.

Musicians

There is very little information on the musicians. Originally the artillery had drummers, but they were replaced with hornists by 1803. Their uniform would have had dark blue swallow nests, with yellow lace and probably an epaulette, as the artillery musicians held the rank of an NCO. The hornists were using *havmaanes* (half-moon horns), these appear to have been replaced with *waldhorns* (hunting-style horns, see Volume 1) when they were converted into the mobile artillery in 1808, the horns had blue cords and black leather straps. In winter they had a dark grey woollen overcoat with blue cuffs and collar.

Arms and Equipment

The gunners lost their muskets in 1803, which were more often than not a hindrance while serving the guns, and from 1804 began to receive new, rather long M1802 cavalry-style sabres, which with their longer blades would be more practical in a fight against attacking cavalry. The NCOs of the artillery were seen as a special class of technicians, but normally they came from the ordinary working classes and did not have much money to spare, so it were decided that in recognition of their services all the NCOs would receive a special 'Artillery NCO sabre M1802', which they would not have to pay for, the sabre being 'owned by the regiment'. By 1808 all Danish gunners had received new sidearms, though some were still lacking in Norway, and there were no stocks available for the new National Artillery.

In 1808 the Danske Artilleribataljon requested 90 M1802 NCO sabres and 1,123 M1802 artillery sabres, which were basically the same with just a minor difference of the hilts, the lion-heads being different. Some 600 M1802 sabres were in stock in Copenhagen and the rest were ordered from the Frederiksværk armaments factory, and delivered before the end of that year. There existed some variation in the form/model of blade, but basically they had same type of blade with a basic length of 78cm for an overall length of 92.8cm.

For the Holstenske Artilleribataljon, sidearms were not so readily available. The M1756 and M1801 infantry/grenadier sabre was therefore used to equip the artillerymen as a stopgap measure, mainly for the fortress and secondary artillery formations, the Holstenske Artilleribataljon and part of the Borholmskeartilleri, and most of the volunteer and town militia units. The artillerymen carried a cartridge box on a shoulder belt which in fact contained tools for the service of the guns. Before 1800 they carried prickers on the shoulder belt, but the belt had since been abolished and the prickers were now carried in a rack on the gun carriage.

The units received some bread bags, but getting water bottles and backpacks was apparently much more difficult and it is not clear exactly when they finally received them. Any other equipment would essentially be the tools and accessories belonging to the gun.

Limber Riders, Artilleriets Stykkuske

As the limber riders were normally part of the company and were considered of the same rank as *Underkonstabel*, they wore the same uniform as their company. Normally they would always have worn blue, later grey riding overalls, high gloves and spurs and they carried a whip.

The 'Kørende' or 'Mounted' Gunners

The 'mounted' artillery batteries were basically ordinary artillery gunners of the normal foot artillery, only differing in having a special sabre scabbard and their mode of transport.

In their operational configuration a mounted gun had a crew of 15: one NCO as commander (mounted), four gunners rode (mounted) on the gun carriage, four gunners were transported (mounted) on the newly converted 3-pdr ammunition carts which now had four wheels, and finally the last two gunners rode on the front side horses of the gun and ammunition wagon. There were no gunners seated on the actual limbers, which were of a special style (see illustrations). The NCO/gun commander rode on a separate horse, and so probably wore cavalry boots with

Danish *Ridende Artilleri* (Horse Artillery)

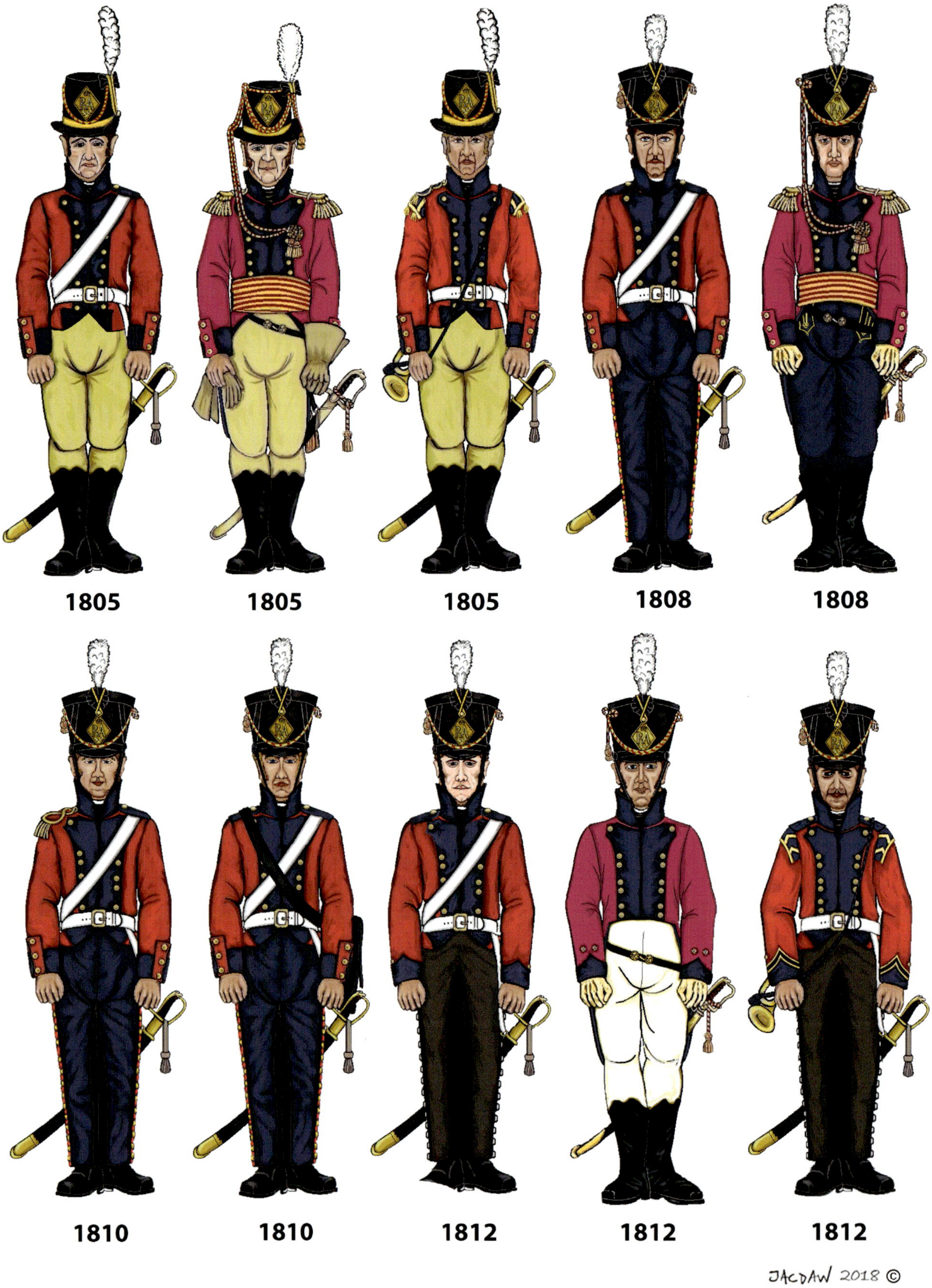

Plate 29. Danish *Ridende Artilleri* (Horse Artillery)

Top row, left to right:
Ridende Artilleri 1805 showing a gunner, officer and trumpeter in full dress.
Ridende Artilleri 1808, gunner and officer in campaign dress.

Middle row, left to right:
Ridende Artilleri, gunner NCO 1810 in campaign dress, gunner 1810 in campaign dress with a satchel of ready-to-use shot over his shoulder, *Ridende Artilleri* 1812, gunner in campaign dress, officer in full dress and trumpeter in campaign dress.

spurs. When they were in action his horse was normally given to one of the gunners mounted on the gun's limber horse, to act as his horse holder, so the NCO could dismount and command his crew.

Uniforms 1808–1814

The officers, NCOs and gunners of the Kørende artillery were all ordinary artillery gunners, and so wore the same uniforms as the rest of artillery. The only difference was that the gunners had a slightly different and more flexible scabbard for their sabres.

Arms and Equipment

The mounted gunners were equipped with a white bandolier with a large black leather cartridge pouch which contained artillery tools etc. They had a white leather waist belt from which hung the M1802 artillery sabre with a lion-head hilt, now their only defence as their muskets had been abolished by this time as already mentioned. The fascine knives with simple wooden grips were kept as tools and later used for fieldwork.

The regimental, Landeværn, 'volunteer' and some of the 'national' foot artillery also carried the M1754 infantry sword *c*.1803–14, when the M1802 was unavailable. However by 1812–13 most must have received new sabres, as in 1815 it is recorded that there had been made some 3,267 M1802 sabres for the artillery gunners, and that also *c*.1,000 of the new M1808 artillery sabres had been bought for their use. Some 1,500 of these M1802 sabres were mounted in the hilts of the old *Faskinknivs*.

According to the artillery archives of the Danish/Holstein artillery, regarding sabre M1802, the number of sabres received ready for use was as follows:

1804–1809	1,899 sabres, mainly old hilts with new blades
1810–1812	1,125 sabres, only newly cast hilts with new blades
1813–1815	243 sabres, only newly cast hilts with new blades

There were still 3,163 sabres in Danish stocks in 1863.

We do not know the figures for Norway but the total number delivered was probably *c*.1,300; at least half had old hilts, the rest had new hilts. There appear to be more variations in the blades used in Norway, a newly cast M1802 hilt and a Solingen-type hussar blade, but this is probably the horse artillery sabre M1807, of which 150 were made and delivered by Frederiksværk 1808–1809, probably for the use of the Norwegian horse artillery.

In 1804 the Danish artillery converted 300 'Scabbards [M1802] with a ring mounting added for use by the Mounted artillery'. The same number of scabbards was converted by the Holstein artillery at same time. We do not know exactly how this modified scabbard was carried.

Artillery Sabres

Although there was only one model of *Artillerisabel* M1802 there were a couple of sub-models of the 4,500 ordered and delivered between 1803 and 1815. The first 1,500 would have had the old hilts from *Faskinkniv* M1777, as only the scabbards and blades were delivered from Frederiksværk. The artillery arsenals then had to mount the new blades themselves. What is strange is that all the books record that only 1,000 M1777 *Faskinknivs* were made and a few of them had the model with a 'helmet hilt' which is thought to have been a special NCO model (these hilts were not reused). The extra 600 were probably those which were sent to Norway and modified there, so giving yet another variant.

Extra models were made with recast hilts right from the start (1804). But in 1808, there were no more old hilts to be found, and as a consequence all the sabres were now made with the newly cast hilts. In 1808 a new type of scabbard was made with a little ring at the top for a new method of suspension, why this occurred is not recorded, possibly they were made especially for the Kørende artillery. This would probably have protected the scabbard and made it easier to handle, probably to hook it up out of the way while serving the guns.

The wagon train never had a clearly designated sidearm, but used old infantry straight swords of Great Northern War vintage; at the time of issue, some of them were at least 100 years old! They were repaired, shortened, given new brown leather scabbards and then issued as the *Train Hirchfænger*.

Danish Artillery Drivers

1805 1808 1810 1805

1811 1808 1811 1812

Plate 30. Danish Artillery Drivers

Top row, left to right:
Fod Artilleri (foot artillery) limber horse rider *c.*1805
Fod and *Kørende Artillery* (foot and mounted artillery) limber horse rider *c.*1808; when mounted they had a habit of turning their hat to the right so it was more evenly balanced when riding.
Danske and *Holstenske Artilleri Batallion*/Danish and Holstein local defence artillery battalions limber horse rider *c.*1810.
Ridende Artilleri/horse artillery limber horse rider *c.*1807.

Bottom row, left to right:
Ridende Artilleri/horse artillery *Stykkusk*/limber horse rider *c.*1810. He carries a M1796 sabre.
Trainkusk/artillery train waggoner 1803–11 shown in a civilian coat and waistcoat, leather breeches and a hat as headwear. As an alternative to the civilian coat, they also made use of old M1785 long tailed infantry coats, generally red with blue cuffs, lapels and turnbacks.
Trainkusk/artillery train waggoner *c.*1811–14 in full dress armed with an infantry sabre.
Trainkusk/artillery train waggoner 1811–14 in field dress.
The last figure carries the so-called *Train hirchfænger*/waggoner short sword. These were old infantry 'straight-swords' which had had the blade shortened by ⅓ of its length.

Whilst the limber riders were considered to be part of the gun crew the waggoners were classed as being with the train.
In 1812 the waggoners of the horse artillery were allowed to wear the same uniform jacket and trousers as the *Ridende Artilleri* gunners and they used the same *Mantelsæk*/valise.

Note: all scabbards were normally made of natural brown leather, probably until after the war, when they were all 'darkened' or blackened.

Regarding the artillery NCO sabre M1802, the following numbers were made (all with new hilts and blades):

1804	143 NCO sabres
1806	156 NCO sabres
No further production of this type	

artillery NCOs also used the M1802 sabre. The number available is not known, but in 1868 there were still 154 in service, so at least that number were used.

The M1809 'Stralsund sabre' was long thought to be booty from the fighting at Stralsund in 1809, but in fact the Danish government had apparently bought 2,000 Dutch infantry sabres, of which at least 1,000, were issued to the artillery, mainly after 1810, for the newly raised Danske and Holstenske artillery battalions. Two versions of this sabre exist, but the other model was mainly used in the navy, which also received 1,000.

The M1756 infantry/grenadier sabre was also used to equip artillerymen as a surplus, but mainly for the fortress and secondary artillery formations including the Danske and Holstenske artillery battalions, the regimental artillery, part of Borholmskeartilleri etc., as well as most of the volunteer and town militia units. The train probably received these sabres as well, as there were at least 3,500 in service, so enough for both them and the regular artillery, but most men probably received old cut-down infantry rapiers.

Other items of kit obviously included the calfskin backpack, on the top of which the greatcoat was rolled and strapped in winter. The men were also issued with a grey/white canvas bread bag and a square metal canteen.

Part of the equipment belonging to the gun was a *Kardustaske* (large shot bag). This was a large black leather satchel-type case lined inside with sheepskin. It would hold either three 3-pdr balls plus charges or two 6-pdr shots and their charges. Two of these were carried on top of each limber box and others in the ammunition wagon.

The Horse Artillery, *Ridende Artilleri*

This artillery corps, formed after Prussian model, was meant as a reserve that could be deployed quickly due to its mobility. It could also move forward to support cavalry attacks or accompany cavalry and light troops in reconnaissance and patrol missions.

The gunners of the horse artillery were all mounted on horses to ensure their mobility. In the artillery regulations from 1804, it was noted that there would be no seats for gunners on limber box; all of the 16 gun crew would ride a horse, so this was a rather expensive battery to man. A gun crew would consist of 12 gunners and four horse holders, and four to six extra gun drivers would also be added to each team. Each company would also have its own *staldetat* (permanent stables), to care for their horses, as they had a

Danish Artillery Swords 1803–1816

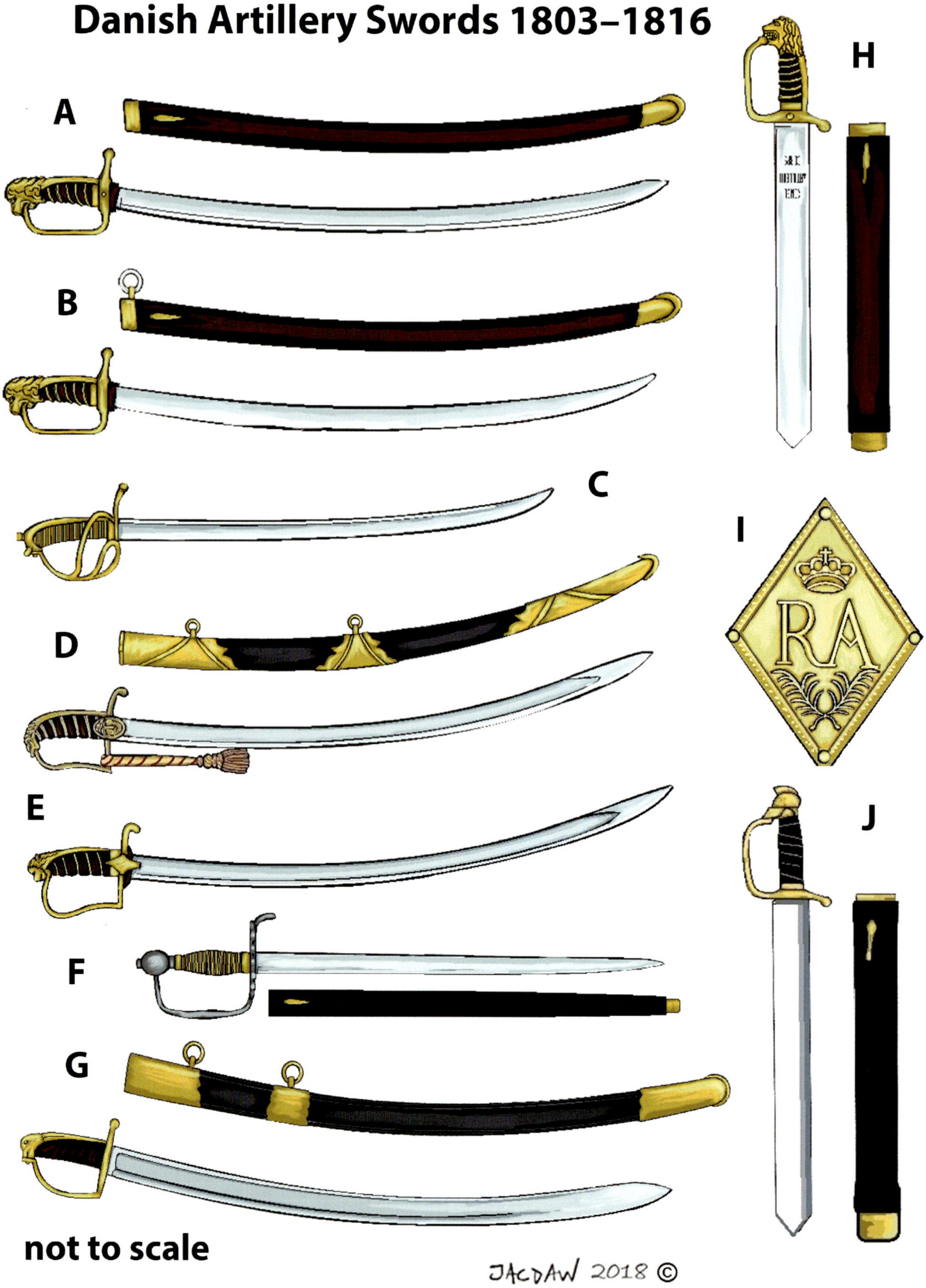

Plate 31. Danish Artillery Swords 1803–1816

A. M1802 artillery sabre. This is the original model M1802, produced from 1804 often with reused 'old' M1777 hilts, but also found with some new hilts. Note the form of the blade, probably the original hussar-type blade with a fuller all along the top edge from Solingen. The scabbard was of natural brown leather. This was a very long sabre (76–79.5 inch).

B. M1802/1808 artillery sabre for the mounted artillery. In 1808 a total of 300 were made for the mounted artillery in Denmark, and as far as we know, the same number was made in Holstein for their mounted artillery. It is basically the M1802 with a few modifications, in 1808 they all had newly cast hilts and a different cheaper-looking blade with a short fuller, stopping some 13cm before the point, it was also lighter, more pointed and shorter. A carrying ring had been added on to the original scabbard, for use of the mounted artillery. With both the hook and ring this would indicate that it could be carried in different ways.

C. The 'Stralsund' sabre M1808, as it is called by collectors. This is the sabre often referred to as the 'M1808 artillery sabre' or the 'Stralsund sabre' or even the 'Holstenske sabre'. In 1808, 2,000 Dutch sabres were bought from a private contractor. One thousand of these were allotted to the artillery, becoming the main sabre of the artillery by 1816. Originally this was an older Dutch model sabre. It had two branched brass hilts which enclosed the hand and it was carried in a black scabbard. Later some of these hilts had their branches removed.

D. Artillery officer's sabre.

E. M1802 artillery NCO's sabre.

F. The so-called *Train hirchfænger*, an old infantry straight-sword which had had the blade shortened by 1/3 of its length.

G. M1796 *Ridende Artilleri* sabre (Former *Husarsabel* M1761).

H. The *Faskinkniv* M1777 with a lion-head hilt, used by the artillery up until the issue of the sabre. Note some were engraved with 'KONLIG / ARTILLERIE/ CORPS' across the blade just below the hilt. A few of these *Faskinknivs* had a helmet at the top of the hilt, an NCO's model, but they were not reused.

I. Hat and shako plate for *Ridende Artilleri*.

J. Fascine knife, *Faskinkniv* M1777 with a helmet hilt.

Main source: Niels M. Saxtorp, 'Hærens Blankvåben på Napoleonskrigens', *Våbenhistoriske Årbøger* (Copenhagen, 1974).

permanent stock, while the rest of the artillery only had a small number of horses for training and received new ones when they were made ready for service in the field.

Until 1798 the main gun of the Danish horse artillery had been the light and mobile 1-pdr *Amusette*. All three horse artillery batteries had 16 x 1-pdr *Amusettes* and 4 x 10-pdr howitzers. But from 1798 the Danish and Holstein horse artillery received 8 x 20 calibre 6-pdr guns, and 2 x 10-pdr howitzers each.

From *c*.1802 the Norwegian horse artillery instead received 8 x 3-pdr 20 calibre M1799 guns, and 2 x 10-pdr howitzers, as these were considered more suitable in the Norwegian terrain.

A typical horse artillery battery was composed of six officers, 18 NCOs, 14 master gunners (*Overkonstabel*), 60 gunners (*Konstable*), 70 junior gunners (*Underkonstable*) and two trumpeters.

Theoretically each battery was equipped with eight 6-pdr guns and two 10-pdr howitzers, but again, 3-pdr guns were also used in Norway. In their operational configuration all the gunners of the horse artillery were mounted on horses, there were no gunners seated on the limbers in Denmark, but the limbers had ammunition chests on them.

Horse Artillery Gunners' Uniforms

Their uniform was virtually the same as the foot artillery, but with some differences akin to the cavalry (yellow breeches, blue overalls, short boots and spurs). Until 1808 they had a round, black felt hat which had a yellow band around it and on the front a brass rhomboid-shaped plate stamped with the crowned letters 'RA', for *Ridende Artilleri* over a wreath. On the left side it had a white plume over a black cockade, with a yellow loop and red and yellow cords and tassels, not always shown on contemporary artwork.

From 1808, the regiment received the same shako as the cavalry, in black felt with a black leather peak and a black leather chin strap with the same plate as before. It had

Danish Artillery Shabraques 1802–1814

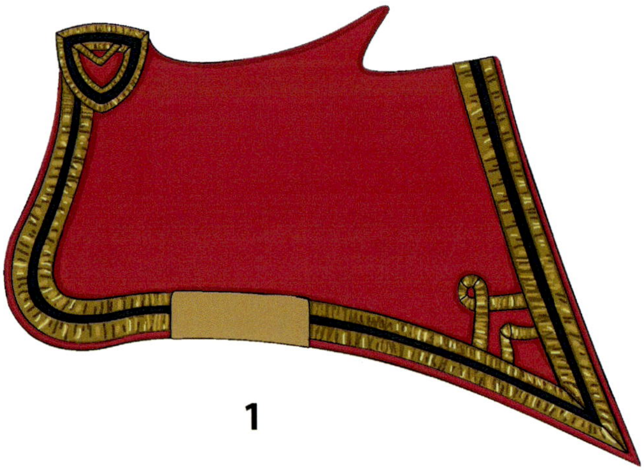

1

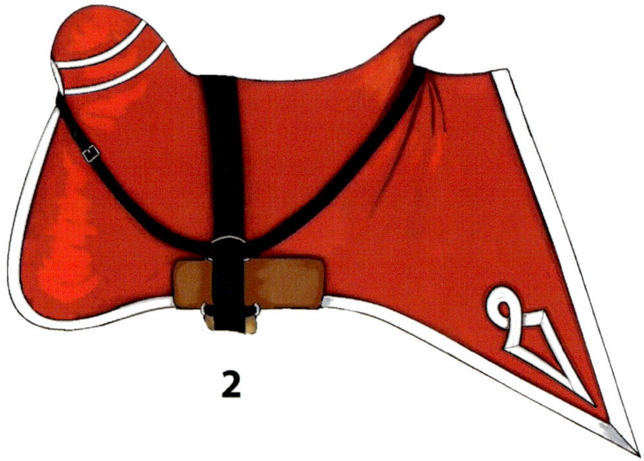

2

3

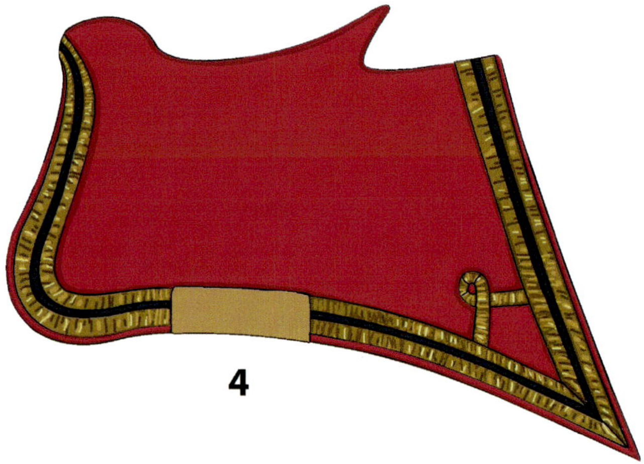

4

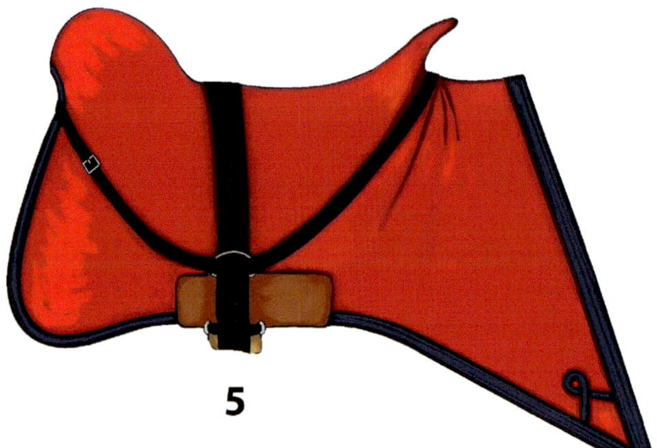

5

Plate 32. Danish Artillery Shabraques 1802–1814

Full dress shabraque of the new model, but with false holster covers sewn on! This is probably a reminiscence of the old 1789 model/style, kept as a special distinction for the *Ridende artilleri* officers. Note it is in the crimson colour of the artillery. After the Brockdorff collection.
The *Ridende artilleri* gunners shabraque is also clearly of the new model too, and although not fully visible, we can see all the lacing. It also has a form of false kind of holster covers, simply by adding two white laces at the top front of the cover (gunners had no 'full dress' shabraques, so this was the 'standard model'). After the Brockdorff collection.
Ridende artilleri officer 1809 by Senn. The original picture is not very clear, but by removing the ADC lace on the front and adding the missing details based on the previous 'full dress' shabraque, this gives a rather accurate reconstruction. Jørgen Koefoed Larsen 2018.

We have no verifiable information on the shabraques of the officers of foot artillery and Kørende (mobile) artillery, but Jørgen Koefoed Larsen feels it is safe to assume that for full dress they used the same basic model as that used by horse artillery officers, but without 'false' pistol holsters. Norwegian artist Andreas Bloch made a convincing reconstruction of a shabraque of a staff sergeant of a Norwegian Kørende (mounted) company in 1814. Bloch is often regarded as misleading concerning Norwegian uniforms, but this was because he mainly used Danish military archives and Tøjhusmuseet a lot of time as very little information could be found in Norway during the period of the (forced) Swedish Union 1814–1905 and most archives have been lost. So his information is nearly all based on Danish sources, which he then have often used without knowing or understanding how (or at all) they were in fact used or modified in Norway. But this also must tell us that as his sources are Danish, most of what he shows is correct for Denmark. It is highly possible that he found a source for this drawing in archives now lost today, and it looks very convincin like a shabraque, as used by the NCOs and trumpeters in Denmark and Holstein of the Kørende or 'mobile artillery'.

a white plume over a black cockade with yellow loop on the front. In full dress, the shako had red and yellow cords and tassels. Note that only the gunners and NCOs of the horse artillery were permitted wear moustaches; they were the only gunners who had this privilege, which was forbidden in the foot and the Kørende artillery.

The horse artillery gunners wore the same coatee as the foot artillery, and they both followed the same evolution in the cut of their coats at the same dates.

From 1804 to *c.*1808 they wore a pair of fall-fronted buff yellow leather breeches and unadorned black leather Hungarian or Hessian boots for full dress, and in service dress they had a pair of dark blue fall-fronted breeches and Hungarian boots.

From 1805, possibly earlier, for campaign or field service dress they now had a pair of fall-fronted dark blue overalls with black/dark brown leather inserts and a red stripe, and small brass buttons down the outside leg. From 1810 they began to receive fall-fronted grey breeches for service dress and fall-fronted grey overalls with leather inserts, red piping and small brass buttons down the outside leg for campaign wear. For foul weather dress they were issued with long grey cloaks.

Equipment and Arms

In 1796 it was decided that all three horse artillery companies (Danish, Holstein and Norwegian) should have 'cavalry type sabres of one common type'. The number of sabres needed was 546. This, the artillery command suggested, could be done by repairing 507 older sabre models in stock from the hussars ('hussar sabre M1761'). Also they would need new scabbards, as the old ones were too damaged. This was approved, and the work begun, but it would not fulfil the number needed, so 60 more sabres were ordered to be made by København swordsmiths. These had newly cast hilts and the blades of the hussar sabre 1792 model. All 567 sabres were delivered to all three horse artillery companies by 1799.

However by 1807 several of the oldest M1796 sabres, were worn out, so the artillery command ordered 150 new M1807 horse artillery sabres from Frederiksværk and they were delivered *c.*1809–10.

So the horse artillery sabre M1796 was made in three different models:

1. The original horse artillery sabre M1761/1796 with new scabbards (507 sabres were delivered 1796–99)

Danish Artillery Fanion and Matros Pennants

not to scale

JACDAW 2019©

Plate 33. Danish Artillery Fanion and Matros Pennants

Top: author's reconstruction of an artillery fanion, probably carried by the artillery commander's headquarters **c.**1814. Dimensions unknown. After the *Faneboger* and an original in the Tøjhusmuseet, Copenhagen, today renamed Krigsmuseet.
Middle: as they were classed as a boat crew, the Matros Company was permitted to carry the same ensigns as a naval vessel. A smaller version of the normal naval ensign was carried as a unit colour. Dimensions unknown.
Bottom: a long pennantwas carried as a secondary (company) colour. Both were carried on (white?) flagstaffs with a (white/yellow) knob as a finial. Dimensions unknown.

2. The horse artillery sabre M1796 with a newly cast M1761 hilt and a blade from the hussar sabre M1792 (60 sabres delivered 1799)
3. The horse artillery sabre M1807 with the newly cast M1802 hilt and blade from 'hussar sabre M1792' (150 sabres were delivered in 1809–10). Generally they had an overall length of 95cm for an 80cm blade and they were carried in a black or dark brown leather scabbard which had brass fittings.

The grip was of brown leather secured with tressed brass wire. It had a whitened or brown leather sabre strap and knot.

The sabres were carried on a white leather waist belt with a brass buckle. They were equipped with a white leather shoulder belt with an unadorned black leather cartridge pouch.

Horse furniture consisted of black leather light cavalry harness and a red 'Hungarian' shabraque with white lace border and knot and probably a blue-grey valise piped white. The lace border may have become blue, as in Norway *c.*1808.

NCOs' Uniforms

As the NCOs were mounted they had the same distinctions as the line cavalry NCOs. From 1812, when the new rank regulations were introduced, the Artillery Corps suggested that their rank distinctions be placed above the cuffs of their uniforms, but the King rejected this idea. The new distinctions were to be placed on the cuffs. The artillery ranks were, starting with the lowest: *Konstabel*, *Overkonstabel*, *Bombarder*, *Sergent*, *Commandersergent*, *Fyrværker*. The *Konstabel*, being the lowest rank, had plain pointed cuffs, but the lower ranks probably did not adopt them until after the war.

Officers' Uniforms

The field officers were supposed to have changed from hats to shakos the same time as the men in 1808, but some officers were still wearing their hats in 1809 and it appears that they may not have changed them until even later, *c.*1810. On the front was a brass rhomboid-shaped plate stamped with the crowned letters 'RA', for *Ridende Artilleri* over a wreath, this plate was carried on both the hats and later on the shakos. The hats had tasselled flounders (or raquettes) on long cords which hung down from the right of the cap to the breast and were looped over a lapel button on the left side, on the third button from the top on the lapel. The hat had a black cockade placed on the side held in place by a gold lace loop and a gilt button, and it had a white plume. When the hat was replaced with the shako in 1809/1810 it also had gold and crimson cords including tassels. The shakos were frequently privately made and made entirely of leather without the 'V' strengtheners on the sides. The shakos had a black cockade now placed at the front and held in place by a gold lace loop and a gilt button, and had a white plume.

The officers wore a crimson coat with dark blue lapels, dark blue lining/coat tails, turnbacks, collar and cuffs of the same cut as the line infantry officers. The earlier coat had thinner lapels with evenly spaced buttons. The new coats of *c.*1808 now had wider lapels and the buttons were placed in pairs. The coat had gold epaulettes until 1812. The coats made under the new regulations of 1812 had pointed cuffs with the new rank distinctions, and the tails were still blue.

In 1804 the officers wore a pair of buff breeches which were replaced on field service by a pair of fall-fronted dark blue breeches which opened down the side with buttons (this vent was piped red), and black leather Hungarian boots. They had the same rank distinctions as the line cavalry officers, including the waist sash which they wore under the coat until 1804 when they started wearing it over their coat.

Their black leather cartridge pouch had a brass badge, originally a crowned 'C7', the cypher of Christian VII; from 1808 it was changed to a crowned 'FR VI' for Frederick VI. It was carried on a gold laced, later yellow shoulder belt which had a pair of prickers on the front. These officers carried the standard artillery or infantry officer's sabre, depending on what was available in the armouries, in a black leather scabbard with brass fittings and a red and yellow/gold sword knot and tassel. Some officers acquired either privately made lion-headed artillery officers' sabres, or hussar officers' sabres.

The shabraques for mounted officers were red edged with two bands of gold lace with a blue lace in between, and a Hungarian-style knot on the tail (see illustrations). From 1813 the lace was silver, although theoretically it should have been in white wool, and the blue lace had gone. This probably reflects shortages, with the officers receiving infantry or light dragoon surplus.

Trumpeters' Uniforms

Details about the trumpeters' uniforms are unknown, but they probably followed the same style as the rest of the army, a trooper's coat with dark blue swallow nests with deep yellow lace trim, and probably an epaulette as most trumpeters had the rank of an NCO. The trumpet would probably have had blue cords or blue and yellow cords (see illustrations for the variants).

Colours

The artillery battalions were not issued with colours, but they did have company pennons or fanions. Unfortunately it is not known to what extent they were used. Later each company/battery was supposed to have carried two, to mark their emplacement, but nothing is mentioned for the period 1803–1814.

The later models, *c.*1814/1815, had a red field with a pair of crossed cannon barrels, under the title 'Der Konelig Artillerie Korps' and a grenade in each angle, all in gold paint.

The Danish Wagon Train, Artilleriets Trainkuske, Ammunition Wagon and Artillery Wagoners

The Danish train wagon *c.*1801–1807, wore old coats with long skirts, probably also coats of the M1785 model, which were in use before the introduction of the M1789. According to the dress rules, train wagoners were to 'bring own waist coat, leather breeches, socks and boots' (until *c.*1808). The army would provide a coat, hat (M1789), spares (if needed), whip and sidearm. By 1810 most wagoners would have received the old, now surplus, short M1802 coatees to replace the old M1785 coats.

In 1811 they received uniforms. These consisted of a shako, although it was more common for them to wear a grey fatigue cap with regimental blue turn-up; also a red, single-breasted coatee with a dark blue collar, cuffs, front turn-ups and shoulder straps. The uniform was to have straight cuffs and it is doubtful if it ever adopted the pointed cuffs of the 1812 regulations before the end of the war, as the men were still wearing their old uniform out, as they were a low priority in the issue of new ones. On the right side of the collar there was a yellow 'K', on left a yellow 'A'. They also had a white waistcoat and a grey infantry model overcoat. They wore a pair of dark blue, later grey cavalry-style overalls with boots with spurs. A pair of gloves and a whip completed this kit.

8

The Ordnance

The Danish system of pressing all usable guns into service, many 30 or more years old, meant that there were a number of different models in use, particularly among the 3-pdr and 6-pdr pieces, including the model 1687 system, used by the mobile costal units from *c.*1808.

The newer models were issued to the frontline units and their older pieces were either reissued to the coastal and militia or sent to Norway, and the even older pieces ended up in the arsenals and fortresses or were issued to town militias. The standard field guns were of the bronze-barrelled 1766/1792 'Carl af Hessen' system, and the majority of the 3-pdr and 6-pdr guns used during the war were based on this system. These pieces were to be remounted on more modern lighter carriages designed to accommodate more modern elevating devices.

The Danish Artillery Reforms 1796–1814

Background

Since 1721 Denmark had had the good fortune of not being embroiled in a major war, but as a consequence this had created a decline in the Danish army. It was not helped by a trio of rather mediocre Danish Kings: Christian VI (1699–1746), who was weak and extremely religious, Frederik V (1723–1766), who was a drunkard, and Christian VII (1749–1808), who was at best mentally unstable if not completely raving mad. So during these years Denmark was ruled mainly by a string of court nobles and ministers, most of whom were not at all interested in matters concerning the army in general and even less in those concerning the artillery.

The threat of a Russian attack on Holstein in 1762 led to a revival of interest in the army, the strengthening and modernisation was directed by the very able (French) General Claude-Louis de Saint Germain (1707–1778). But once the threat was gone court intrigues soon got rid of him.

The new commander of the artillery (from 1765 at the age of 20) and soon the de facto army commander (1766) was the nephew of the Danish king and the brother of the Duke of Hesse-Kassel, Prince Carl of Hesse-Kassel. He was charming, active, and very interested in science and military matters, but was more of a martinet and simply did not have either the knowledge or the education for such a grand position. However, Denmark was lucky as he brought with him a number of very able and outstanding German officers, and more were to follow – this became the backbone of the later army reforms. This also led to a very direct military cooperation between the state of Denmark and war-experienced Hesse-Kassel, not least in matters of artillery. The most influential of those German officers (and future military professor of Prince Carl) was the former commander of Frederik the Great's artillery, General Heinrich von Huth (1717–1806). Today he is all but forgotten, but in his day he was reckoned as one of the most outstanding artillery officers and military reformers of his time.

His ideas and planning reformed the Danish artillery first (from 1766–1806) and then the army from1789–1806. Huth was also responsible for the actual plans used during the court coup in 1784, and he formed, as Prince Frederik's military tutor, the thinking of the new de facto ruler, the Prince Regent. Without the sound foundations of Huth, the Danish army would not have become as effective as it was both during the conflict of 1807–14 and subsequently in 1848–50.

The Reforms of the Artillery

General von Huth reformed first the artillery of Hesse-Kassel and then the Danish artillery, mainly from what he had learned during the Seven Years War. He subsequently created a unified artillery system only differing in the details for both Denmark and Hesse-Kassel, which was also studied and copied by some of the other German states.

However between 1766 and 1794 Prince Carl meddled in several ways in both the production and organisation of the Danish army, with disastrous results. He planned, for example, to form large 'mixed' batteries with several different types of gun within the same company, which would have been a logistical nightmare.

By 1794 the Prince Regent had lost his faith in him and slowly began to take over the command of the army in person, reducing Prince Carl (now his father-in-law) to a mere figurehead and making him director of the Frederiksværk – another job he messed up in the end.

Danish 3-pdr 22 Calibre Regimental Gun M1766, System 'Carl af Hessen', on M1794 Carriage

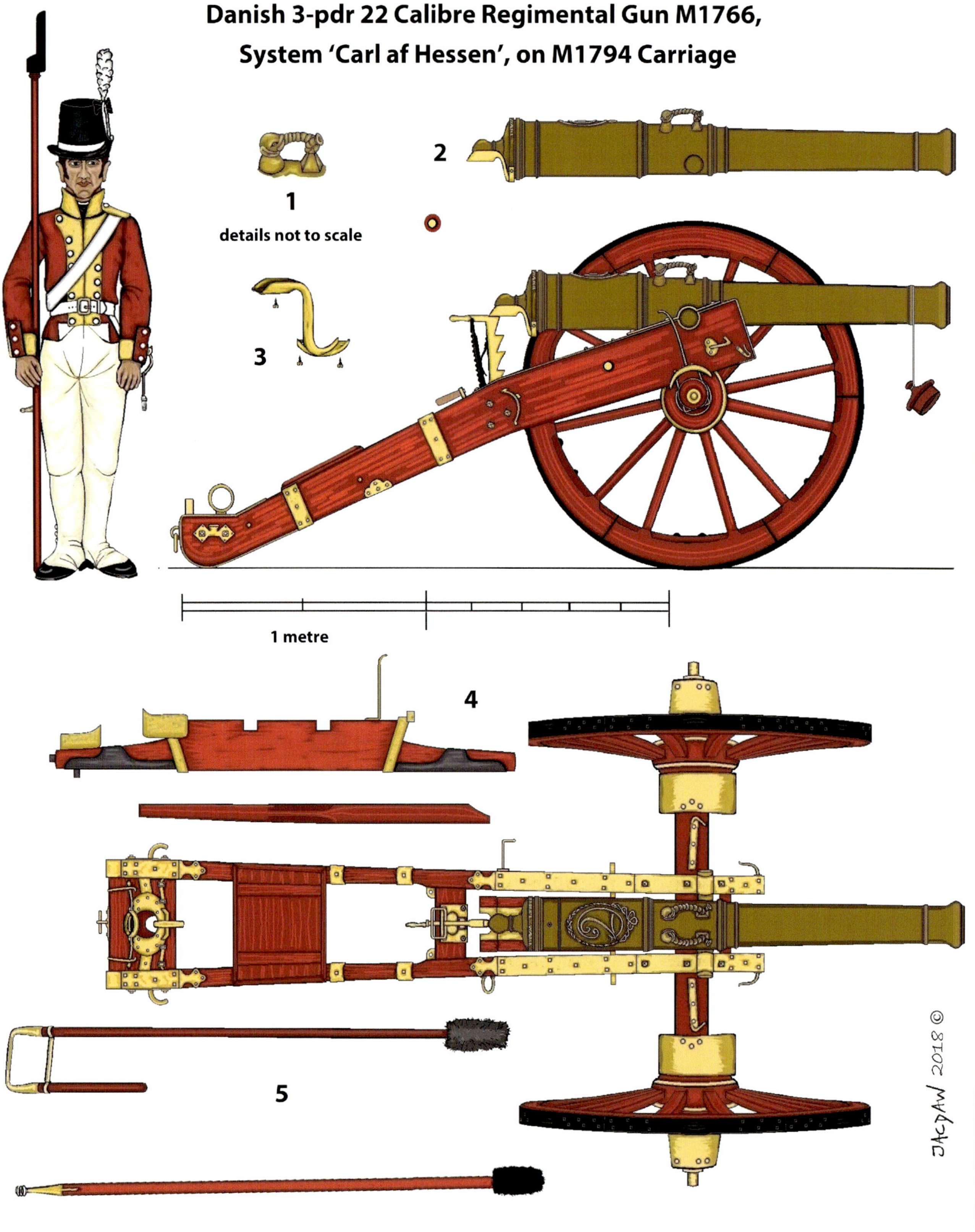

Plate 34. Danish 3-pdr 22 Calibre Regimental Gun, System 'Carl af Hessen', M1766/M1799

The gun is shown mounted on a 1794 model bracket carriage as used by the regimental artillery. The barrel bears the older monogram with the 'C7' within a wreath, which tells us the barrel was cast between 1766 and 1799. A total of 88 were made, a rather high number as each infantry regiment would have needed only four, so 48 would have been sufficient, but apparently at the same time the Prince Regent was planning to double the strength of the army by creating a reserve, the Landeværn (home guard), and as they were to have regimental artillery as well, the extra guns which were made were probably destined for their use. Note the tompion to protect the piece from the elements when not in action.

1. Elephant head and trunk lifting handles, typical Danish style.
2. The M1766 22 calibre gun barrel, note the added tooth or wedge bracket under the knob of the cascable, to fit into the elevating device (*Tandem stille maskine*). Later barrels had this tooth cast on directly at the foundry.
3. Detail of the 'tooth' and bracket.
4. Details of the wooden axle showing the steel sleeves and the mud guards, a Danish peculiarity.
5. Gunner's equipment; top, the trail spike (*baksebomme*) to manoeuvre the gun, it was painted red for the regimental artillery. Bottom: the sponge (*Krumvisker*) and a combined sponge and wad hook (*Krumsætter*).

The loading and cleaning tools appear to have been stowed on the left-hand side of the carriage and the manoeuvring tools and trail spikes were strapped to the right-hand side when looking forward from the rear of the gun.

Source: after an original barrel and plans conserved in the Tøjhusmuseet, Copenhagen, now called the Krigsmuseet; and various artillery manuals/and artillery cadet drawings. The gun is shown with a regimental artilleryman of the Danske Livregiment holding a powder ladle made of wood or copper (*ladeskuffe*) during the Siege of Copenhagen in 1807 for scale. By 1810 powder ladles were rarely seen in the field, only in the fortress or coastal batteries.

By 1794 the Prince Regent, ably assisted by General von Huth and the capable commander of the artillery, Major General Ezechais Gustav von Mecklenburg, started the major reform in organisation, training, arms and equipment of the Danish artillery. This was done by closely studying the experience gained in the American and French revolutionary wars. The casting of large numbers of new gun barrels (usually referred to as 'pieces' in English terms) was not economically viable (the economy between 1796 and 1806 being rather stretched), but Huth considered that most gun tubes were good enough for the service. However the guns needed to be more mobile and the equipment more standardised. Several foreign artillery systems, such as the Austrian 'Lichtenstein' system (1744), the Prussian 'Holtzmann' system (1745), the French 'Gribeauval' system (1765) and the British 'Congreve' system (1792), were studied and several details were copied. The priority, as agreed in 1794, was first to reform the regimental artillery, then the horse artillery, and lastly the field artillery.

In 1797 a clear plan for the future organisation of the field artillery in Denmark, Holstein and Norway was also laid out. This standardised the equipment in each artillery company, based around one type of gun. Also, as Denmark would concentrate mainly on 3-pdr guns, 10-gun companies became the normal complement to guarantee that the Danish always had plenty of guns available in battle. Also the Danish artillery should fight after the rule: 'Go forward, aim well and there is no shame in losing a gun which has been well served in battle, as the Standing Orders for the Artillery officers from Prince Frederik put it.

In the end, the most influential of the foreign carriage systems from 1796 was the 'Gribeauval'. After field testing, the English single-pole carriage 'Congreve' system was rejected as the single-pole carriage was simply not strong enough to support the weight of the rather heavy Danish 6-pdr guns. The system could only support the Danish 3-pdrs, which were very close to an English 6-pdr in both weight and calibre. Until after the end of the Napoleonic wars the main disadvantage of the English system' was that it could only carry a rather light piece (maximum *c.*600kg)! However, the Danish did build some of these 'English

Danish 3-pdr 22 Calibre Field Gun, System 'Carl af Hessen', M1766 on 1796 Carriage

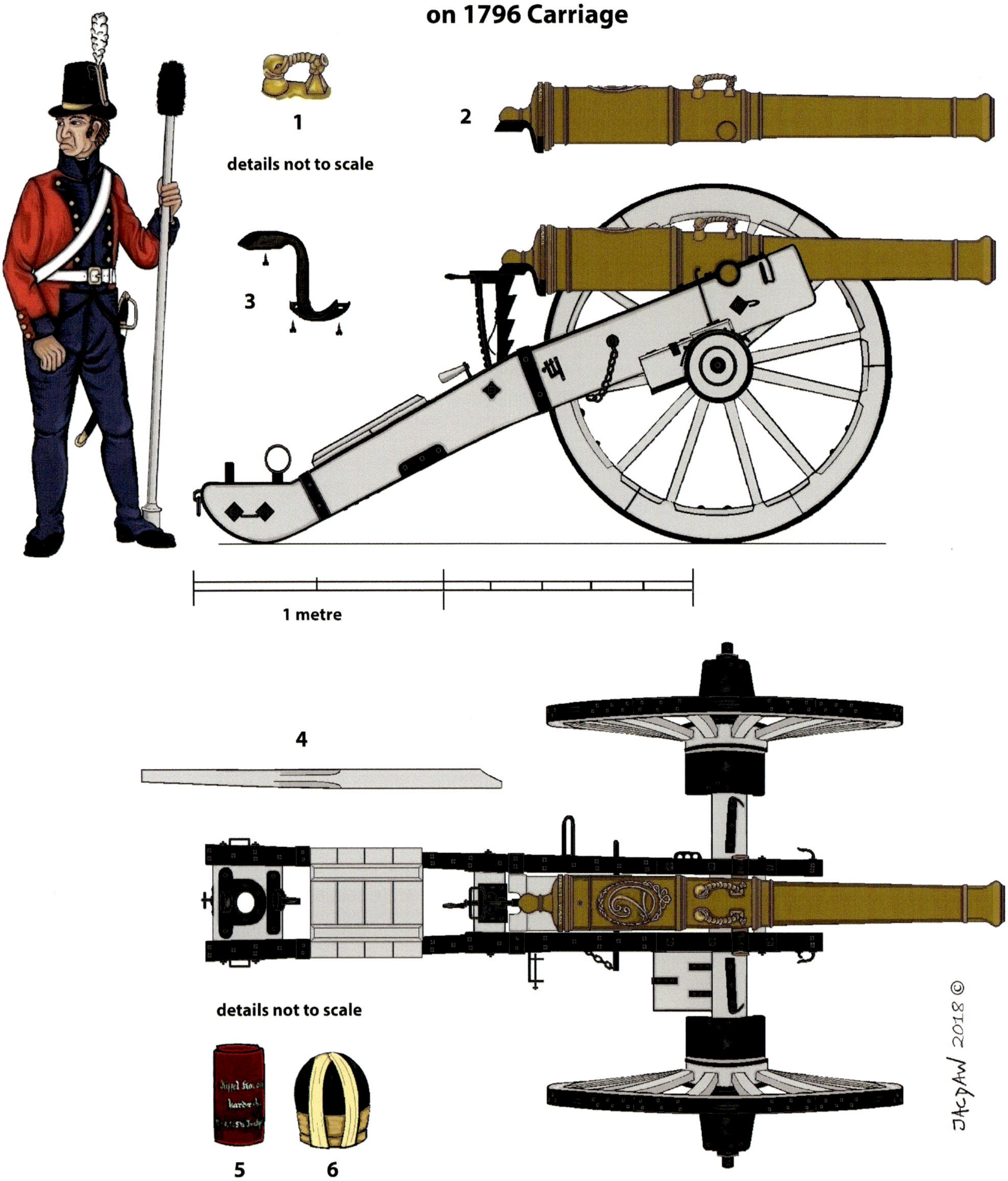

Plate 35. Danish 3-pdr 22 Calibre Field Gun, System 'Carl af Hessen', M1766

The gun is shown mounted on a new carriage which was based on the French 'Gribeauval' system and was drawn with a Prussian-based limber which was used as light field artillery until 1814, although they were mostly relegated to the artillery reserve after 1808.

1. Elephant head and trunk lifting handles, typical Danish style.
2. Barrel, note the added tooth or wedge and bracket fixed under the button of the cascable, to fit into the new elevating device (*Tandem stille maskine*). Later barrels had this tooth cast on directly at the foundry.
3. A clearer view of the bracket and tooth or wedge which was bolted fixed under the button and the cascable.

4. The trail spike (*baksebomme*) to manoeuvre the gun, painted pearl grey to correspond with the gun.
5. Canister case.
6. Round shot with sabot attached.

Note, the loading and cleaning tools appear to have been stowed on the left-hand side of the carriage and the manoeuvring tools and trail spikes were strapped to the right-hand side when looking forward from the rear of the gun.

Source: after an original barrel and plans conserved in the Tøjhusmuseet, Copenhagen, now called the Krigsmuseet, some full scale models found at the Fredericia Fortress, and a drawing found in the Hessisches Staatsarchiv, Marburg, Germany. The gun is shown with a foot artillery gunner *c.*1804, for scale. Near wheel removed for clarity.

carriages' for export to Turkey and, as the original text says, 'The Barbaric [Arabic] states'!

The result was the Danes' own unique system using a combination of features, principally based on the 'Gribeauval' and Austrian systems, but with Prussian, English and Hessian influences together with some Danish-designed improvements.

All three models had slightly different gun carriages, different mainly in the form of the trails, probably as an effort to reduce the recoil of the regimental and field guns, and lessen the ground pressure.

All of the carriages used during this period were of the bracket-type M1794/1796 carriages, but some older versions for the heavier 12-pdr guns continued to be used, especially in the fortresses. A project to produce some light, iron-barrelled 3-pdr and 6-pdr field guns in Sweden were abandoned due to the war.

The Technical Details of the Ordnance

Another major modernisation of the artillery was the new elevating device first introduced in 1798. Firstly the 'Gribeauval screw' had been considered and was actually used on a few fortress guns, but in the end a Danish device was chosen, called the *Tandem stille maskine*. This new system necessitated the addition of an iron bracket with a 'nose' or 'tooth' to be fixed under the breech and cascabel button, to enable it to function on the older pieces. The mechanism consisted of a cog and a winding handle with curved lifting bar and a toothed ratchet. There appears to have been two versions of this mechanism.

It was mounted in a square iron gear box with two cogs inside which were operated by a handle called a *Svingel* (turn-handle). In turn this was bolted onto a transom. The handle wound a slightly curved cogged bar either up or down, called the *hævestang* (lifting bar), and in turn this was attached to a heavy-duty ratchet. This raised or lowered the piece and was curved with the same radius as the rear of the gun would move in during operation on the same axis.

This was used for the finer adjustments of the sightline. All firing was carried with 0.5 degrees as the lowest sight line and 15 degrees as the highest. Firing at either a higher or a lower angle than this would mean that the shot would not graze the ground correctly and fly on to the target, but just bore itself harmlessly into ground. In the case of howitzers a higher angle was normally used, so the shell would only roll a short distance before exploding on target. Too high an angle would often mean that the shell would also bore itself into ground, and the following explosion, if it did explode, would have less effect. One turn of the handle would change the sightline around one degree either up or down.

Danish 3-pdr 20 Calibre Field Gun, System 'Carl af Hessen', M1766

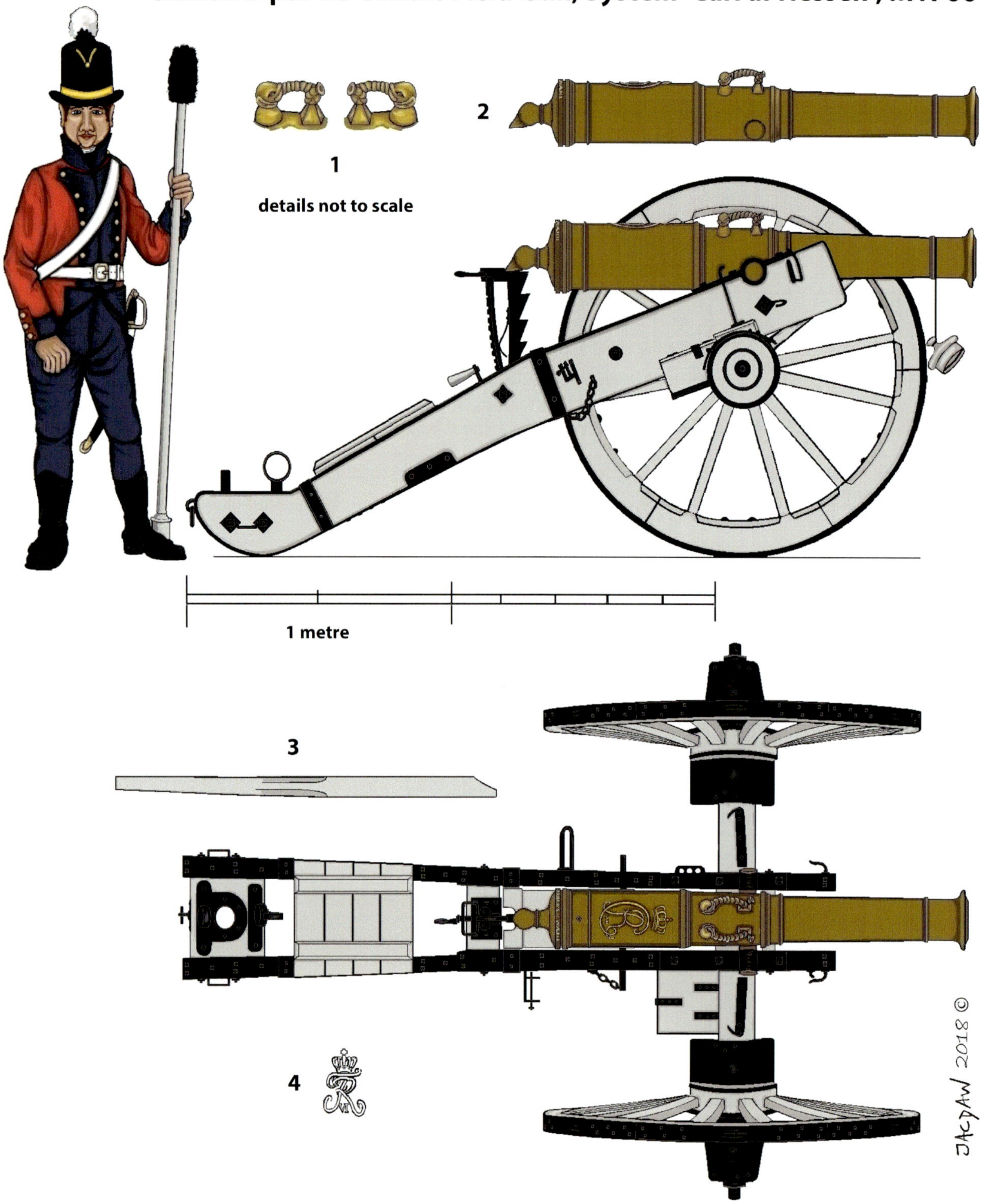

Plate 36. Danish 3-pdr 20 Calibre Field Gun, System 'Carl af Hessen', 1766

The gun is shown mounted on a 1796 model bracket carriage as used by the foot artillery. The barrel bears the new monogram with the 'CR' with 'VII' underneath which tells us the barrel was cast between 1799 and 1806. Note the tompion, which was found on all the guns, which was usually attached to a cord wrapped around the barrel.

1. The elephant head and trunk lifting handles, typical Danish style.
2. The M1766 20 calibre gun barrel, note the added tooth or wedge under the knob of the cascable, to fit into the elevating device (*Tandem stille maskine*). This later piece had this tooth cast on directly at the foundry. Calibre 20, bore diameter 76mm, bore length 152cm, total length of gun barrel 167.2cm, number cast 144.
3. The *baksebomme* (trail spike) to manoeuvre the gun painted grey for the foot artillery.
4. The monogram of Frederik VI as found on the later pieces, cast after 1808.

This gun is mounted on the new M1796 gun carriage based on the 'Gribeauval' system. The limber was also redesigned after the Prussian and Austrian model in 1799. At same time a new horse battery had been built with the same carriage and limber, but with a newly cast 3-pdr 20 calibre M1766/97 gun barrel. It had been made for Norway. This barrel was shorter and had a new short, disc-shaped muzzle to improve accuracy, as there had been problems with 'overshooting' with the old M1766/22 calibre barrels, and no more barrels of this type were cast. A new tooth was also cast on the button of the cascable for the new 'elevating device'.

In 1800 it was decided that in future the artillery would use the new 3-pdr 20 calibre M1799 barrels, and that all new guns cast would be of this model. Subsequently the existing 3-pdr foot artillery and later regimental artillery should be re-armed with this model when possible. This would give the artillery a slightly lighter gun which would be more manoeuvrable and easier to aim correctly. It is not clear from the sources if or when this actually happened, but by 1813 a total 122 new barrels had been cast for the horse artillery in Norway, the field artillery in Denmark and the regimental artillery (most cast 1809–14), so probably some had changed barrels by 1814, but most of those which were converted into M1808 mounted artillery guns in 1808–09, still had the older model 22 calibre barrel.

Note, on the bottom left of the carriage there are three 'loops', this is probably where they placed the vent prickers and drills used when serving the gun, as mentioned in regulations. Spare ones, and probably when they were moving, would have been placed in a tool box. The loading and cleaning tools appear to have been stowed on the left-hand side of the carriage and the manoeuvring tools and trail spikes were strapped to the right-hand side when looking forward from the rear of the gun.

Source: after original barrel and plans conserved in the Tøjhusmuseet, Copenhagen, now called the Krigsmuseet, and a drawing found in the Hessisches Staatsarchiv, Marburg, Germany. The gun is shown with a foot artilleryman from a Holstein national battery company holding a combined sponge (*Krumvisker*) and rammer *c.*1807, shown for scale. Near wheel removed for clarity.

Danish 3-pdr 22 Calibre M1766/1799 System 'Carl af Hessen' Field Gun on M1808 Kørende Carriage

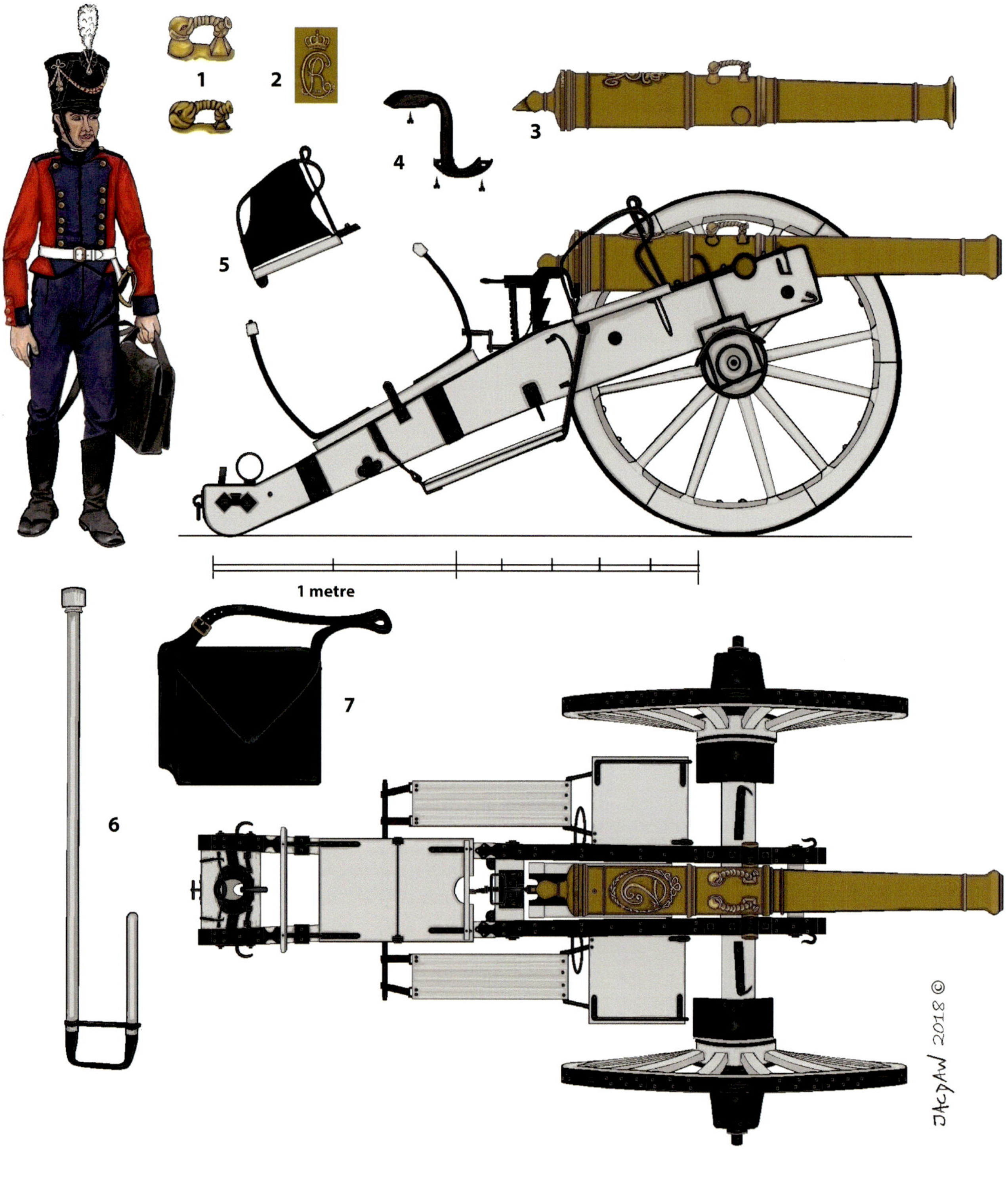

Plate 37. Danish 3-pdr 22 Calibre Field Gun, System 'Carl af Hessen', M1799

Mounted on an M1808 Kørende gun carriage with seating for four gunners, a gunner seated either side of the gun above the axle and two on the trail, one facing each side. The barrels cast from 1808 to 1814 bore a new monogram, that of Frederik VI 'FRVI', those cast between 1799 and 1808 bore the late version monogram of Christian VII 'CRVII' (crowned script). Not all the 'remodelled' guns used were the new 20 calibre M1766/M1799 gun barrels, some were converted from the preceding model, mainly for the newly raised Danske and Holstenske artillery battalions formed in 1808, from the disbanded Landeværns artilleri. Besides the M1687 3-pdr guns they also used surplus 22 calibre M1766 barrels, but with the new tooth cast on and the new elevating device.

1. Different models of elephant heads and trunks used for lifting rings.
2. The late version of Christian VII 'CRVII' monogram.
3. A new lighter 20 calibre piece cast after 1808 may also have been used. They all had the monogram of Frederik VI.
4. The bracket with the tooth or nose which was fixed on to the older pieces so they could function with the elevating device.
5. The gunner's seat shown with the leather/canvas seat coverings.
6. Ramrod with a wooden head (*Krumsætter*)
7. Satchel with ready-to-fire shot, it contained three pieces of shot with the sabot and charge tied together for the 3-pdr guns or two shots for the 6-pdr guns.

Contrary to many modern interpretations the gunners did not sit astride the gun carriage. The first plans for the mounted artillery gun clearly shows that the two gunners were intended to sit sideways each one facing opposite sides of the carriage. The two frames are arm rests, not back rests. Sitting sideways allowed the gunners to mount and dismount quickly as well as having a good view of what was going on (see diagram). The seats on the axle had a black leather cover attached to the back bar for the back rest, no doubt to protect the gunners from mud thrown up by the wheels. The loading and cleaning tools appear to have been carried on the left-hand side of the carriage and the manouvering tools and trail or hand spikes were strapped to the right-hand side when standing at the rear of the gun looking forwards. A drag rope seems to have been stowed on each side. The 22 calibre pieces were inscribed with their weight on the heads of the left-hand trunnions, in this case 620 Danish pounds. The seats and foot boards would be dismounted when the piece was in action.

Source: after the original barrel, model and plans conserved in the Tøjhusmuseet, Copenhagen, now called the Krigsmuseet; also a contemporary illustration conserved at the Fredericia Fortress. For scale the gun is shown with a gunner of the Kørende (mounted) artillery carrying an ammunition satchel. Near wheel removed for clarity.

Danish Elevating Systems, *Tandem Stille Maskine*

Plate 38. Danish Elevating Systems, *Tandem Stille Maskine*

Left: the standard model used for the 3-pdr guns.It was first approved in 1798 (thus 'M1798'), and first produced in 1798–99.
First made for the 88 'regimental' guns on carriage M1794, delivered to the Copenhagen arsenal in 1799 before delivery to infantry regiments.
Right: another model from a contemporary drawing, probably the original Model 1766.

Source: illustrations made after originals conserved in Norway, the Fredericia Fortress and the Tøjhusmuseet, Copenhagen, now called the Krigsmuseet; together with drawings found in the Hessisches Staatsarchiv in Marburg, Germany, and several near-contemporary drawings made by cadets.

At the bottom of the bar there was a 'stop', to avoid winding it too high. If for some reason the line of sight had to be changed in a hurry, another bar called the *Aftrækkeren* (trigger bar) was mounted. This was connected to the ratchet, which had either three or four large teeth, generally four, so it could move up and down, with a strong heavy spring in the middle maintaining the pressure against the tooth. At the top was a bar, connected to a handle and sitting in a groove, where it would stay under normal adjustments. When the firing angle needed to be changed rapidly the handle could be pulled back, which pulled the tooth out of its groove and the piece could fall down some five degrees to the next tooth of the ratchet.

All of the newly cast 3-pdrs from 1800 onwards were shortened from 22 calibres to 20 calibres (Model 1766/1800) and were given a flatter dish-shaped muzzle, and the knob of the cascabel had this tooth cast on to fit the elevating device.

General Notes on Casting, and the Decoration Cast on the Pieces

From 1757 all the Danish cannons were cast in the foundry at Frederiksværk. They were cast solid and then drilled out; this was one of the reasons why the foundry was situated in Frederiksværk, as here the water could be channelled and large watermills built to turn the large drills and other machinery used in the fabrication of the cannons.

All the barrels were cast some 3–4mm larger than needed and were then ground smooth, except for where the handles, the royal monogram and the breech lettering were situated. These were roughly cast and then chiselled out, sanded and polished manually by craftsmen.

The M1687 barrels simply had the text 'FRIDRICS WÆRK' (one word on either side of the vent). Just below the royal monogram there was an elaborate field where the year of casting was inscribed. Most of those used were cast after 1760, so they had the double monogram of Frederik V until 1766.

Most barrels of the M1766 system had the place and year cast marked on them and by this time they were all cast in the foundry in Frederiksværk. From 1789 they were inscribed with '17 FRIDRICS WÆRK 89' on either side of the vent. The early monogram of Christian VII was a head within a wreath.

Some guns could be cast with a special text on them commemorating a dignitary such as Carl of Hessen, written in Latin on the 6-pdrs cast for Norway:

Carolus Landgran Hassia
Generalisimus Regis

This lettering could also be found on some howitzers and guns of the M1766 system. The howitzers would have had another version of the monogram of Christian VII on the chase, a crowned 'CR' with a small '7' in Roman numerals within the 'C', and any other lettering on the field between the first and second reinforce. The cannons would have it the other way round, here the lettering could be found on the chase.

Twelve 6-pdr guns found in Norway had this variation of the text:

Carolus prince Landg. Hassia
Cass Summ: Rer Torment Dux
Dan Direct

Another eight 6-pdr guns had the following variation:

Carolus prince Landg.
Prorex Norveg Rex Milit

Some 6-pdr and 12-pdr guns found in Denmark, together with a few in Norway, had the following text:

Christianus septi
Mux Rex Dan: Nor

All the guns cast between 1799 and 1814 were more simply decorated, they now only had the monogram, the place of casting (Frederiksværk) and the year inscribed on them,

Danish 6-pdr 22 Calibre Field Gun, System 'Carl af Hessen', M1766 on M1796 Carriage

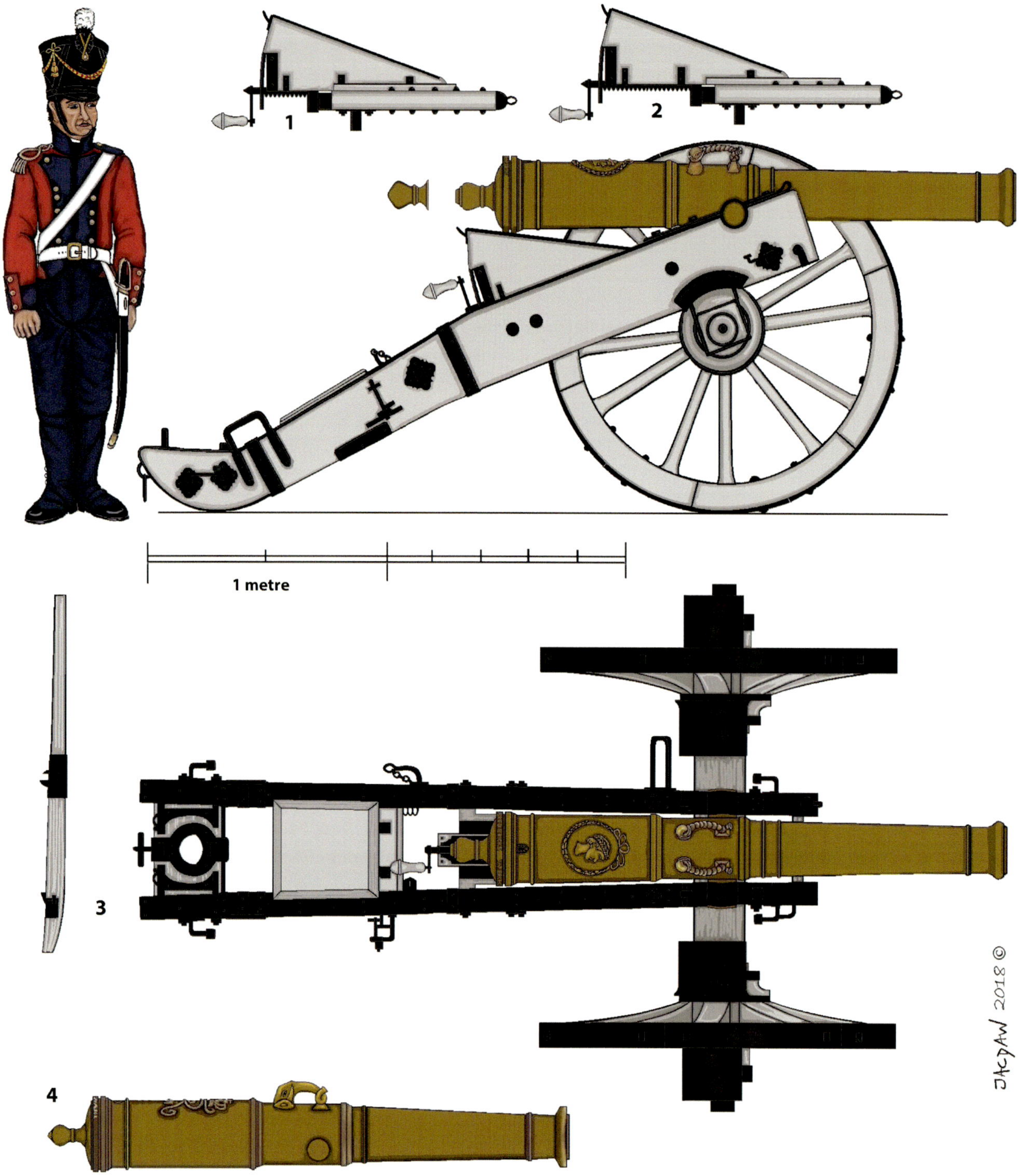

Plate 39. Danish 6-pdr 22 Calibre Field Gun, System 'Carl af Hessen', M1766

This piece was used mainly by the foot artillery. These gun barrels were used in Denmark, Holstein and Norway until 1814, the first series cast had the full 'Emperor's head' monogram. The same barrels were used in Denmark until 1806 at least, when they started to be replaced with the newly cast 20 calibre barrels.

1. The elevating or aiming device. All the various 6-pdr guns used the Prussian-influenced elevating system, which had been improved by the Danes, called a *Kielwinde* in German or a *Donkraft* in Danish. The improvements were important enough for the Prussians to refer to the system as 'After the Danish model'. The wedge is shown in the wound forward position as when used for standard horizontal firing range.
2. The wedge is shown in the wound backwards position, as when used for elevated maximum firing range.
3. The *baksebomme* (trail spike) to lift or manoeuvre the gun, variant. Not a variant of the button of the cascable.
4. The 20 calibre M1800 6-pdr piece.

All these tools were made in different sizes to correspond to the different guns. The Danish artillery book *Dansk Artilleri I Napoleonstiden* claims that the mops were not used with the 6-pdr guns and above because they were too long and heavy to use, however modern-day tests show differently, so they may have been used by the 6-pdr gun crews after all. We know for sure that the 6-pdrs (two companies) stationed on Zeeland probably received new 20 calibre barrels, probably sometime in 1810 or a little later as we know that only 27 were cast in 1808–09. Again, none of these barrels were delivered to Holstein or to Norway. The loading and cleaning tools appear to have been stowed on the left-hand side of the carriage and the manoeuvring tools and trail spikes were strapped to the right-hand side when seen from the rear looking forward.

Source: after an original barrel and plans conserved in the Tøjhusmuseet, Copenhagen, now called the Krigsmuseet, and contemporary drawings found in the Hessisches Staatsarchiv, Marburg, Germany**.** For scale, the gun is shown with an NCO of the foot artillery wearing a shako *c.*1810. Near wheel removed for clarity.

no doubt linked to the economy drives. Christian VII used another monogram between1782–1806; it was a 'C7' within a floral wreath, joined at the top with a ribbon. Between 1806 and 1808 he used the crowned 'CR' with a small '7' in Roman numerals within the 'C', as used on the howitzers.

Note that the lifting handles or 'dolphins' on Danish cannons were actually elephants' heads with the trunk forming the handle or lifting ring, probably influenced by the Danish Order of the Elephant. On the earlier pieces, *c.*1762, the elephants look back towards the cascabel, after this they look forward towards the muzzle.

All the carriages were all made of oak, as were the wheels, except for the felloes (the outer rim of the wheel, to which the spokes were fixed) which were made of *Bøgetræ*/ beech wood.

Another particularity of the design of Danish wheels was the spacing of the spokes, which were always mounted in pairs. The joints of the felloes were situated between the pairs, and this reinforced the joint and lessened the stress on them. This form of construction was used on all wheeled vehicles, gun carriages, limbers, military wagons and carts.

Munitions

The Danish artillery appears to have used the same basic types of munitions as used by other nations, solid iron round shot, in all three of the basic calibres (1-pdr, 3-pdr and 6-pdr), all three also used their version of grape or case shot. This was a cylindrical thin metal tin containing up to 50 small balls. Bursting shells, or grenades as they are sometimes called, were only used by the howitzers. They appear to have started to use spherical case shot towards the end of the war. All the munitions were delivered to the batteries with a wooden sabot and powder charge strapped to the munitions.

The Danes used a particular fuse (called a *Fængrør*) to fire their pieces; it was similar to an English reed, but with a funnel on the top, filled with gun powder which was covered in greased paper.

Danish 6-pdr 20 Calibre Horse Artillery Gun, System 'St Germain', M1762 Mounted on a M1796 Carriage

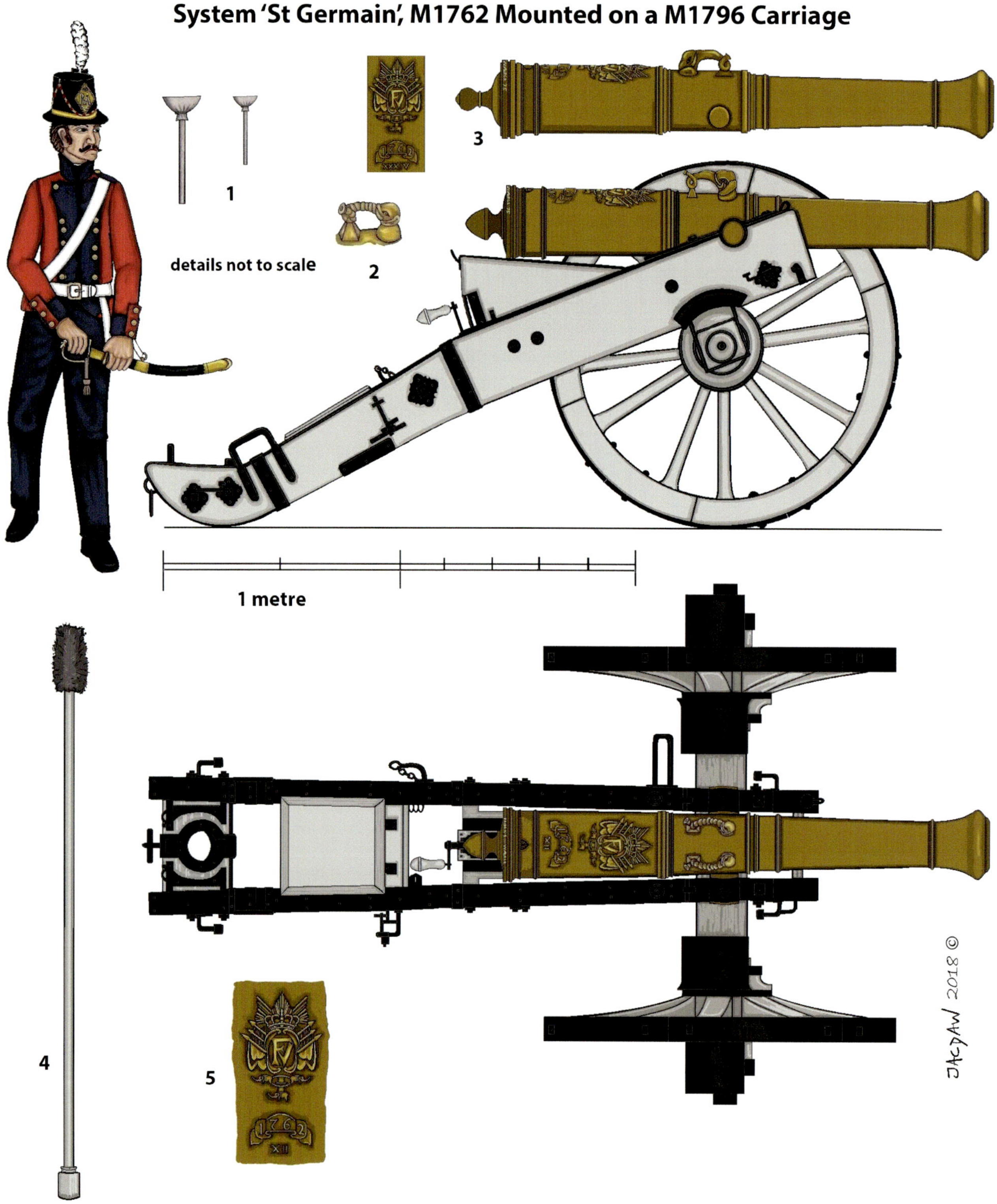

Plate 40. Danish 6-pdr 20 Calibre Horse Artillery Gun, System 'St Germain', M1762

This piece was mounted on a modified M1796 carriage and was only used by the horse artillery in Denmark and Holstein, not in Norway. A total of 46 pieces of this model were cast between 1762 and 1766, during the reign of Frederick V. As a special distinction the elephant's heads are looking towards the rear.

1. The fuses (called quills in England) as used by the Danish artillery.
2. The 'elephant' lifting handle.
3. A 6-pdr 20 calibre piece cast during the early part of the reign of Christian VII. A few of the last of these models cast in 1766, probably no more than eight, had the elephants' heads in the usual position.
4. The standard combined sponge and ramrod (*Visker og ansætter*) tool. All these tools were made in different sizes for the calibre of the different guns.
5. A better view of the monogram of Frederick V, 'FV', as found on the barrel.

The loading and cleaning tools appear to have been carried on the left-hand side of the carriage and the manoeuvring tools and trail spikes were strapped to the right-hand side when seen from the rear looking forward.

Source: after an original barrel and plans conserved in the Tøjhusmuseet, Copenhagen, now called the Krigsmuseet, and contemporary drawings found in the Hessisches Staatsarchiv', Marburg, Germany. For scale the gun is shown with a horse artilleryman *c.*1806. Near wheel removed for clarity.

Danish Artillery According to the Organisational Reforms of 1797 and Later Changes

First of all, a clear distinction was made between the regimental artillery and the regular or brigade artillery.

The regimental artillery had now had two 3-pdr guns allotted to each infantry battalion, and when possible and appropriate, 1-pdr guns – principally in Norway.

These were allocated in pairs to each of the single infantry battalions, who themselves trained and mastered the handling of the guns for every manoeuvre. The gun carriages were lightened and towed with limbers, and for the 1-pdr guns/*Amusettes*, limbers were not required as they were of the galloper model. All the wooden parts were painted red, 'The same colour as the red uniforms of the infantry', with the metal painted yellow to distinguish them from the other branches of the artillery.

The brigade artillery mustered the regular batteries. Every infantry brigade of two regiments had a light battery attached.

The medium 6-pdrs were normally part of the divisional reserve artillery. Each Danish/Holstein/Norwegian field artillery battery usually had 10 guns and howitzers of the 'Carl af Hessen' system M1766. The pieces were 3-pdr and 6-pdrs. The howitzers used were 10-pdrs and 20-pdrs.

A heavy 12-pdr field company/battery was to be composed of eight 12-pdr guns, four 36-pdr howitzers, and four 1-pdr *Amusettes*.

A medium 6-pdr field company/battery was to be composed of eight 6-pdr guns and two 20-pdr howitzers.

A light 3-pdr field company/battery was to be composed of eight 3-pdr guns and two 10-pdr howitzers. In Norway two 3-pdr companies used barrels of the M1766 system and the two (national) companies used tubes of the M1687 system. In 1813 the 3-pdr guns revealed themselves, in some situations, to be of limited effect, so they were, where possible, replaced with 6-pdr guns.

A light 1-pdr *Amusette* company/battery was to be composed of eight 1-pdr *Amusettes* (these were guns formerly used by the horse artillery 1788–99 and now surplus, but intended for the use of the light infantry and light cavalry).

A horse artillery company/battery was to be composed of eight (short) 6-pdr guns and two 10-pdr howitzers. In Denmark and Holstein, the horse artillery used barrels of the 'St Germain' system from 1762. In Norway the horse artillery company/battery was to be composed of eight 3-pdr 20 calibre guns and two (short) 10-pdr howitzers.

The 'Kørende' or 'Mounted' Artillery Batteries

In 1807–1808, after studying of the performance of the artillery in the Continental wars and seeing that the brigade

Danish 10-Pdr Howitzer System M1766/M1789, Mounted on a Modified 3-pdr Carriage M1796

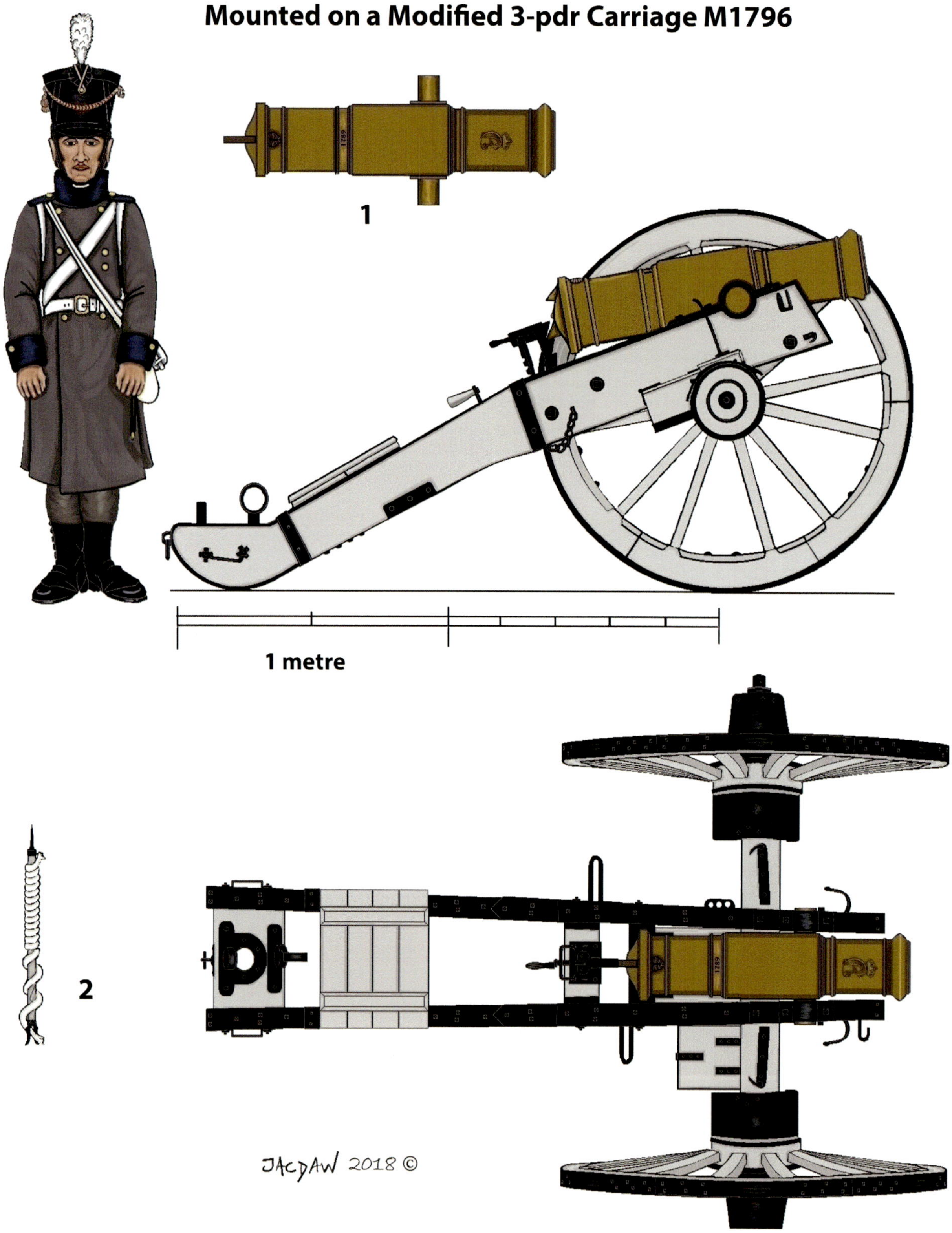

Plate 41. Danish 10-pdr 7¾ Calibre Bronze (Long) Howitzer, System 'Carl af Hessen', M1766/M1789

The Model 1789 howitzer was used mainly by the horse, foot and mounted artillery in Denmark and Holstein. For use in Norway there was a shorter version (6⅓ calibre) of the same howitzer (only 16 of these were cast, all shipped to Norway).

1. Barrel
2. Linstock (*luntestok*)

The loading and cleaning tools appear to have been carried on the left-hand side of the carriage and the manoeuvring tools and trail spikes were strapped to the right-hand side when seen from the rear looking forward. The gun is shown with a foot artilleryman *c.*1813, wearing an overcoat.

These guns were used by the Norwegian horse artillery company and two 'light' national foot companies. In 1809, two 'mounted artillery companies', were formed, which used the same model of howitzer. In 1811 two more light national companies were formed and all four were converted into Kørende (mounted) artillery. Further in 1811 six 'national artillery companies' were formed and all were converted into Kørende (mounted) artillery, which also used the same model howitzer.

Tactically, in the Danish artillery the howitzers were not just used for lobbing grenades over hills or other obstructions, or setting fire to buildings or demolishing obstacles during sieges. The howitzer was considered the main defence against close-range infantry and cavalry attacks, as its short but large calibre barrel could fire a large and effective canister round in a wide arc, blunderbuss style; the short barrel could be loaded quickly. Also used for street fighting or fighting in close terrain, it was this weapon which was normally put to the fore, because of its relative lightness, and effectiveness at close range.

Source: after original barrel and plans conserved in the Tøjhusmuseet, Copenhagen, now called the Krigsmuseet. The gun is shown with a foot artilleryman *c.*1813, wearing an overcoat. Near wheel removed for clarity.

artillery proved to be highly skilled in manoeuvring and very efficient, the regimental artillery was deemed to be superfluous and was accordingly abolished in 1808.

Instead, after mainly studying the new very mobile Swedish M1804 artillery, a battery of mounted (Kørende) artillery was formed (not to be confused with the horse artillery), which was to be composed of eight 3-pdr guns which were converted from the regimental artillery, and two 10-pdr howitzers from the regular artillery's arsenals. They were to be attached to each brigade of infantry.

When moving, some of the gunners were mounted on the gun carriages, four rode on the gun carriage of which two sat sideways, each one facing opposite directions and one gunner was seated either side of the barrel, when in action the two axle seats and foot plates were removed and laid aside.

There were no gunners seated on the limbers which were of the old style, see illustrations.

So the Danish artillery was based on the slightly outdated, but solid 'Carl af Hessen' M1766 system heavy pieces, but during the period 1794 to 1808 both the pieces and carriages were modernised.

The gun carriages and all other types of equipment of the Danish Field Artillery were painted pearl grey, similar to the colour of the British artillery of the period, with metal in black. The barrels were in bronze and in the field they were left unpolished. From 1799, after experience was gained, the lids of limber ammunition boxes and ammunition carts/wagons were painted dark grey or dark blue – all to avoid the equipment from appearing too visible and easy to spot when deployed in the field.

Reform of the Regimental Artillery 1794–1799

The 'old' 3-pdr M1687/1748/57 regimental gun was used by all the Danish Infantry regiments until *c.*1800. Then 45 of the best that remained were repaired and shipped out to the island of Bornholm, for further use there, and the rest put in store in the arsenals. These pieces were mounted on 'limon' carriages (called 'galloper guns' in English).

Danish 20-pdr Howitzer System 'Carl af Hessen', M1772/M1789, Mounted on a Modified 6-pdr M1796 Carriage

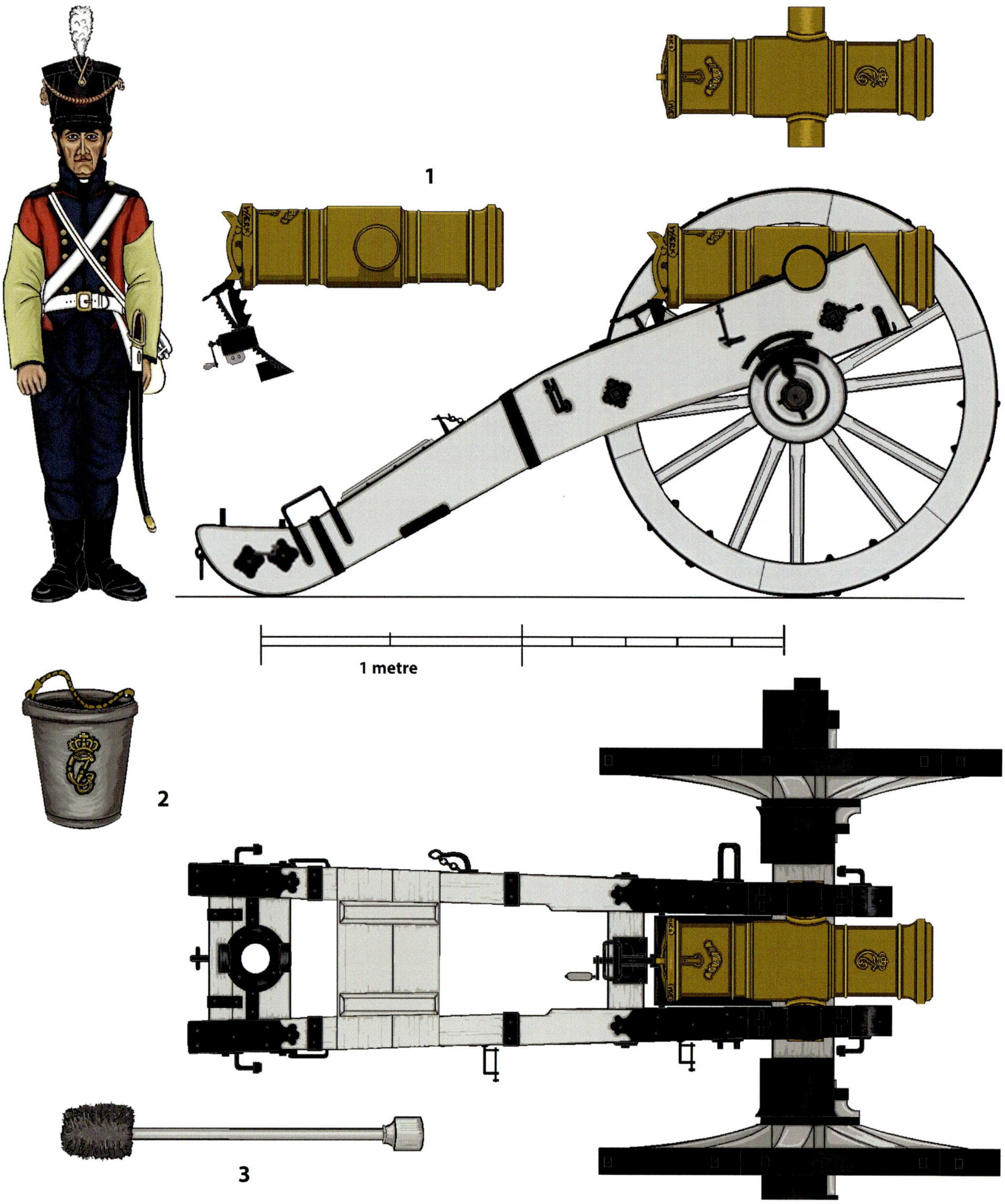

Plate 42. Danish 20-pdr Bronze Howitzer, System 'Carl af Hessen', M1772/M1789

Details of barrel
1. Artillery corps leather bucket (*svalespand*), painted grey and decorated with the royal monogram
2. Howitzer model short sponge and rammer

Source: after original barrel and plans conserved in the Tøjhusmuseet, Copenhagen, now called the Krigsmuseet. For scale the gun is shown with a no. 2 howitzer gunner *c*.1812. He is wearing the special canvas oversleeves issued to howitzer no. 2 loaders to protect their uniforms whilst sponging and loading, as they had to put both their arms inside the howitzer barrel during both operations. Near wheel removed for clarity.

In Norway a number of light field batteries were formed after 1800–1810, using the same barrel put into the new carriage M1796, and made locally. But this took time, and as late as 1808 parts for the elevating device were apparently still missing and they were ordered 'to be made locally'. In Denmark after 1808, the M1687 pieces were also mounted on M1796 carriages and was used by some of the Danish and Holstein artillery battalions' light artillery companies, *c*.1808–1814.

The first proposal for a new carriage in 1794 was based on a Hesse-Kassel design (from 1788), probably proposed by Prince Carl. It would reuse the M1687 piece, have an ammunition box on the trail, an old-style limber and an M1766 elevating device. This design was revised, although the basic design was in the main respected.

The new regimental Model 1794 gun was finished and delivered by 1799. It was built using a 3-pdr 22 calibre M1766 piece mounted in the new model 1794 carriage. This had a trail which was clearly inspired by the Austrian design. A total of 88 were made, rather more than was really necessary as each infantry regiment would only need four, meaning 48 should have been enough; however apparently during the same period the Prince Regent was planning to double the strength of the army by creating the Landeværn (home guard) reserve, and as this was to have regimental artillery as well, these extra guns were probably made for it.

In 1800 it was decided that in future the regimental artillery would, when the new 3-pdr 20 calibre M1799 pieces had been cast, be rearmed with them when possible. This would give a slightly lighter gun and also a gun more easily aimed correctly. It is not clear from the sources if or when this happened, but by 1813 in total 122 new pieces had been cast for the horse artillery in Norway, the field artillery and regimental artillery in Denmark, so probably some had by then changed their barrels. However several of those converted into M1808 mounted artillery guns in 1808–09 still had the older model 22 calibre piece, which necessitated the addition of a bracket with the nose or tooth under the cascabel for the elevating device.

In Norway several of the preserved 3-pdr 22 calibre pieces also have what can be described as a nose or tooth on a bracket bolted under the cascabel for the elevating device, whether this was also done in Denmark is unclear, but it is very possible.

For limbers the M1799 limber was chosen, a Prussian/Austrian based model, with a rather large ammunition box on the limber as the standard model. These limbers were the basis for all future limbers, only differing in size, and the size of the ammunition box. In the 3-pdr batteries the wheels were nearly the same size.

The ammunition wagons used by the regimental artillery were older two-wheel carts.

The New Carriages and Limbers for the Horse Artillery, 1796–1799

Until 1798 the principal piece used by the Danish horse artillery had been the 1-pdr *Amusette*, and all three horse artillery batteries had 16 1-pdr *Amusettes* and four 10-pdr howitzers. In his army reforms of 1789 Prince Carl had wanted 'mixed batteries' of eight 1-pdr pieces, eight 3-pdrs, four 10-pdr howitzers. This were not accepted by the Artillery Corps, by Huth or by the Prince Regent, as they all wanted 10-gun batteries built around one main gun type, the 6-pdr. So in 1796, tests were carried out for new pieces and new carriages. Finally it was decided the carriages would be modified M1796 carriages and the pieces would be the 6-pdr 20 calibre 'St Germain' M1762.

In 1797 a new organisation was ordered, and from 1796–1799, new and more modern guns delivered. There are few details of the actual form of these new carriages, specially made for the horse artillery in 1798, and designed after plans first made in 1796.

The plans for a new mounted 6-pdr system were influenced by the Swedish mounted artillery M1804, and were tested in Denmark 1805–06, but not accepted because they were too expensive. This was the basis for the carriages and limbers of the horse artillery, but with seats added.

Danish M1799 Artillery Limber, with Ammunition Chest for 3-pdr Piece *c.*1805

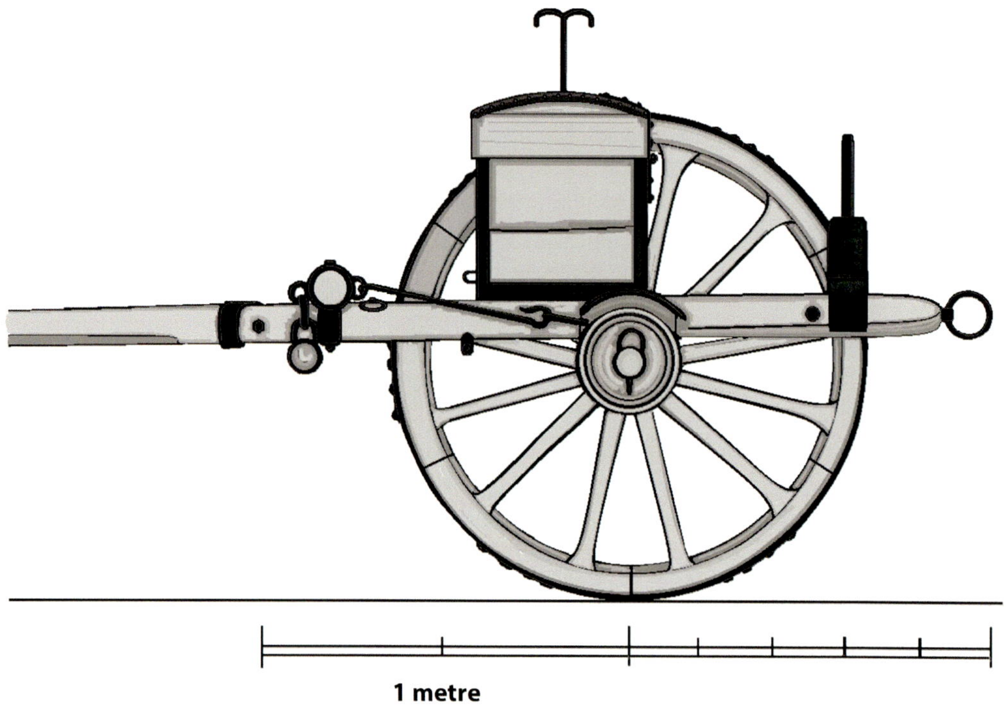

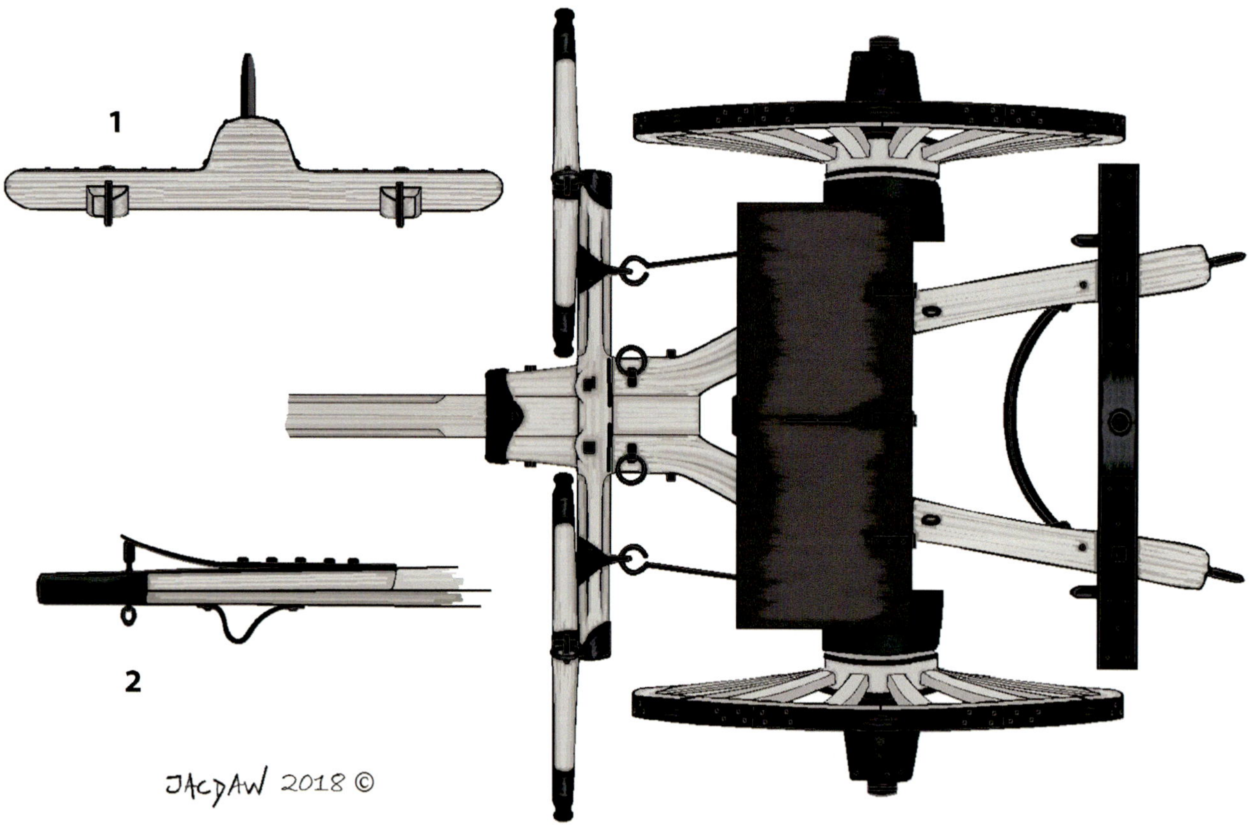

Plate 43. Danish M1799 Limber, with Ammunition Chest for 3-pdr Piece *c.*1805

Used throughout the period in both Denmark and Norway by the foot and horse artillery. This was the standard model for 3-pdr guns, but there were different sizes of ammunition chests, the one is shown is the smaller model. The 6-pdr limber had a larger chest placed more evenly astride the axle. The horse artillery in Denmark also used this model for extra mobility. For the regimental artillery it would have been painted red with the metal fittings painted yellow. This model did not have the gunners sitting on the chest, but from 1810 seats were added to the models found in Norway, for their Kørende Artilleri, as this was both formed and equipped differently to the Danish unit. Seats may also eventually have been added to the limbers used by the Danske and Holstenske artillery battalions.

1. Pintle bar, note variant shape. It was a fairly common practice to wrap spare ropes around the two fork shafts which protrude from under the pintle bar.
2. Head of centre shaft with fittings for the couplings for the lead pair of horses

Source: after plans found in Tøjhusmuseet, Copenhagen, now called the Krigsmuseet, a drawing found in the Hessiches Staatsarchiv, Marburg, Germany, and photographs of a preserved limber in Norway. For scale, shown with an NCO of the foot artillery 1802–1808, note the pleats on the rear of the coatee and the buttons which also kept the belt from sliding down. Near wheel removed for clarity.

Removing seats accordingly, must show how a horse artillery gun actually looked. As seen from above, the gun carriage resembles more the 'Gribeauval' system than the M1794 carriages made for the regimental artillery, and is also close to those carriages made for the Field Artillery 1800–06.

In 1796 the Crown Prince told his chief of artillery production, Von Mecklenburg, that the 'Gribeauval' carriages would be made in a 'modified Danish model' and this was to be the norm in the future, and also for the construction of the carriages for the horse artillery from 1798.

The iron strake bands on the wheels were part of the older guns, but were probably kept to strengthen the wheels and to give a firmer grip when moving at speed in rough terrain.

The limber was the M1799, but again with iron strake bands on the wheels and a smaller ammunition box (the horse artillery teams were to be followed by four-wheeled ammunition wagons). The four 10-pdr (long) howitzers were also part of the battery, and used the same carriage in a slightly modified form.

For the Norwegian horse artillery after several other suggestions had been tried, and it was finally decided to cast a new 3-pdr 20 calibre M1799 piece and use this together with two (short) 10-pdr howitzers.

The carriages were of the M1796 design. The two howitzers of the battery used the same carriage but modified to accommodate the barrel. Later this model was also chosen as the basis for the future 3-pdr foot artillery piece.

The 3-pdr Field Artillery, 1801–1806

It was decided to use the new carriage M1796 for the five 3-pdr line batteries in Denmark and the two 'heavy' 3-pdr batteries in Norway, with the M1798 elevating device and M1799 limber, but to continue to use the old 22 calibre gun barrel until the new 20 calibre pieces could be cast, probably due to the poor state of the economy and the lack of space in the foundry in Frederiksværk. On those older barrels, a bracket ending in a nose or tooth was bolted onto the cascabel to be used for the M1798 elevating device. Also an improved separate rear sight and new sighting techniques were tested and employed on those guns which had been converted. The older types of royal monograms were still to be found on most pieces, as they were all cast before 1800.

The woodwork of the pieces of the line batteries was painted light grey with the ironwork painted black, but it was normal that the 'blueprints' always showed the carriages in 'natural wood'. This colour scheme included the limbers and wagons.

The planned new 3-pdr 20 calibre M1799 piece was 'to be used by all 3-pdr artillery in the future', but only by 1814 had enough had been cast (122 pieces) due to delays both in production and the lack of funds.

The M1799 limber was the basic limber used by the field artillery. With different versions, either large or smaller ammunition boxes were used. Also from 1799 all the lids of the ammunition boxes were to be painted dark grey or black to reduce their visibility in the field. The large model ammunition box would hold 60 complete 3-pdr munitions.

Denmark had during this period two models of 10-pdr brass howitzers. The 10-pdr M1789 howitzers used

Danish Kørende Artillery Limber M1799/M1808 for 3-pdr Guns, *c.*1808

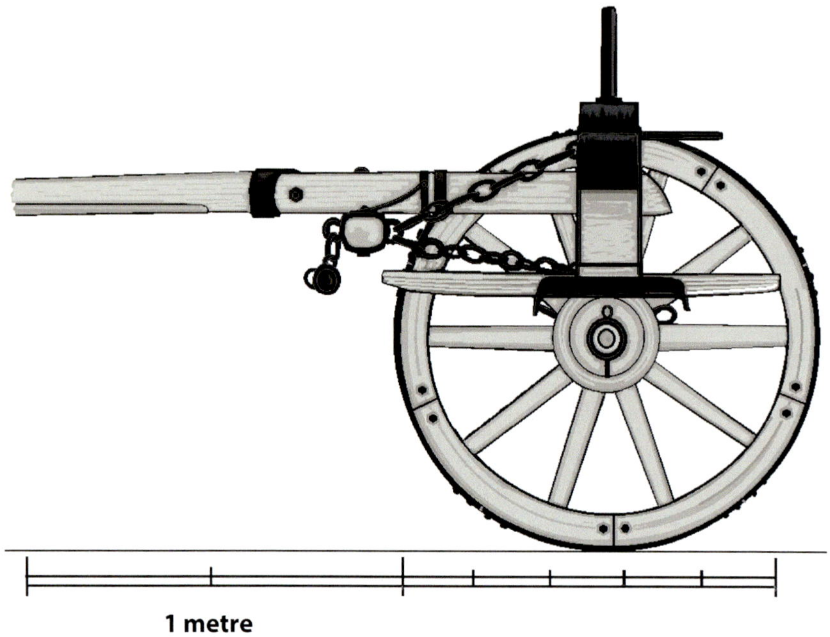

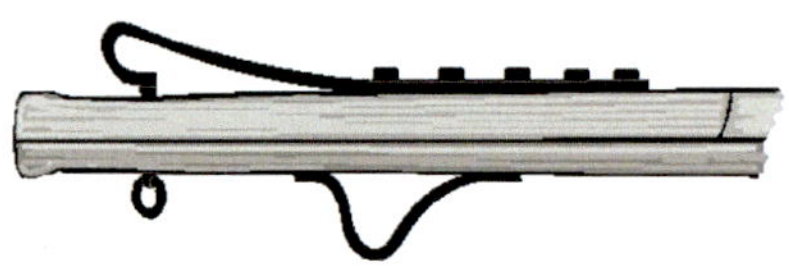

2

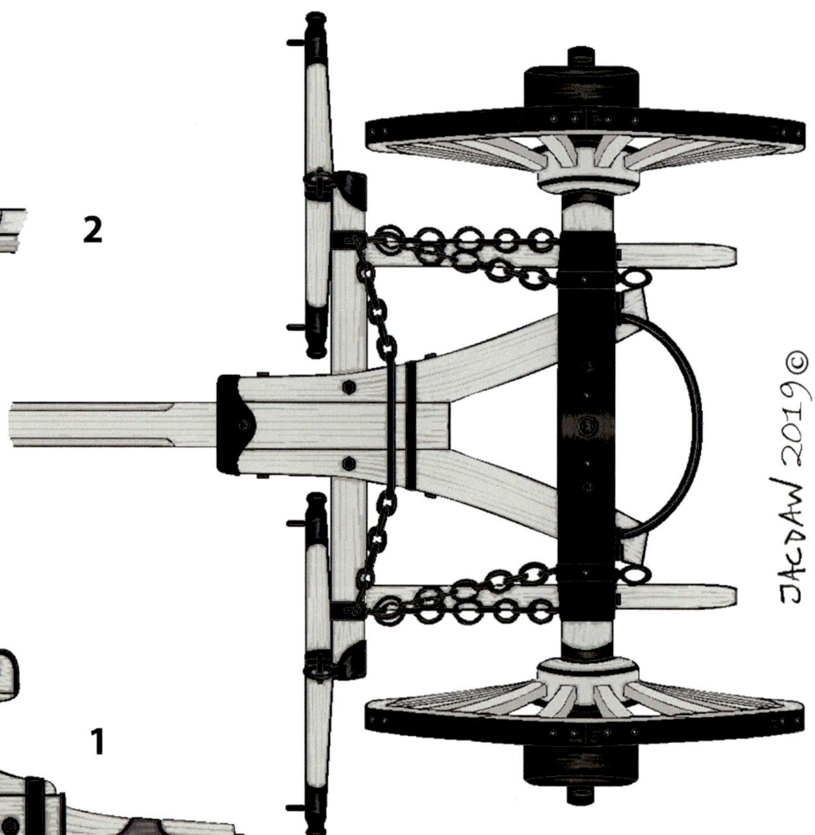

1

Plate 44. Danish Kørende Artillery Limber M1799/M1808 for 3-pdr Guns, *c.*1808

1. Cross section of the axlebed/axle tree and pintle
2. Head of the shaft with hook for the draught horses.
3. Alternative cross section of the axlebed/axle tree and pintle, after a period sketch.

Source: after a model found in Tøjhusmuseet, Copenhagen, now called the Krigsmuseet; also drawings and a couple of photographs of an original limber, since lost, taken in 1864. For scale, shown with an Over constabel (lance corporal) of the mounted artillery *c.*1814, redrawn after a sketch made by G. Shäfer. Near wheel removed for clarity.

an M1799 limber with the smaller ammunition box. The 10-pdr (short) M1789 field howitzer, calibre 13cm, length 83cm was to be used by the light and horse artillery. Finally only 16 were cast, 1789–91; eight were issued to the Danish and Holstein horse artillery and the other eight were for the Norwegian horse artillery and two light batteries. Those of the Danish/Holstein horse artillery were replaced in 1799 by four long howitzers and the other eight short howitzers were then sent to Norway as well.

The 10-pdr (long) M1789 field howitzer calibre 13cm, length 101cm was issued to the foot artillery (65 were cast 1789–91). This was the main howitzer of the foot artillery/horse artillery until 1800–1804, but those of the 6-pdr foot artillery batteries were then replaced by the heavier 20-pdr M1772 howitzers.

In 1795–96 several tests were carried out to find the best carriages to be used by the howitzers in the future. It was decided that for the 10-pdr howitzer a slightly modified 3-pdr M1796 carriage was to be used.

In 1806 the 3-pdr field artillery batteries began receiving the new 3-pdr M1805 ammunition wagons. Previously the 3-pdr field artillery batteries had used a combination of the older two- and four-wheel ammunition wagons. In 1805 a new model ammunition wagon was built and issued. This was a two-wheel ammunition cart with a new longer and stronger frame connecting it to new style limber, making it effectively a four-wheel wagon, but as the front wheels could pass under the rear, a tight turning radius was still possible. On top of the new frame two standard (small) ammunition boxes were mounted for extra ammunition and extra kit.

Although the economy was tight, the Prince Regent worked hard to modernise the artillery, and by 1806 the Danish and Holstein artillery had received new carriages and limbers. It is unclear whether the Danes also received eight ammunition wagons as well, as the sources are unclear about this point. But they probably did and they would then have been part of the 'artillery park', providing ammunition when needed during battle, not directly part of the battery, but placed at a central point close to the battle line, providing ammunition for all (four) batteries from there. They used the limber of the old M1792 'Gribeauval' model. In 1813 it was rather outdated, but still in use by some mainly French reserve batteries but also by several horse batteries because of its (relative) lightness. Most French 6-pdr foot batteries, had by 1813 changed to either the new M1808 limber or the even more modern M1813 limber by mid 1813, freeing up older materiel to be donated to several allies such as Denmark.

The 6-pdr 22 calibre barrel mounted in a 6-pdr carriage M1796 and the standard model aiming device M1774 for 6-pdr cannons slightly modernised. The planning for a new 6-pdr carriage started in earnest just before 1800, and at the same time they also tested the 'Gribeauval screw' elevating device, but in the end, a modernised version of the old M1774 *Kielwinde/Stillekile* (wedge device) was used. The 'Gribeauval screw' aiming device was later used for the lighter fortress guns, and first in 1834 it was taken in use generally by all the heavier field artillery too (see drawing in the Tøjhusmuseet).

The new 6-pdr 20 calibre M1806 piece was to be cast and used by the foot artillery in Denmark, Holstein and Norway. But in reality only 27 were cast 1808–09 and were only issued to the 6-pdr foot artillery batteries in Denmark, but not in Holstein or Norway.

The 20-pdr howitzer M1772 calibre 17cm, length 93cm (64 cast 1772–84) was the main howitzer used by the 6-pdr batteries from 1803. In 1796 several tests were carried out to find out which carriages were to be used in the future. It was decided, after reflection, that a slightly modified 6-pdr carriage M1796 was to be used for the M1772 20-pdr howitzer. No pictures are to be found of this carriage. Note the both 20-pdr and the 10-pdr howitzers had a special conical-shaped powder chamber.

It had been intended that Norway would only use the short 10-pdr howitzers. The 6-pdr companies were equipped the standard 20-pdr howitzers.

The limber M1799 used for the 6-pdr artillery was similar to a standard M1799 limber, but was slightly larger and more strongly built model to absorb the extra weight with an ammunition box.

In 1806, the 6-pdr field artillery batteries began receiving the new 6-pdr M1805 ammunition wagons. Previously the 6-pdr field artillery batteries had used the

Danish M1799 Limber for 6-pdr Guns, with Large Ammunition Chest

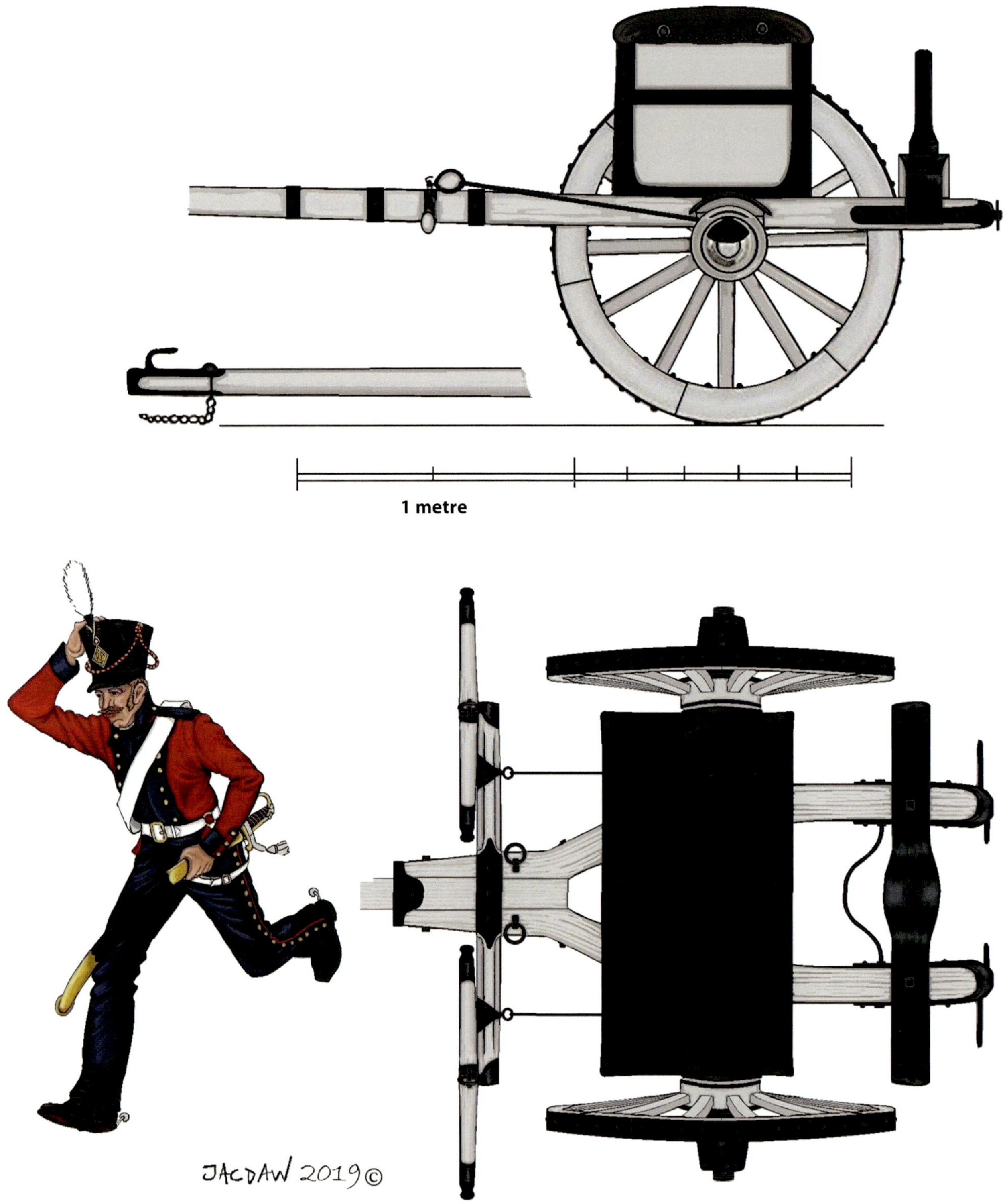

Plate 45. Danish M1799 Limber for 6-pdr Guns, with Large Ammunition Chest

Used throughout the period in both Denmark and Norway by the regimental and foot artillery. The 6-pdr limber had a larger chest placed more evenly over the axle. The same type was used by the regimental artillery, because it could hold more ammunition and mobility was not so important in the regimental artillery. This model did not have gunners sitting on the box, but it probably had seats added after 1808, as are found on a preserved model limber and drawings in Norway.

1. Pintle bar
2. Head of centre shaft with fittings for the couplings for the lead pair of horses. It was a fairly common practice to wrap spare ropes around the two fork shafts which protrude from under the pintle bar.

Source: based on a model and drawings found in Tøjhusmuseet, Copenhagen, now called the Krigsmuseet, and a drawing found in the Hessisches Staatsarchiv, Marburg, Germany. For scale, shown with a horse artilleryman. Near wheel removed for clarity.

old rather cumbersome four-wheel M1765 ammunition wagons. In 1805 a new model ammunition wagon was designed and built and issued. It was based on a modified old four-wheel ammunition wagon M1765, but with same new-style limber as that used by the M1805 3-pdr ammunition wagon, so that the front wheels could pass under the chassis, and so a tight turning radius was now possible increasing considerably its manoeuvrability. It could carry 130 ready-to-use munitions.

In 1808 it was decided to discontinue the regimental artillery, but to use its pieces and carriages to form seven new *Kørendebatterier* (mounted batteries) of eight 3-pdrs, either with the 22 calibre M1766 tubes or the new 20 calibre M1799 tubes in an improved M1794/1808 carriage, and adding a new M1808 limber. Also each battery was to have two 10-pdr howitzers M1789 mounted on M1796 carriages, with seats added from the stores of the regular artillery.

The new M1808 ammunition wagon for the mounted artillery should hold either 108 x 3-pdr complete munitions or 52 x 10-pdr howitzer munitions.

Further Developments 1813–14

Experience gained during the first part of the campaign in northern Germany led to the conclusion that the two mounted 3-pdr batteries, although fast and flexible, had too little 'punch', while the two 6-pdr foot batteries, although firing an effective shot, were neither very fast nor manoeuvrable. So a reform was made in the field. Only one 3-pdr 'mounted battery' was kept, but now in the role as a light and flexible 'horse battery' (Gønners Battery – named after its commander, as was normal practise in the Danish artillery).

The other 3-pdr 'mounted battery' (Koye's Battery) exchanged its guns for four French 6-pdr pieces of the 'Year An IX' system (all cast 1813), one Dutch 6-pdr piece cast in 1790, and one Austrian 6-pdr piece of the 'Lichtenstein' system (cast 1807), along with two 24-pdr howitzers of the 'Year An IX' system (all cast 1805). The battery kept its two Danish 10-pdr M1789 howitzers as well.

The French guns were all supplied with limbers of the old M1792 model (all formerly from the French 50th 'mobile division', in Hamburg). The four guns and two howitzers came from the French 11/8e Artillerie à Pied. The Austrian and Dutch guns were surplus pieces from the regimental artillery of the French 105e Ligne.[1] Denmark kept all the ammunition wagons M1808 (with seats), and provided extra horses for rest of the gunners. This in effect transformed the battery into a 6-pdr mounted battery. Also the 6-pdr Gerstenberg Battery received more horses and limbers and ammunition wagons were crudely modified so the gunners could ride on them while on the march. But the gunners would as before be expected to march on foot beside their guns when in battle. The last foot 6-pdr Friis Battery was not reformed, but kept with the same organisation and number of horses, and was to be used as a standard foot battery. On several occasions the Danish artillery showed its worth, during the many large and small encounters during the campaign, earning praise from its French allies on several occasions, and always used to its maximum effect, without regard for its own losses.

The Cannons of the 'Light Companies' of the Danish and Holstein 'National Battalions'

In Denmark and Holstein a number of light batteries (normally four to eight pieces) were formed after 1808, by using surplus 3-pdr 16 calibre M1687/1748/57 gun barrels, mounted on the new M1796 carriage. After 1808 also some 3-pdr 22 calibre M1766 pieces were also mounted on mainly locally produced M1796 carriages, and were used by the Danske and Holstenske artillery battalions, which had

1 The drawings in the Hessen-Darmstadt archives are dated 1804.

been formed from the artillery companies of the disbanded Landeværn's artillery. They were all used for mobile coast and fortress defence, often to good effect.

Fortress Carriages M1800

The M1766 3-pdr 22 calibre piece and 6-pdr M1765 iron piece were both mounted in a fortress carriage M1800. Also, as part of the fortress artillery, they were modified with new carriages after the specifications ordered in 1796 and produced from 1800 onwards. They were built more simply and stronger, with fewer iron parts (no dust shields and iron bushings etc.) and were less manoeuvrable than standard field guns. The bronze 3-pdr pieces normally used the 'Gribeauval Screw' elevating device, as did some other 6–12-pdr bronze pieces. Most of the others, including all the iron guns, still used wooden wedges for height adjustments /aiming.

The Ordnance

The 1-pdr *Amusette* system 'Carl af Hessen' Model 1766 was used mainly in Norway by the regimental artillery until 1814, and the horse artillery until 1796. It was designed by Huth, the director of the Danish artillery of the time, as a light and manoeuvrable gun, originally conceived as experimental horse artillery. The Norwegian army used it from *c*.1770–80 until 1814 principally as a regimental gun. Here the lightness of the piece was seen as an asset, in broken and steep terrain, yet the effect of its shot was not impressive. It was never used much in Denmark, being considered far too ineffective in the more open fields of the mainland. A number were stored in the arsenal (see Volume 3).

The system had some unique futures. It was originally intended that the gunner could aim and fire the gun while still seated on the seat provided (this was not a 'driver's seat' as is frequently assumed; modern day re-enactors have carefully avoided this experiment). Theoretically this was to provide a well-aimed shot. The gun was capable of being fired whilst still harnessed to the draught horses (this must have involved a lot of training for the horses!)

On the 1-pdr gun of the M1766 system, the barrel could be swivelled and aimed to both sides from within the gun carriage. From the start the barrel had a little triangular tooth or wedge cast at the end of the knob or button of the cascabel, intended for the new elevating and traversing system on the carriage. A handle placed at the back of the carriage could thereby be turned by the gunner's left hand to swivel left or right. On the right side of the carriage there was another handle, which could only be used by the right hand; this was to move the barrel up and down. This handle operated in a tandem arrangement with a vertical bow with notches. There was a little triangular tooth mounted on an iron bracket bolted underneath the cascabel button and the breech that would fit into these notches.

A gun of same type and appearance was apparently used by the Hessian artillery, two of which ended up in the hands of the Hanoverian Feldjæger Corps who used them against the Danes in 1813!

Following are the technical details of the 1-pdr *Amusette* in service with the limber and ammunition cart.

1-pdr bronze cannon, system 'Carl af Hessen', Model 1766
Calibre: 53mm
Length of bore: 116cm
Total length of gun barrel: 127.2cm
Weight of barrel: 100kg
Number of barrels cast: 191 (sources differ as to how many were sent to Norway, 60 to 80)

Monogram of Christian VII on the breech. There were no lifting handles on these barrels. The trunnions were positioned below the bore. A triangular tooth mounted on an iron bracket bolted underneath the cascabel button and the breech to function with the lifting device.

Gun Carriage
Model reference: M1766
Wheel diameter: 131cm
Length of gun carriage: 126cm
Width of gun carriage front: 15cm
Width of gun carriage rear: 20cm
Length of draught poles: 375cm
Width of carriage including wheels: 181cm

Two-wheeled ammunition cart: also used for the 3-pdr guns
Diameter of wheels: 131cm
Length of ammunition box: 115cm
Width of ammunition box: 45cm
Height of ammunition box: 45cm
Width of carriage including wheels: 181cm
Total length of wagon including hay rack: 37cm

Following are the technical details of the different models of 3-pdr cannons in service, together with their limbers and ammunition carts.

3-pdr/16 calibre bronze cannon, system 'Harboe', Model 1687/1748/1757, for use by the Danish regimental light artillery (Regiments Artilleri) 1757–1803/08, by the coastal Bevægeligefeltbatterier1809–15, and by the field artillery Fodbatterier and the horse artillery in Norway. The same piece was also mounted on a sledge carriage in Norway in the winter.

Calibre: 7.6mm
Length of bore: 123.2cm
Total length of gun barrel: 138.6cm
Weight of barrel: 198–202kg

Number of barrels cast: 200. There were in fact in two main models, 60 cast in 1748, mainly for Norway, and 142 cast in 1757–62, again some were for Norway giving a total of some 110 guns for them, the other 90 or 92 were issued to the Danish regimental artillery.

The M1687/1748 had a standard button on the cascabel, and later when some of these barrels were laid into the M1794 gun carriage and had to use the new elevating device, a little triangular tooth mounted on an iron bracket was bolted underneath the cascabel button and the breech. The Danish model was normally the 1687/1757 version; there was only a slight difference in appearance.

An elevating device of same type as the one later used on the 1-pdr M1766, was also used for some of these 3-pdr M1687/1748/57s, of which 142 had been cast and used by the regimental artillery up to 1799. They had the King's monogram on the field between the breech and the second reinforce. The earliest models would have had the monogram of Frederik IV; the later cannons had a simple version of the reversed 'F5' crowned monogram of Frederik V and a simpler wreath of leaves; it also had a small shield or cartouche added beneath with the year of casting cast on to it, sometimes in Latin. Around the breech base ring there was an inscription, 'FRIDRICS WÆRCK'. The piece had an elephant head and trunk lifting rings; the muzzle swell was flared. The trunnions were positioned below the bore and the one on the left hand side was stamped with 'C' on the end and that on the right had an 'F'.

Gun Carriage

Originally these pieces were mounted in a rather simple limon-type 'galloper gun' model carriage, pulled by one horse between the shafts and a second horse in tandem, but they were found to be 'Unstable, as the guns tended to overturn'. From *c.*1800 they were all fitted with a trail transom equipped with a towing ring and were now pulled by a standard (pre-1796) limber with a pair of horses. This was probably the model used in Bornholm. They initially used wooden wedges for elevation. A number were placed into new carriages after 1794 with the new elevating device, mainly in Norway.

Model reference: M1796
Wheel diameter: 137.5cm
Length of main carriage: 250cm
Width of carriage front: 38.4cm, uniquely the supporting brackets
Width of carriage rear: 54.2cm, uniquely the supporting brackets
Width of carriage including wheels: 199.2cm

Gun Limber

Model reference: M1799
Wheel diameter: 126.7cm
Length of limber including shafts: 5.0m
Length of main limber (Y frame): 181cm
Width of limber front: 181cm
Width of limber rear: 181cm
Length of ammunition box: 51.7cm
Height of ammunition box: 51.6cm
Width of ammunition box: 110cm
Width of limber including wheels: 199.2cm

3-pdr/22 calibre bronze cannon, system, 'Carl af Hessen', Model 1766/1794 for the foot artillery.

The standard 3-pdr M1766 22 calibre, cast until 1799 and used by the foot artillery, had a standard knob on the cascabel. The earlier models cast before 1800 had a triangular iron tooth mounted on an iron bracket which was bolted underneath the cascabel button and the breech to function with the new lifting device. These guns were used until 1808, when the Kørende artillery was created and the pieces were remounted in new carriages.

Calibre: 76mm
Length of bore: 167cm
Total length of gun barrel: 186.4cm
Weight of barrel: 305kg
Number of barrels cast: unknown

Monogram of Christian VII on the breech. The piece had an elephant head and trunk lifting rings and a flared muzzle swell. The trunnions were positioned below the bore and the one on left hand side was stamped with 620 on the end.

Gun Carriage

Model reference: M1794
Wheel diameter: 137.5cm
Length of main carriage: 250cm
Width of carriage front: 38.4cm
Width of carriage rear: 54.2cm
Width of carriage including wheels: 199.2cm

Gun Limber

Model reference: M1799
Wheel diameter: 126.7cm
Length of limber including shafts: 5.0m
Length of main limber (Y frame): 181cm
Width of limber front: 181cm
Width of limber rear: 181cm
Length of ammunition box: 51.7cm
Height of ammunition box: 51.6cm
Width of ammunition box: 110cm
Width of limber including wheels: 199.2cm

3-pdr/20 calibre bronze cannon, system 'Carl af Hessen', Model 1766/1796/1799 for use by the foot and Kørende artillery as well as the regimental artillery.
In 1797–99 a major overhaul of the regimental artillery was carried out. This led to directives for a new range of 3-pdr M1766/99 guns.

The gun barrel was to be shortened by 'two cannonball lengths' reducing the total length to 167.2cm. The swell of the muzzle of the gun was no longer flared, but made more parallel and the muzzle mouldings and lip were shaped like a disc. This was done to improve aiming, as aiming along the back to front sight point on the older guns would often make the shot overshoot at closer ranges. The sight line was thus reduced by half a degree. With the new type of gun carriage, a new improved version of the elevating gear box (Tandem stille maskine) was made.

To fit into this, a tooth was cast on the knob or button of the cascabel on all guns subsequently cast (the same 'elevating gear box', was installed on the 10-pdr howitzers according to Dansk artillerii Napoleons tiden (Tøjhusmuseet), and later on the 20-pdr howitzers as well.

All these improvements were applied on the 122 guns of the 3-pdr M1766/99 cast between 1799 and 1813. Initially these new guns were to have been used to re-equip the regimental artillery until 1808, but few if any were actually issued; they were reassigned on their formation to the Kørendebatterier.

Calibre: 76mm
Length of bore: 152cm
Total length of gun barrel: 167.2cm
Number of barrels cast: Unknown

Monogram of Christian VII on the breech. An elephant head and trunk lifting rings.

Gun Carriages
Model reference: M1796
Wheel diameter: 137.5cm
Length of main carriage: 250cm
Width of carriage front: 38.4cm
Width of carriage rear: 54.2cm
Width of carriage including l wheels: 199.2cm

Model reference: M1808 Kørende gun carriage with seating for four gunners, a gunner either side of the gun and two on the trail. The first plans for the mounted artillery gun clearly shows that the two gunners were intended to sit sideways, each one facing opposite sides of the carriage. The two frames are arm rests, not back rests. Sitting sideways allowed the gunners to mount and dismount quickly as well as having a good view of what was going on (see diagram).
Wheel diameter: 137.5cm
Length of main carriage: 280cm

Gun Limber
Model reference: M1803
Wheel diameter: 126.7cm
Length of limber including shafts: 5.0m
Length of main limber (Y-part): 181cm
Width of limber front: 181cm
Width of limber rear: 181cm
Length of ammunition box: 51.7cm
Height of ammunition box: 51.6cm
Width of ammunition box: 110cm
Width of limber including wheels: 199.2cm

Following are the technical details of the different models of howitzers in service, together with their limbers and ammunition carts.

10-pdr, 7¾ calibre bronze howitzer, system 'Carl af Hessen', Model 1789, to be used by the foot artillery in Denmark. A shorter version of the same howitzer was used Norway (6⅓ calibre).

Calibre. 13.0cm
Length of bore: 101cm
Total length of gun barrel: 114cm
Weight of barrel: Unknown
Numbers cast: 65
These pieces had the monogram of Christian VII on the muzzle, not on the breech.

Gun Carriage
Model reference: M1796
Wheel diameter: 137.5cm
Length of main carriage: 250cm
Width of carriage front: 46cm
Width of carriage rear: 55cm
Width of carriage including wheels: 199.2cm

Gun Limber
Model reference: M1803
Wheel diameter: 126.7cm
Length of limber including shafts: 5.0m
Length of main limber (Y Frame): 181cm
Width of limber front: 181cm
Width of limber rear: 181cm
Length of ammunition box: 51.7cm
Height of ammunition box: 51.6cm
Width of ammunition box: 110cm
Width of limber including wheels: 199.2cm

10-pdr bronze howitzer M1789 as used by Kørendebatterier, 1808–1814. No picture or plans exist of the 10-pdr howitzers in the new M1808 carriage. There is a Danish 10-pdr howitzer barrel from a *Kørendebatteri*, which was left spiked by the Danish and taken as a trophy by the Swedish at Bornhøved in 1813, and preserved in a collection in Sweden. Unfortunately the carriage was not preserved, nor are there any pictures of it in Sweden. It would probably have used a modified Model 1796 howitzer carriage with the same seats as used on 3-pdr gun. We have only the following specifications.

10-pdr/7¾ calibre bronze howitzer, system 'Carl af Hessen', Model 1789 for the use of the foot artillery in Denmark

Calibre: 13.0cm
Length of bore: 101cm
Total length of gun barrel: 114cm
Weight of barrel: Unknown
Numbers of barrels cast: 65, the same as the preceding model.

These pieces had the monogram of Christian VII on the muzzle, not on the breech.

Gun Carriage
Model year: 1796/1808
Wheel diameter: 137.5cm
Length of main carriage: 250cm
Width of carriage front: 46cm
Width of carriage rear: 55cm
Width of carriage including wheels: 199.2cm

Gun limber: limber without ammunition box
Model year: 1808
Wheel diameter: 95cm
Length of limber including shafts: 5.0m
Height of limber: 111cm
Width of limber front: 181cm
Width of limber including wheel: 199.2cm

Following are the technical details of the different models of 6-pdr cannons in service with their limbers and ammunition carts.

All the different 6-pdr guns used the Prussian-influenced elevating system called a *Kielwinde* in German or a *Donkraft* in Danish. In English this means a wound wedge.

6-pdr/22 calibre bronze cannon, system 'Carl af Hessen'
Calibre: 96mm
Length of bore: 211cm
Total length of gun barrel: 231cm
Weight of barrel: 611kg
Number of barrels cast: 190

The first 6-pdr M1766 22 calibre cannons which were cast had a bas relief showing the head of King Christian VII as a Roman emperor, but this was replaced with the more usual 'C7' monogram of Christian VII on the breech on all later cast 6-pdr cannons. They had an elephant head and trunk lifting rings.

6-pdr/20 calibre bronze cannon, system 'St Germain', Model 1762
A total of 46 pieces were cast between 1762 and 1766, during the reign of Frederik V.

As a special distinction the elephants' heads are looking towards the rear. The last eight had the elephant heads in the standard position looking forward.

6-pdr/20 calibre Model 1766/1806, as for use by the foot artillery, later by the mobile artillery.
Length of bore: 192cm
Total length of gun barrel: 211cm
Weight of barrel: 605kg
Number of barrels cast: 27

Monogram of Christian VII on the breech on the first cast, but replaced with the monogram of Frederik VI. These pieces had an elephant head and trunk lifting rings.

We know for sure that in 1803 and 1809–10 some 27 new 6-pdr 20 calibre M1800 pieces were cast and delivered, probably to those two 6-pdr foot companies stationed on Zealand and perhaps also the company in Jutland. The first were probably in 1810 or later as we do not know any other details; from the date of an official order/or M1803 from first trial models cast, there were probably only three or four, the rest cast in 1808–09. However none these were delivered to either Holstein or Norway.

Gun Carriage
Model reference: M1796
Wheel diameter: 152cm
Length of main carriage: 288cm
With of carriage including wheel: 190.4cm
With of carriage front: 40cm
With of carriage rear: 53.6cm

Gun Limber
Model reference: M1799
Wheel diameter: 126.7cm
Length of limber including the shaft: 5.0m
Length of main limber (Y Frame): 181cm
Width of limber front: 181cm
Width of limber rear: 181cm
Length of ammunition box: 51.7cm
Height of ammunition box: 51.6cm

With of ammunition box: 110cm
With of limber including wheel: 199.2cm

Note: the model used by the horse artillery did not have seats, but these limbers as used by the mobile artillery in Norway had two seats added to them.

6-pdr/20 calibre bronze cannon, system 'St Germain', Model 1762, for use by the horse artillery in Denmark and Holstein only.
Calibre: 96mm
Length of bore: 192cm
Total length of gun barrel: 211cm
Weight of barrel: 477kg
Number of barrels cast: 44

Monogram of Christian V on the breech. These pieces had elephant head and trunk lifting rings which looked back towards the breech.

Carriage: Model 1796.

20-pdr bronze howitzer, system 'Carl af Hessen', Model 1772/96.
Calibre: 17cm
Length of bore: 93cm
Total length of gun barrel: 110cm
Weight of barrel: 380kg
Number of barrels cast: 64

From 1796 they were mounted on same carriage as the 6-pdr guns ('Gribeauval' style), but in a reinforced version which had wider and slightly shorter double trails. Monogram of Christian VII on the muzzle.

Gun carriage
Model reference: M1796
Wheel diameter: 152cm
Length of the main gun carriage: 288cm
Width of carriage including wheels: 190cm
Width of carriage front: 49cm
Width of carriage rear: 64cm

Gun limber
Model reference: M1799
Wheel diameter: 126.7cm
Length of limber including the shafts: 5.0m
Length of main limber (Y-part): 181cm
Width of limber front: 181cm
Width of limber rear: 181cm
Length of the ammunition box: 51.7cm
Height of the ammunition box: 51.6cm
Width of the ammunition box: 110cm
Width of limber including the wheels: 199.2cm

Ammunition

Table V shows the ammunition supply available for all the common gun types in use in the Danish army, according to the general regulations as written in the general rule book.

From 1804 all the 3-pdr and 6-pdr guns when preparing for action in the field should always have at least 200 munitions in the 'first line supply' (with the gun, the ammunition wagon and the centrally so-called 'Flying Park', and note, in the case of the 3- and 6-pdr guns, some have more. Howitzers generally have less, they would only fire when needed, so normally used less ammunition.

All the canister or case shot (*Kardæsk*) tubes were painted deep red. All the calibres of canister contained 100 'balls', it was only the size of the balls which changed depending on calibre. The canister was made of tin. The round shot (*Fuldkugle*) were painted black. For both, the bagged powder charge would be attached to the sabot. The howitzers had a greater selection of ammunition: other than canister they also had shells, both the common explosive type and shrapnel, and also an incendiary shell which completed the range.

There was also a version of a shrapnel canister shell. This was a shell with 10 smaller shells inside, each with its own fuse, horribly effective when used correctly.

Not mentioned, but obviously carried with the ammunition as well, were the fuses or 'quills' as they were called in the British artillery.

Service

The service of the howitzers deserves a mention. Firstly the Danish instruction manual confirms the use of two oversleeves by No.3 gunner for loading. These separate oversleeves served to protect the gunner's uniform from the residue in the howitzer, as during the loading process he had to place his arm/arms completely inside the howitzer barrel.

No. 2 sponges out the chamber and barrel, cleaning with the sponge end

No. 3 inserts the cartridge with the LEFT hand into the chamber

No. 2 Then uses the rammer end to push the cartridge fully into the chamber.

No. 3 Pushes the grenade into the barrel, with the RIGHT hand, pointing the fuse/detonator in the middle facing to the front (the left hand supports from below, keeping a firm grip on the carriage)

No. 3 Straightens the (two) fuse (ends on top) and aligns them (makes sure that the fuse will be lit, when howitzer is fired):

In Denmark the shell and the charge were always loaded separately, because there were three different powder charges for different distances (short-range, middle-range, long-range). Basically this was the same procedure for mortars.

Table V. Ammunition Available for Common Gun Types in the Danish Army			
Type of Gun	Ammunition with the Gun (Box & Limber)	Ammunition in the Caisson	Ammunition Reserve with the Park
1-pdr *Amusette*	-	160 x 1-pdr shot + 64 x canister	160 x 1-pdr shot + 64 x canister
3-pdr regimental piece	60*	70 x 3-pdr shot and canister	normally did not have a park
3-pdr foot artillery pre 1804	60	70 x 3-pdr shot and canister	70 x 3-pdr shot and canister
3-pdr foot artillery post 1804	36	108 x 3-pdr shot and canister	210 x 3-pdr shot and canister
3-pdr 1808	10(?)**	168 x 3-pdr shot and canister	210 x 3-pdr shot and canister
10-pdr howitzer	8(?)**	92 x 10-pdr shot and canister	90 x 10-pdr shot and canister
6-pdr horse artillery	30	130 x 6-pdr shot and canister	130 x 6-pdr shot and canister
6-pdr foot artillery	46–50 (?)	130 x 6-pdr shot and canister	130 x 6-pdr shot and canister
20-pdr howitzer	6(?)**	70 x 20-pdr shot and canister	70 x 20-pdr shot and canister

(?) Details are scarce or conflicting, and where some guesswork has been included here. Concerning the howitzers, the 'shot' noted here were probably explosive shells, the main type of ammunition for howitzers.
*Normally a mix of ⅓ canister and ⅔ shot
**This was probably canister shot only, but the number of shots may be higher, as we have no clear details

Howitzer Tactics

Danes preferred to use howitzers to defend themselves against close range infantry/cavalry attacks and during street fighting. They found howitzers much more effective here than ordinary guns.

The reason for canister and shell canister to have round bottoms was that when the howitzer was charged, the shell or canister was positioned just where the (conical) charge chamber began, this placed it on top of the charge and in contact with the same. For this obvious reason 'ready shells' with sabots were not used for howitzers, until after this time period.

Notes on Artillery Equipment

The 'sponge combined with the ramrod' called in Danish Viskerkolber og sætter always had a straight staff, but to protect against a back blast while sponging out and to speed up loading, 'crooked handling tools' were used. These were originally a Swedish invention, later adopted and refined in Germany, and further refined in Danish service.

Crooked sponges/cleaners (*Krumvisker*) were part of the handling tools of all 1-, 3- and 6-pdr guns. They were intended to be used primarily with one arm only, and to protect against 'back-blast'. In emergencies they could also be used to insert loose canister shots.

Crooked rammers (*Krumsætter*) were only part of the equipment of 1-pdr and 3-pdr pieces. It was felt that the weight of a 6-pdr ball with a fixed charge was too heavy to insert properly with the use of just one arm, so 6-pdrguns used a standard ramrod/rammer to ram the charge home, using both hands.

Limbers, Teams and Harness

The 3-pdr foot artillery pieces were usually drawn by teams of four horses; the two nearside horses ridden by gunners. The 3-pdr mounted artillery pieces were usually drawn by teams of six horses; the three nearside horses and the offside lead horse were ridden by gunners. The 6-pdr pieces were pulled by six horse teams; the three nearside horses were ridden by gunners. The 12-pdr guns were usually drawn by 10 horse teams.

The 10-pdr howitzers were pulled by four horses; the two nearside horses were ridden by gunners. The 20-pdr howitzers were pulled by six horses; the three nearside horses were ridden by gunners. The 36-pdr howitzers were drawn by teams of eight horses.

The siege and heavy field guns were rarely seen in the field during these wars.

The different wagons were drawn by a four-horse team and the two-wheeled ammunition carts were drawn by a two-horse team in tandem, where at least the lead horse was mounted by a driver. The harness and saddles were made of black or dark brown leather, the horse blankets were dark grey.

The gun teams were always in rather mixed colours and around 25 percent of the horses were white or greys. As the cavalry preferred red, brown and black horses they had the first choice and the artillery mainly got the leftover colours. They were all different, including red and browns,

Basic Danish Gun Teams

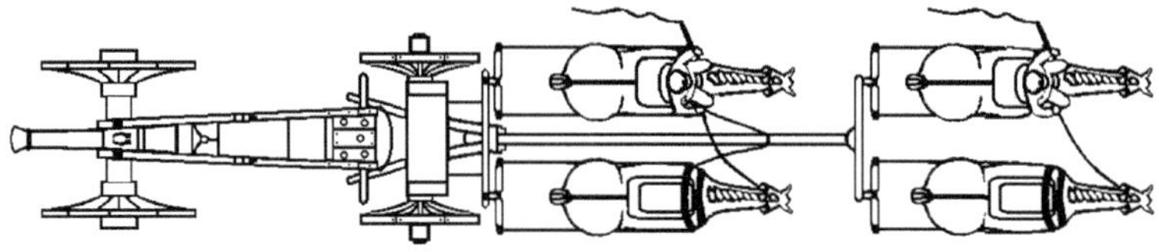

3-pdr Foot Artillery & Team

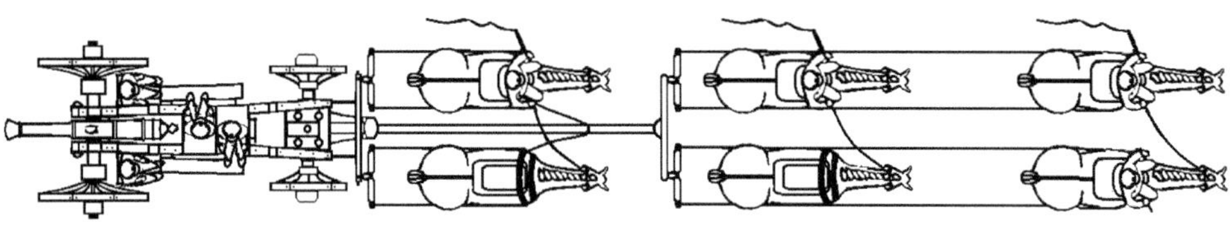

3-pdr Kørende Artillery Team

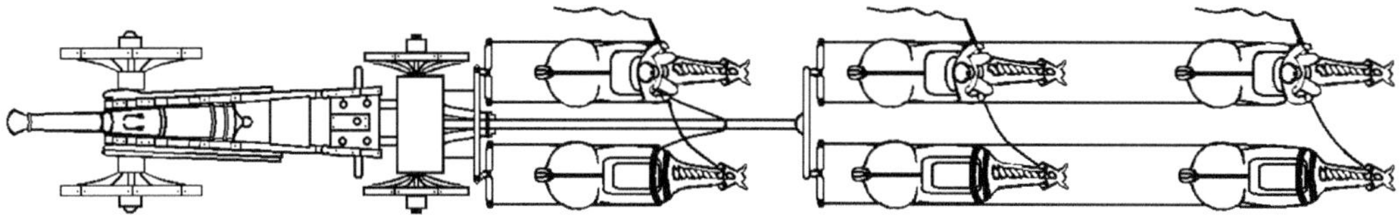

6-Pdr Cannon & Team

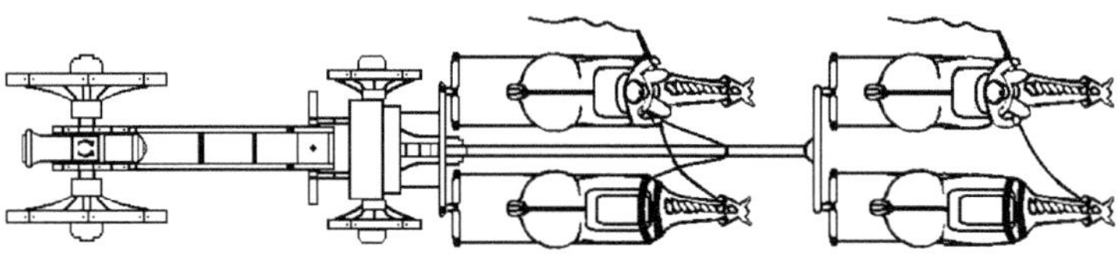

10-pdr Howitzer & Team

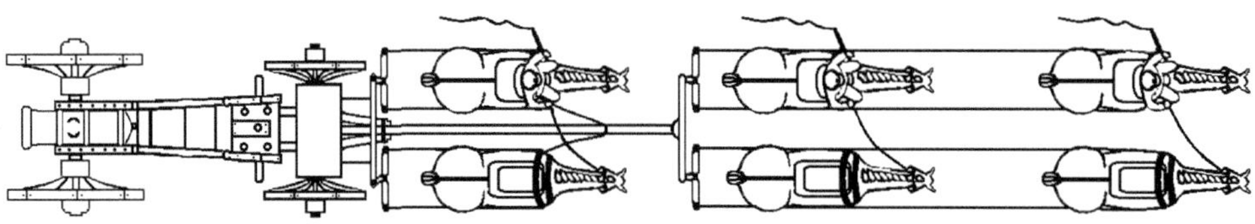

20-pdr Howitzer & Team c.1804–1805

but it looks like the light brown colour is also dominant, blacks much rarer. Holsteiners were probably the dominant breed, as they were larger and stronger but also the largest and strongest Jyske were used as well.

Artillery, Infantry and Cavalry Ammunition and General Supply Wagons and Carts

In 1765 General von Huth had standardised the transport wagons for ammunition, supplies and general baggage for the infantry and cavalry. From then there were two basic models of wagons, the two-wheeled ammunition carts and the larger, four-wheeled heavy wagons. There all underwent modifications and improvements over time.

The Two-Wheeled Wagons

The two-wheeled model which was used for the 1-pdr Amusettes (mainly in Norway by this time), the 3-pdr regimental and foot artillery guns and howitzers and apparently for the regimental musket ammunition reserve as well. The basic two-wheel cart was also the basis of a number of other types of wagons, such as a 'Field forge after the British model' still used by the artillery 1800–1814, in a slightly modernised version with new wheels and fittings.

1. The original M1766 model contained 160 x 3-pdr or 224 x 1-pdr shots. There was a separate arrangement for the howitzer munitions.

These two-wheeled carts all had the same basic design, but the interior was made in several different versions which had different compartments arrangements for the different types of gun or howitzer ammunition.

However, it quickly became obvious that the two-wheeled carts had several design flaws. They were too high and narrow, and from start they overturned much too easily off road or in hilly terrain. This was made worse by being loaded with too much ammunition, in several layers, making it even more top heavy and with too much weight to the rear which also tired the horses unnecessarily.

To lift these carts back onto their wheels when they overturned required a great deal of effort by the crew, and often the ammunition was damaged as well. The easiest way to right the cart was obviously to remove the ammunition first, but as it was originally loaded in two open boxes and two smaller boxes, closer in design to trays, this was difficult, and quite often the ammunition was damaged by the elements and water during this manoeuvre.

So frequently the gun had to make do with the 20–30 shots in the detachable ammunition box placed on the gun carriage, not enough for a prolonged action (The 1-pdr *Amusette* had no ammunition at all kept with the gun). So during the reform of the artillery 1796–1800 these two-wheeled carts were rebuilt.

2. The revised Model 1800 now only contained 108 x 3-pdr or 144 x 1-pdr shots.

Now the carts were to have six boxes inside, of the same size, of which the two middle ones were closed ammunition chests (*Kantiner*) which could be taken out if needed and kept the ammunition fully protected, and could be brought forward to the guns if necessary. Also all six could more easily be taken out if the cart overturned, and be put in more quickly. Now all the ammunition was stored in just one layer.

In the case of the 1-pdr ammunition carts, it was suggested that all six boxes should be of the *Kantine* model so that in hilly or broken terrain, the boxes could be taken out and strapped two each to a horse and two on the gun carriage.

Nevertheless, the artillery command still had strong reservations about these two-wheeled carts, and in 1805 a new version of the 3-pdr wagon was designed and the wagons started to be modified. They now had four wheels and were generally considered as manoeuvrable, light and very stable. Most of the two-wheel carts of the artillery were rebuilt in this way 1805–14. They contained the same quantity of ammunition as before (108 shots).The fore carriage had smaller wheels which gave a better turning arc.

These were to be used by 3-pdr foot artillery and light coastal defence artillery of the National Artillery, from 1808.

3. Revised Model 1805 light four-wheel 3-pdr ammunition wagon of the foot artillery, with room for 108 x 3-pdr shots.

The final version came in 1808, with the model for the new mounted artillery (Kørende Artilleri), slightly longer and with two extra 30-shot ammunition boxes with seats for four gunners. All the two-wheel carts of the former regimental artillery (disbanded in 1808) were so converted. This wagon now contained a total of 168 shots, 108 in the main caisson with 30 additional munitions under each of the seats.

4.Revised Model 1808 light four-wheel 3-pdr ammunition wagon, with seats, of the Kørende (mounted) artillery, with room for 168 shots.

The Four-Wheeled Wagons

Until 1800 they were mainly the M1765, a four-wheeled chassis upon which different carriages and boxes could be added, the first modular military innovation.

These boxes could either be the *würst*-type ammunition wagons or open topped or covered baggage wagons, field forges (called a *Smedevogn*) or ambulances etc.

At first all the wheels were the same size, but in 1800 the front wheels were made smaller. The rear wheels still had a diameter of a 146cm, but now the front wheels had a

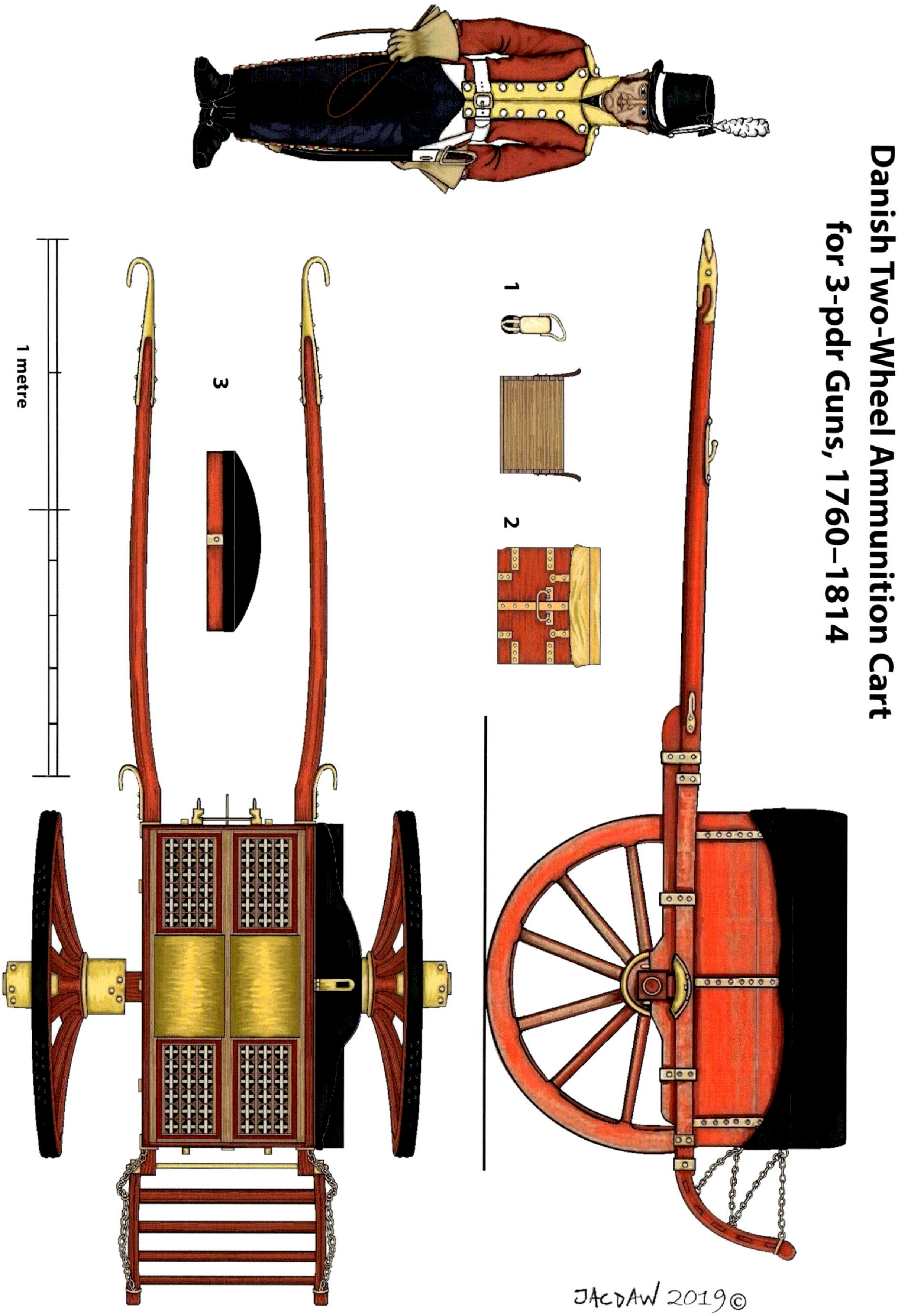
Danish Two-Wheel Ammunition Cart
for 3-pdr Guns, 1760–1814
1
2
3
1 metre
JACDAW 2019©

Plate 46. Two-Wheel Ammunition Cart for 3-pdr Guns and Regimental Munitions, 1760–1814

1. A 3-pdr shot with wooden sabot and charge and 'tray'.
2. Chest for 3-pdr munitions including, ball, canister and empty trays. It could contain up to 108 x 3-pdr shots and canisters or 52 x 10-pdr howitzer shells and/or canisters.
3. The shape of the lid.

A plan view of the ammunition cart showing the six individual 3-pdr ammunition chests, each containing 18 individual munitions shots or canisters. There were four separate trays and two fully closed chests placed inside the box on the cart. Two of these smaller chests had a lid and they were lined with sheepskin to keep the munitions dry and protect them from the cold.

Sources: the original plans in Tøjhusmuseet, Copenhagen, now called the Krigsmuseet. For scale, shown with a regimental artillery driver. Near wheel removed for clarity.

diameter of only 115cm. The smaller front wheels gave the vehicle a better turning radius.

After 1800 the undercarriage was made more flexible by introducing a new front part of the same type which had already been introduced for the artillery limbers, and making them interchangeable with the limbers. Further modifications were made to modernise it in 1805.

A very rare and preserved example of this type of wagon (M1765), can be seen in the Defence Museum of Norway. This version is fitted out as a general supply wagon. With a different box, the same wagon could also be converted into an ammunition wagon.

Both the regimental wagons and normally those commandeered locally, had an inscription written on them, detailing to which unit they belonged to, regiment battalion and company.

In 1803 as an experiment, a padded and sprung 6-pdr ammunition wagon, was made for use by the horse artillery. In the end this was not adopted, as it was seen as too expensive. Unfortunately there is only one picture in the archives of a 6-pdr ammunition wagon; there is one other technical drawing in the army archives, dated *c.*1806–08. It was among the resolutions, not in the artillery archives.

Instead, all the four-wheeled ammunition wagons were given round wooden lids, footboards and iron rails at the front and back, 'to be used if necessarily as transport'. The wagons were all generally lightened and modernised. A large canvas top cover was added for protection. This was 'to be painted in the same Dark Colour (Black) as the top lid itself, so as not to be all to be easily spotted by the enemy, while in action'. In 1805–09, all the 6-pdr ammunition wagons of the 6-pdr foot artillery batteries were fitted out this way. Most of the wagons had a hay rack fitted at the rear.

Specifications:
Model year: 1765/99/1805
Ammunition capacity; 130 x 6-pdr shells and/or canisters, 80 x 20-pdr howitzer grenades and canisters
Diameter of front wheels: 115cm
Diameter of rear wheels: 146cm
Length of the ammunition box: 325cm
Width of ammunition box: 75 cm
The height of the ammunition box: 60cm
Length of 'front limber' including the shaft: 350cm
Length of wagon including the shaft and hay trays: 450cm
The width of wagon including the wheels: 190cm

As mentioned above, this chassis was also used to mount a heavy field forge.

The ammunition box could also be mounted on a sledge, for use by Norwegian ski units from 1789, again showing the remarkable simplicity of the system. The same box could be fitted to the standard M1765 type of chassis, turning it into an ammunition wagon. This is probably of the type used by the 3-pdr batteries, which could carry 210 ready-to-use shots.

The 6-pdr version was apparently a little longer, but of the same general appearance, and could hold 130 ready-to-use shots. Also the covered curved lid (opening to the left) enabled the artillery men (and skiers) to 'ride' on the lid when they were not in action, being provided with handles, front and back for a better grip (see Volume 3 for more details and drawings of the ski equipment).

Field Forges, *Smedevogn*

There were two basic types of field forges, a two-wheeled version destined for the cavalry and a four-wheeled model for the artillery companies.

The two-wheeled cavalry version was referred to as being after 'the English model'; although designed in the 1730s it continued to be used both during and after the Napoleonic Wars. It was virtually identical to the contemporary British forge.

Danish 3-pdr Kørende (Mounted) Artillery Ammunition Wagon, c.1808–1814

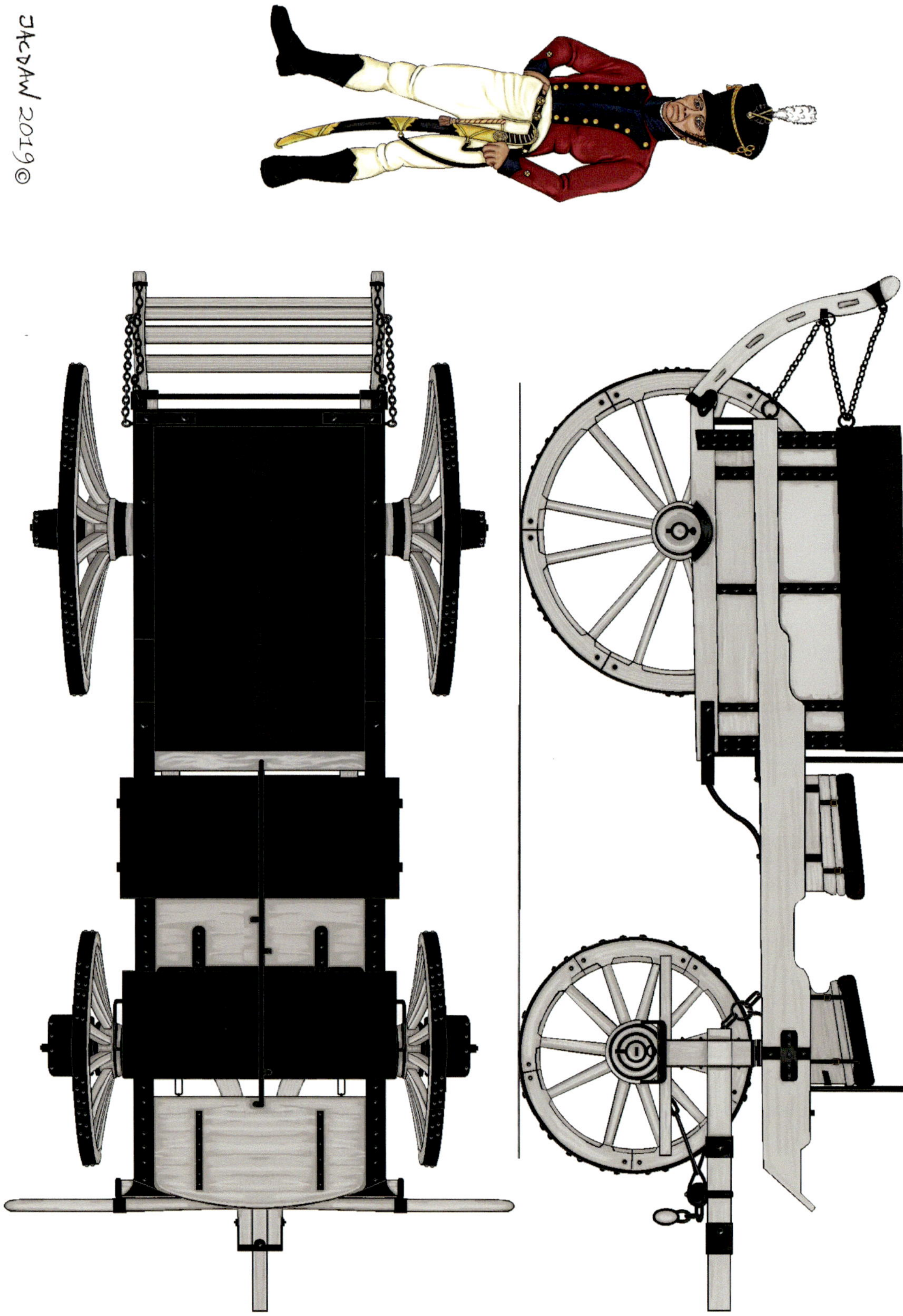

Plate 47. Danish 3-pdr. Kørende (Mounted) Artillery Ammunition Wagon, *c*.1808–1814

This was the standard two-wheeled ammunition cart, converted into a four-wheel wagon to increase stability. This was the second such modification; this version had seating for four gunners. Note the central rail with hand grips. This wagon, combined with the 3-pdr Kørende cannon with the four gunners seated on the gun created a fully mobile team. The foot artillery had used a variant of same model, where the two front seats were replaced with ammunition boxes and they did not have a foot board at the front. These were later used by Danske and Holstenske artillery battalions.

Source: an original plan from the Tøjhusmuseet, now called the Krigsmuseet. For scale, the wagon is shown with an officer of the mounted artillery *c*.1812. Near wheels removed for clarity.

The four-wheeled field forge used during these wars was designed in 1765, replacing the 1730 model which was generally known as 'of the Dutch model'. The new model was based on the general service wagon. The M1765 field forge was a much better design as it was lighter and more compact, and the bellows, tools, coal and forge were better protected against wind and rain.

Here is an extract from one of the few books detailing the artillery in this period, *Forsøg til en praktisk artilleri håndbog*, J.T. Lundbye, 1823. The field forge ('Smedevogn'), was 'to have the same undercarriage and wagon body [kaross] (including the canvas tarpaulin), as the 'Brødvogn'/ supply wagon [M1765]. But it has at the front inside lockers for tools and coal, near the rear a bellows, and on the tailgate there is a forge/furnace. On the side there is a locker for a detachable anvil, which can be placed on the ground.'

The blacksmiths (Smed) were civilian craftsmen, not soldiers hired by the regiment and as such they did not have a designated uniform, but wore civilian clothes supplemented with old leftover uniforms. Normally they brought their own tools and basic working clothes (although they could also have been former soldiers taking work, and so have some old items of uniform) but were not as such under military discipline. However, normally rations and some items of working clothes would constitute part of their pay.

This would normally include stockings, breeches/ trousers, shoes, shirts, a work gown or leather apron, and maybe a simple uniform coat and hat/fatigue cap. But again, these were not regulated, and depended on the contract the regiment had made with the blacksmith.

Only the *Kursmede*/blacksmiths, part of the three horse (*Ridende*) companies, received the same uniform under the same terms, as an *Underkonstabel*/gunner, but not any sidearms.

Pontoons

Due to the number of rivers in their country, the Danish army also had a well-organised pontoon system, transported on the standard four-wheeled service wagons with a modified bed. There was even a version which could be transported on two-wheeled wagons, presumably being lighter and more rapid.

Artillery Colour Codes

Until 1808 the carriages of Danish regimental artillery were painted red, with the metalwork painted pale yellow, and the foot and Kørende artillery should have been painted pearl grey with the ironwork and fittings painted black.

There is a vast amount of confusion about the colours of the Danish artillery, much of this is due to old field guns being retired to the arsenals and then being repainted in the colours of the fortress artillery, which was still red with the ironwork and fittings painted yellow

The siege guns had red carriages and the metalwork was painted black. The fortress artillery retained its traditional red carriages with the metalwork painted yellow. These colour codes were also applied to their respective limbers, caissons and wagons and all other wheeled vehicles.

Horse, foot and Kørende artillery: Pearl-grey wood and black iron fittings (this 'pearl grey' is often described as a 'bluish grey' but would fade to a warm grey in time). This included the gun carriages, limbers and ammunition wagons.

Fortress, coastal and regimental artillery: Red wood and yellow iron fittings. This included the gun carriages, limbers and ammunition wagons.

Siege artillery: Red wood and black iron fittings. This included the gun carriages, limbers and ammunition wagons.

Plate 48. Artillery Limber and Wagon Harnesses

3-pdr Kørende limber and team showing a nearside horse with a saddle and an offside wheel horse without a saddle, but with a saddle pad and baggage, feed etc. Normally this team was composed of six horses, only two are shown, the centre and wheeler, the lead horse (ridden) not shown. The 3-pdr foot artillery harness only had four horses and this harness would also have been used for the wagons.

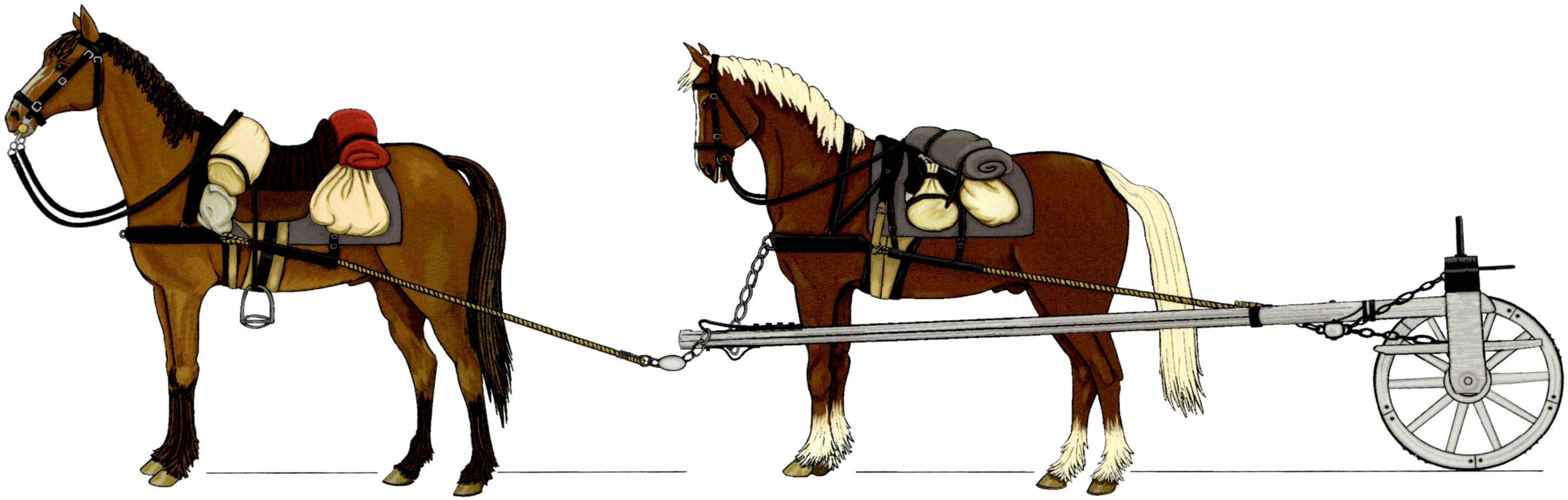

3-pdr Kørende Limber & Team, Showing a Nearside Horse & an Offside Wheeler

Plate 49. The Arillery Limber and Wagon Harnesses II

6-pdr limber and team, showing the offside. The nearside horses were ridden, so obviously they would have had saddles.

6-pdr Limber Team, Offside

Danish Limber and Wagon Harness

Danish Four-Wheel Ammunition Wagon M1765/99/1805

Plate 50. Danish Four-Wheel Ammunition Wagon M1765/99/1805

This wagon was used by the 3-pdr foot artillery park and the 6-pdr foot artillery, in the field and park from 1806, and in a slightly modernised version for the reserve ammunition park for the Kørende (mounted) artillery. To begin with they all had the same basic undercarriage and main parts as the supply wagons M1765, but with a different upper body. In 1799, it were decided that all ammunition wagons would change their wheels to a new type. Here the front pair of wheels were smaller (115 cm), and the rear pair kept the standard size (146cm). This system, which had been experimented with from *c.*1800 onwards on ammunition wagons, was to ensure that all the wagons , including the light artillery wagon from 1808, should have the tightest turning circle possible. At the same time front limbers were standardised, so as to be interchangeable. The basic idea was that front wheels should always have room under the wagon or gun carriage, so as to have the maximum turn, but they were equipped with a stop chain connected to wagon or gun, to avoid the limber turning too tightly and going right under and causing the wagon to keel over. This made all limbers and ammunition wagons very mobile.

Source: an original plan, and model of the original M1765 ammunition wagon in the Tøjhusmuseet in Copenhagen, now called the Krigsmuseet and plans of the M1799/1805 model found in the Hessisches Staatsarchiv, Marburg, Germany. For scale, the gun is shown with a foot artillery driver *c.*1806. Near wheels removed for clarity on side view, and the front hay rack on the plan view also removed for clarity.

Plate 51 (overleaf). Danish M1765 and Norwegian M1765/1789 Four-Wheel General-Purpose Wagon, *c.*1804

This wagon and body is the standard M1765 general service wagon, which using same chassis and general parts, with the necessary interior fittings, could be made into an ambulance, Baggage, forage, general supplies, bread wagon, for baggage, and even a field forge, just adding the necessary fittings. When they were transporting wounded the lid would be propped up as shown above the wagon. In Norway, an improved model (M1765/1789), was built with some parts copied from a Swedish supply wagon captured during the war in 1788. The Norwegian roads were generally bad to nonexistent (like most roads in Sweden), Sweden had copied the same Prussian design, as had General Von Huth, in Hesse/Denmark, and both had improved on it. The Hesse/Denmark version was improved on for more simplicity, usability and lightness, but Sweden had improved its version for extra strength. And so in 1789 the Norwegians had combined both models into a new supply wagon/ambulance, more suitable for the poor Norwegian roads and terrain. Note the reinforcing struts above the wheels, not found on the original M1765 design, and the shorter wheelbase, no doubt to better support the heavier charge. Also the horses could draw it in another configuration, more suited for a heavy load.

Sources: the original plans in Denmark and Norway, an original M1765/1789 wagon conserved in the Museum of Oslo and a near-contemporary model of a M1765 Wagon (field forge version) conserved in the Tøjhusmuseet, Copenhagen, now called the Krigsmuseet. For scale the wagon is shown with an artillery baggage train driver *c.*1810. Near wheels removed for clarity.

Danish Four-Wheel General-Purpose Wagon M1765, c.1804

Infantry and cavalry supply carts and wagons: Dark red wood and dark red iron fittings. Note: their reserve ammunition was only carried in the two-wheel carts.

Note also that the red colour could vary. The 'old red' was slightly darker in colour, but later that of the regimental was ordered to be of a 'much brighter (new) red', also to be used for the new fortress and coastal guns.

The siege and train units mainly used a variation of the 'old red' which could vary from light red to a darker brownish colour. Note that all ammunition wagons had black tops, but all the other types of supply wagons had either plain red or white canvas tops (or none at all). Some ammunition wagons of the general army train even had their canvas tops painted red as well.

Identification Markings on Wagons

All artillery ammunition wagons were marked with the type of wagon and its number, and what it carried, for example '3 pds. Ammunitionsvogn No. 5', '10 pds. Haubits ammunitionsvogn No. 2', normally written in white paint on the front and back of the (black) canvas top cover, or sometimes in black on the rear or sides of supply and other types of wagon if they did not have tarpaulin covers.

1. All the artillery wagons of the artillery would have painted upon the rear the ammunition type (ball or howitzer shell) and their number in the gun line (1–10). All painted in white paint on the black canvas.

The number in the gun line was important so the commander of the ammunition wagons could always be sure that the cannon had the right ammunition, and that they had it from the same wagon, so the gun commander was always sure how much ammunition he had ready.

2. All the ammunition wagons belonging to the infantry and cavalry would have the name of the regiment and the company number written on the back of them, so as not to mix rifle/musket ammunition, for example 'Holstenske Regmt. Patronkærre', or 'Slesvigske Rytter Rgmt. Feldtsmedie'. All painted in white paint on the black or red canvas cover.

3. According to the order of 1760, all other wagons would be painted with the name of the regiment, type of wagon (and possibly a number, though this may have disappeared before 1800). As most general service wagons found here had white canvas tops, the text would logically be painted in black, and if open at the back, painted on the side of the cover.

The letters were small (around 10cm high) and generally in a script-type of font. Today this lettering is only known from a very few examples preserved in Norway (none have survived in Denmark) and no exact guidelines can be found in any archives, so the examples given above are pure reconstruction made from the few known guidelines.

List of Names of the Carts/Wagons in Use by the Danish Army

Artillery ammunition supply wagon: *Amunitionsvogn*
Infantry ammunition supply wagon: *Patronkærre*
General food supply wagon: *Brødvogn*, literally the bread wagon
General forage supply wagon: *Fouragevogn*
General transport wagon for spares and equipment: ***Rekvesitvogn*** (They could be open-topped or have wooden lids or more generally canvas tops)
Field forges for use by blacksmiths: *Smedevogn*
Carts for medical supplies: *Hospitals kærre*
Carts/wagons used for transport by regimental and general staff: *Stabsvogn*

9

The Heavy Field and Siege Guns

This small chapter is just for completeness, as the heavy artillery or siege train rarely if at all made it into the field during this war. One of the main reasons for abandoning the invasion of Scania in 1808–09, was the impossibility of transporting proper siege artillery over the ice. If Denmark were to take and keep Scania, it would need to attack both the fortresses of Malmø and Landskrona (at least) and that had already been shown difficult in 1710, when a lack of a siege train had led to disaster in the end. In 1808–09 it would even be more difficult with no help available from the navy following the capture of the fleet by the British Royal Navy. With the ice gone and several fortresses still in the possession of the Swedes, an attack on Scania 1808–09 would have been a death-trap (and with the French already in possession of Jutland/Funen even more so!)

There was no official 'train of siege artillery', so when it was needed it had to be formed. The pieces, mortars and howitzers reserved for its use were stored in the arsenals.

The carriages were to be painted red, a darker shade than the other arms and with black metalwork. The carriages were of the heavier old models and it were not modernised much between 1786 and 1816.

The gunners were to be taken from the ordinary artillery companies, again only when needed. The only formal organisation plan for the train's use was made in 1786, and this was apparently the organisational plan used throughout the period.

> 'Plan for the Siege Artillery Train (Brigade)':
> 42 siege pieces (a mix of 12-pdrs18-pdrs and 24-pdrs)
> 16 howitzers (20-pdrs and 36-pdrs)
> 20 mortars(100-pdrs)

It would need to be served by 776 gunners, 66 'fireworkers' and five engineer officers.

To move it would need 1,551 train and gun drivers, 660 wagons and 4,670 horses, more resources than available or obtained to the detriment of both the home defences and the field army.

The Danish M1766/1769 12-pdr Piece

This bronze piece were originally issued to the foot artillery (*Fodartilleri*) from 1769 and stayed in its service until 1803 when these guns became part of the siege artillery (*Belejringsartilleri*) 1803–15.

A new lighter and shorter gun carriage was designed and used from 1800 onwards in the field. These guns were designated as system M1766/1800. All the 12-pdr guns used the Prussian-influenced elevating system (*Kielwinde*) or in Danish a *Donkraft* as already described.

Calibre: 12.2cm (22 calibre)
Length of bore: 268.4cm
Total length of gun barrel: 292.8cm
Weight of Barrel: 1,200kg
Number of pieces recorded as cast: 75

The first 12-pdr M1766 22 calibre cannons which were cast had a bas relief showing the head of King Christian VII as a Roman emperor. They had an elephant head and trunk lifting rings. A number of these guns were distributed to the fortresses as well.

The Danish M1766 36-pdr Howitzer

The 36-pdr 5 calibre bronze howitzer, known as the 'Carl af Hessen' system, Model 1766, was designed for use by the field, siege and fortress artillery. A new shorter and lighter gun carriage was designed and produced from 1800(although most surviving pieces are still mounted on the older carriages).
Calibre: 20cm (5 calibre)
Length of bore: 100cm
Total length of gun barrel: 130cm
Weight of barrel: 690kg
Number of pieces recorded as being cast: 82

It had the monogram of Christian VII on the muzzle end, not on the breech.

The Fortress and Coastal Pieces

The fortress and coastal guns were somewhat of a mixture of different pieces. There were some 12-pdr iron-barrelled guns on field type carriages with spoked wheels. They had 36-pdr howitzers on heavy carriages and with solid block wheels. From 1802 new truck-type carriages was built in large numbers, they were placed on pintle-mounted wheeled casemate ramps. They were known as the 'Gribeauval' system, the carriages had three wheels, two medium to smallish spoked wheels at the front and a central solid block wheel at the rear, but there were a few variations on this type.

Amongst other notable guns were some iron-barrelled 18-pdr cannons mounted on four-wheel truck carriages on pintle-mounted casemate ramps. The carriage had four large, primitive-looking iron-bound solid wooden wheels.

The most important guns used by the fortress and coastal artillery were:

An 8-pdr iron piece, system 1692
Calibre: 107mm
Overall length incl. cascabel: 225cm
Bore: 194cm

An 18-pdr iron piece, system 1692
Calibre: 138mm
Overall length incl. cascabel: 246cm
Bore: 202cm

A 24-pdr iron piece, system 1692
Calibre: 153mm
Overall length incl. cascabel: 314cm
Bore: 276cm

A 36-pdr iron piece, system 1692
Calibre: 175mm
Overall Length incl. cascabel: 340cm
Bore: 297cm

The system of 1692 was originally intended for use on naval vessels, but after 1802, and in particular after 1807, many guns were transferred instead to the fortresses and coastal artillery.

12-pdr iron piece, M1753 'System Reitzensteins'
Calibre: 122mm
Overall Length incl. Cascabel: 298cm
Bore: 268cm

18-pdr Iron Piece, M1753 'System Reitzensteins'
Calibre: 138mm
Overall Length incl. Cascabel: 300cm
Bore: 282cm

24-pdr Iron Piece, M1753 'System Reitzensteins'
Calibre: 153mm
Overall Length incl. Cascabel: 351cm
Bore: 313cm

36-pdr Iron Piece, M1753 'System Reitzensteins'
Calibre: 175mm
Overall Length incl. Cascabel: 359cm
Bore: 315cm

300 guns of this system were cast in Norway, and 250 more in Sweden. The Swedish guns were of particularly high quality.

6-pdr Bronze Piece, M1687 'System Harboe'
Calibre: 98mm
Overall Length incl. Cascabel: 232cm
Bore: 209cm

12-pdr Bronze Piece, M1687 'System Harboe'
Calibre: 122mm
Overall Length incl. Cascabel: 347cm
Bore: 317cm

18-pdr Bronze Piece, M1687 'System Harboe'
Calibre: 134mm
Overall Length incl. Cascabel: 245cm
Bore: 212cm

24-pdr Bronze Piece, M1687 'System Harboe'
Calibre: 149mm
Overall Length incl. Cascabel: 259cm
Bore: 222cm

The 18-pdr and 24-pdr pieces used the 'old calibre', so fired a smaller solid shot from old stocks. The 6-pdr and 12-pdr had been cast in the 'new calibre'. The number cast is unknown.

6-pdr Bronze Piece, M1766 system 'Carl af Hessen'
Calibre: 98 mm
Overall Length incl. Cascabel: 217cm
Bore: 212cm

12-pdr Bronze Piece, M1766 system 'Carl af Hessen'
Calibre: 122 mm
Overall Length incl. Cascabel: 298 cm
Bore: 268cm

Cast in two versions, a heavy 12-pdr M1766, 76 pieces; and 75 light 12-pdr M1766.

18-pdr Bronze Piece, M1766 system 'Carl af Hessen'
Calibre: 138mm
Overall length incl. Cascabel: 351cm
Bore: 317cm

14 of these pieces were cast.

Danish Field Forge M1765/1802 (Artillery Corps)

Plate 52a (left). Danish Four-Wheel Field Forge, M1765/M1802

The Field Forge (*Smedwagon*) wagon was based on the standard M1765 general service wagon. The bellows were housed inside. On one side there was a pull-down bench and the anvil (*Ambolt*) was probably stowed here. On the other side there was a rack for a water bucket. All other materials were stored inside (tools, iron bars and coal). There appear to have been a number of variants of these forges, but unfortunately we do not have enough detail to be more exact.

Source: author's reconstruction based on various plans, and a contemporary model conserved in the Tøjhusmuseet in Copenhagen, now called the Krigsmuseet. This wagon is definitely a 'lighter' Danish vehicle (M1765) as it does not have the extra reinforced struts over the axles, which appear to have been exclusive to the Norwegian vehicles (M1765/1789).

Plate 52b (below). Danish Four-Wheel Field Forge, M1765/M1802

This small illustration shows the rear of the field forge wagon (*Smedwagon*) with the forge deployed shown with two blacksmiths (who were not soldiers, but civilian employees) wearing some items of old discarded uniforms which the regiment gave them as part of their remuneration.

Danish Field Forge M1765/1802 (Artillery Corps)

Danish 12-pdr 22 Calibre Bronze Piece, M1762, on Field Carriage

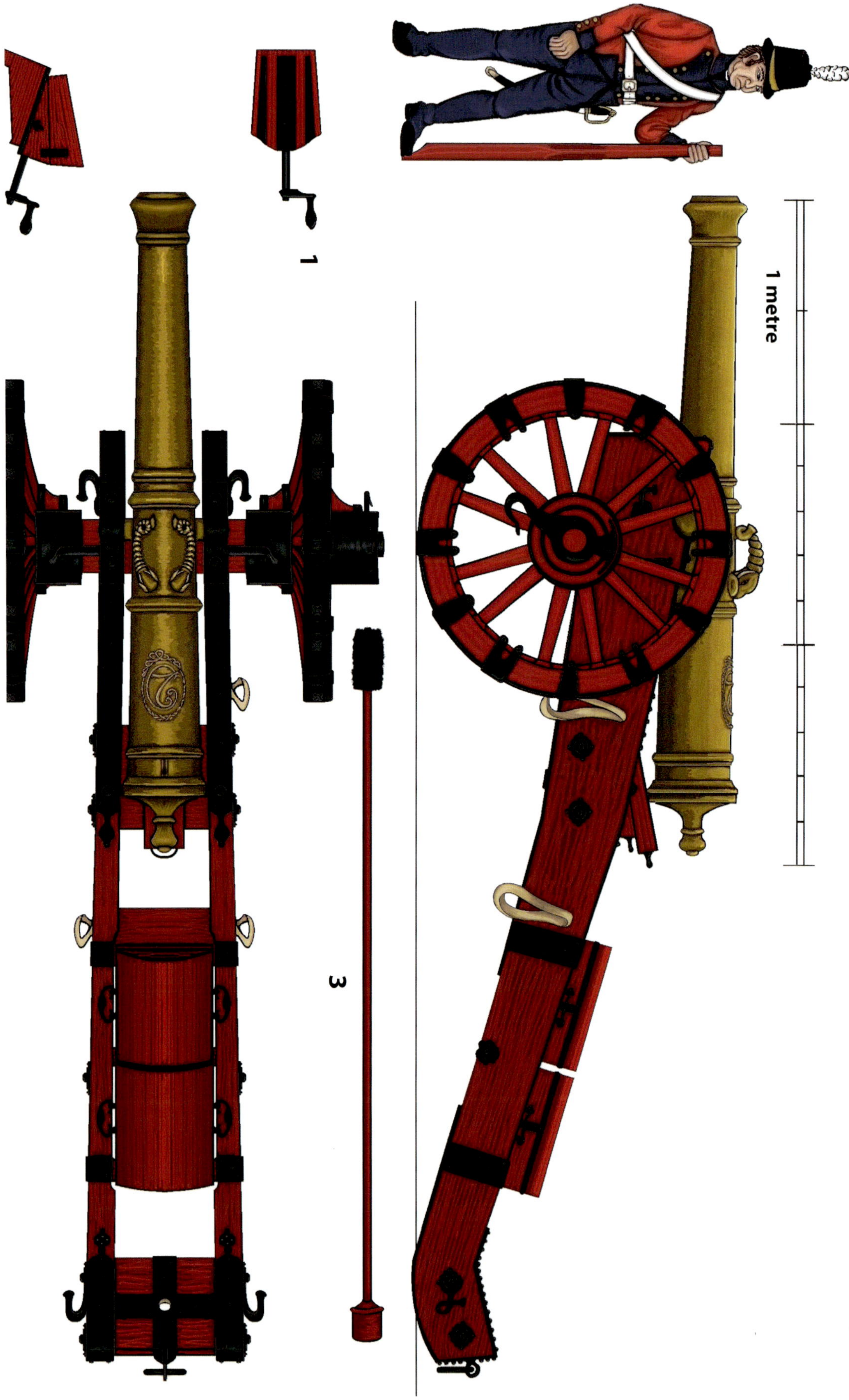

Plate 53. Danish 12-pdr 22 Calibre Bronze Piece, System 'Carl af Hessen', M1766/69

Piece shown mounted on an old model field carriage for use by the *Belejrings artilleriet* (siege artillery) and the *Befæstnings artilleriet* (fortress artillery). A new carriage was designed and produced from c.1802 for the pieces used in the fortresses. This new fortress carriage (M1802), was based on the same design as the field artillery M1799 carriages, but more simple and sturdier, also it was a little shorter. This piece is shown in the earlier colour scheme used for siege pieces; the red was of a somewhat darker shade. Later a much brighter shade of red was used. Calibre 12.2cm, length of bore 268.4cm, total length of gun barrel 292.8cm, weight of barrel 1,200kg, numbers cast 75.

1 & 2. The system of elevation was originally done with wedges, but it was eventually replaced with the elevating or aiming device which was called a *Kielwinde* in German or a *Donkraft* in Danish, c.1806.

Source: based on drawings found in the Tøjhusmuseet, Copenhagen, now called the Krigsmuseet. For scale, shown with an artilleryman.

The Fortress Howitzers

These had a small 12-pdr movable iron howitzer M1787, for use in coastal fortresses. It could be carried by four men using the four carrying handles. The calibre was 120mm; 128 of these were cast. Some 20-pdr howitzers were also mounted on an improved wheeled fortress truck carriage M1788, used generally from 1802. The carriage had four rather large diameter solid wooden wheels, two larger ones in front and two smaller ones to the rear.

The Mortars

There were a number of mortars available, including 10-pdr brass movable siege and fortress mortars that could be manhandled into position by just four men.

Another mortar type was a 50-pdr brass siege and fortress mortar Model 1794, which had a calibre of 230mm. Sixteen of these were cast. Other models included a heavy 150-pdr siege and fortress mortar, and a 200-pdr fortress mortar.

The Rocket Corps, *Raket Corpset*

The Danes had also created some rocket companies (*raketbatteri*).The Danish development of rockets and carriages to fire them was carried out in great secrecy, but due to that, very little can be found in the archives and only a few warheads bear witness to their existence today.

Following the 'terror bombardment' of Copenhagen in 1807, partly with rockets, Denmark decided to form its own rocket corps. It was made up of both sea and land service rockets of different kinds, including the invention of firing multiple weapons based on the 'Roman candle' principal (this led to the invention of the so-called *Espingoler*, which was used with some effect during the wars of 1848–50 and 1864). The officers were mainly drawn from the artillery and engineers, the gunners and craftsmen from the navy and some soldiers from three different battalions. The first Danish rockets were produced on the uninhabited barren island of Hjelm in a workshop directed by a Kaptajn Schumacher. The first active use was a rocket division assisting the gun boats (they were never fired in anger, but took part in a number of diversionary expeditions).

In 1813 two rocket batteries for land service were created and shipped to the Isle of Fyen, but the war was over before they could be used in action (some sources claim they had eight rocket carriages each, other sources give only two). Their crew was drawn from the workers from the rocket factory and from Marine gunners.

We have no contemporary drawings of the carriages, only sketches of much later models, and there is a single eyewitness account from 1813. When comparing them to the English rocket batteries fighting against the Danes in northern Germany, we are told that: 'They are lighter and more mobile[than the English carriages]. They are fired from a light two-wheel carriage with two rocket tubes, and can easily be moved by two horses.' These early carriages were clearly influenced by the carriage of the 1-pdr *Amusettes*, and like them were intended to be drawn in tandem by one or two horses. This type of carriage had also been made at Frederiksværk, where production of rockets and carriages, was carried out.

Uniforms

The officers wore a new blue uniform and bicorn in 1813 (with a very naval appearance). The bicorn was black, with a black cockade and a gold loop and tassels. Their short-tailed double-breasted coat was dark blue with a bright medium blue collar, pointed cuffs and lining, the turnbacks and the buttons were brass or gilt. This coat used the new

Plate 54. Danish 18-pdr M1753 Iron Fortress Piece, System 'Reitzensteins', on Fortress Carriage M1788

This iron piece is shown mounted on a truck-type fortress carriage M1788. It is shown on an angled board floor to help to ease the recoil and to reposition the piece. The boards were probably mounted on joists keep them in position. It is shown with a tompion and a roof over the touch hole, placed on the piece when not in action to preserve the piece from the elements. This piece had a calibre of 138mm and the barrel measured 300cm in length. A total of 300 pieces of the 'Reitzensteins' system were cast in Norway and 250 more were cast in Sweden including 12-, 18-, 24- and 36-pdrs. Those cast in Sweden were of particularly high quality. How many of each calibre were made is unclear.

Source: based on models and drawings found in the Tøjhusmuseet, Copenhagen, now called the Krigsmuseet, originals found in Norway, and several full scale reconstructions in both Denmark and Norway. For scale, shown with a national artilleryman.

Danish 18-pdr M1753 Iron Fortress Piece

rank markings. The breeches were dark blue worn with black Hessian boots with a black tassel. The arms were an officer's sabre with a brass hilt, gold sword knot and the scabbard was black with brass fittings.

The Danish sailors attached to the rocket corps wore a uniform very similar to the *Matros compagni*, consisting of a black hat a dark blue double-breasted coatee, with a red collar and square cuffs with two vertical buttons. All the buttons were brass. The long, large fall-fronted trousers were dark blue and the sailor carried a brass-hilted marine sabre in a brown leather scabbard, with brass fittings, on a black leather belt with an open square brass buckle.

Fireworkers and Craftsmen's Uniforms

These men wore the same dress as the foot artillery but with a special craftsmen's sabre (*håndværkerhirschfänger*). The hat is sometimes shown with a white band.

The King's Engineer Corps, Det Kongelige Ingeniørkorps

The Engineers Officers Corps (*Kongelige Ingeniørkorps*) was attached directly to the Artillery Corps and never had more than 25 officers. It was obviously vastly understrength for the number of missions its men had to accomplish.

They were spread out mainly in all the major fortresses in Denmark, Norway and Holstein and did not handle military matters alone, but also planned roads, canals, public buildings and water supplies. Generally a field army would be accompanied by one or two engineer officers. They were assisted by a number of civilian aides (clerks, foremen etc.) and had at their disposal on Zealand and the surrounding islands the corps of sappers (Sappørkorpset) who had four companies to carry out their work as well as work detachments from the different infantry regiments.

There was also an ammunition production company (fyrværkerkompagni) of 112 men and an independent company of 106 civilian craftsmen (håndværkerkompagni).

Engineer Officers' Uniforms

The Engineer officers had a black felt round hat with a gold band around the base; on the left side it had a white plume over black cockade with a gold loop and red and gold cords and tassels.

From 1808, these officers were issued with the same shako and with the same ornaments as the infantry. Some senior officers still wore bicorns at the start of the period, which had a white plume, a black cockade and a long gold loop with a button and gold tassels at each end.

Their uniform was a scarlet red long-tailed cloth coat, with white turnbacks and lining. It had a black collar, lapels and cuffs with red flaps and gold buttons, all piped gold/yellow. Their rank epaulettes were the same as the line infantry. Around their waist they wore the traditional sash. There is only one detailed picture, from 1804–08. This confirms several portraits showing what is a probably a service uniform coat with two rows of buttons, which was worn without the sash when overseeing fieldworks, fortifications, digging trenches etc. Note that you can see the white inside lining made of silk, and they were allowed to wear officers' hats.

The other uniform was the formal field/parade dress, which resembled that of the infantry and artillery officers' uniforms in general.

From 1812 the scarlet red cloth coat was replaced with madder red, although officers who could afford to buy it with private funds were allowed to continue to use scarlet cloth. Although there is no record of it, they probably switched to pointed cuffs after 1812, but the 1817 uniform definitely had pointed cuffs.

They wore a pair of fall-fronted yellow breeches in 1809 in full dress, and had received fall-fronted off-white breeches by 1811. For service dress they had a pair of fall-fronted dark blue breeches. which from 1812 were probably grey, but there are no contemporary illustrations to confirm this; white breeches on a building site would not be very practical. They had black leather Hungarian boots with black lace and tassel.

They were equipped with a black leather waist belt with lion-head clasps and carried an infantry officer's sabre with a red and gold sabre strap and knot. The model of sabre probably varied, with a number of privately made sabres also being carried.

Their horse furniture consisted of black leather harness and a red Hungarian-style shabraque with a yellow or gold laced border.

Civil servants wore civilian clothes until 1808, when they received a uniform. It was similar to the engineers, minus the officers' attributes, and worn with black bicorn and blue breeches. They were unarmed, so no belt.

Det Kongeligevej Corps

This was a semi-military/civilian unit mainly of former or inactive serving engineer officers posted over different parts of Denmark to oversee and plan the construction of new roads and maintaining existing roads. Normally the actual work was carried out by civilian workers, but military units were sometimes commandeered to help do the job as well.

The roads outside of major towns were often just dirt tracks, but major work was carried out to improve the road network, at least between the major towns.

The corps uniform is unknown, but as former officers the men probably wore their old service uniforms and the inactive officers their old service dress as well, and the others probably wore civilian dress.

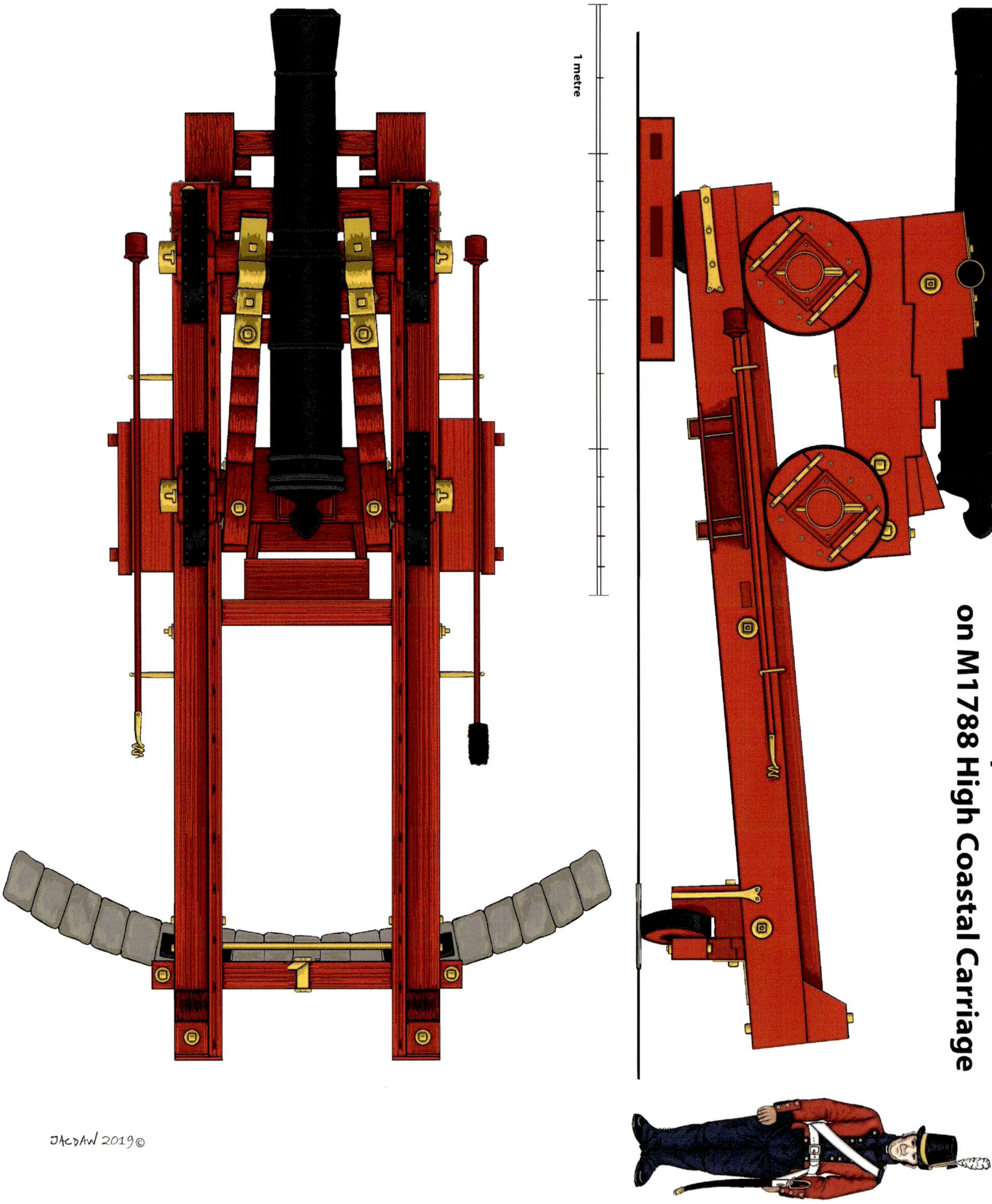

Danish 24-pdr Iron Piece M1753 on M1788 High Coastal Carriage

Plate 55. Danish 24-pdr Iron Piece M1753, System 'Reitzensteins', on M1788/1802 High Coastal Artillery Carriage

This is the original version of the M1788 carriage with four wheels, but a new steeper undercarriage. But this steeper angle of gun carriage also made it more difficult to adjust the gun in height. This was not so much a problem for coastal artillery, where mainly 'ricochet shooting' was used, but it was a problem in fortresses, where the terrain was often more varied and different methods had to be used for shooting. The calibre of this piece was 153mm and the length of the barrel including the cascable 351cm. A total 300 guns of this system were cast in Norway, and 250 more in Sweden. Those cast in Sweden were of particularly high quality. Most of the Swedish pieces appear to have been sent to Denmark.

Source: based on models and drawings found in the Tøjhusmuseet, Copenhagen, now called the Krigsmuseet, some original pieces found in Norway, and several full-scale reconstructions made in both Denmark and Norway. For scale, shown with an artilleryman.

Corps of Sappers (*Sappørkorpset*)

This was a new formation raised in 1808. It was four companies strong, each of 200 men, giving a full strength of 800 men, but the corps was reduced to one company in 1814 and then disbanded. They are best described as volunteer work battalions and they were intended to form a work force under the command of the Engineer Corps to help build and maintain fortifications and other public works wherever they were needed, principally on Zealand and the surrounding islands. They were to enlist men aged between 20 to 50 years old, living in either the towns, or peasants who had drawn lots to be free of military service or had already performed their six years of military service from Zealand, Lolland; Falster and Möen. All were to be able-bodied and strong. They were not to be trained as a proper military unit and were to receive only rudimentary military training and some basic training in the use of their sidearm. Instead they trained to build military and civilian constructions.

Because of the war, many young men found themselves unemployed, and many of them enlisted. Also, several towns encouraged their unemployed to enlist as they received a wage, clothing and food, so very quickly they had more personnel than they needed.

In 1809 the youngest and fittest were asked if they would be willing to enlist in a new volunteer sharpshooters company (*Skarpskytte kompagni*), officially as an independent 5th company of the 1st Battalion of the *Sjællandske Jæger Corps*. The officers and NCOs would be transferred from the *Sjællandske Skarpskytte Corps* and would wear their uniform, and the company would serve as the permanent garrison on the small island of Sejerø, in the Great Belt. Soon a company was raised with a strength of 160 men, and after training they were transferred to the island of Sejerø together with an artillery detachment equipped with two 3-pdr cannon and two small mortars. The Island of Sejerø did not have a garrison between 1807 and 1809, and the island had been raided on several occasions by passing English and Swedish ships and heavy looted. This was now stopped and the company did fine service protecting the island, and beat off several attacks and landings.

In 1815 both the *Sappør Corpset* and the independent *Skarpskytte kompagni* were disbanded.

Uniform

In 1808 the sappers still wore around, black felt hat with a white metal base band and white plume; this was later replaced by a shako with a green plume. They wore a tunic without lapels in red cloth; the front of the coat was piped white and closed by a single row of white metal buttons with straw-yellow upturned front corners. It had an orange collar and cuffs all piped white. They wore a pair of fall-fronted grey breeches, and black leather belts completed their dress.

In 1808 the officers begun to wear the new shakos with a white plume, and carried a standard officer's sabre with a gilt guard and scabbard fittings. They wore black Hessian-style tasselled boots.

The NCOs carried an M1753 infantry sabre. The ordinary sappers only carried a fascine knife (*Faskinkniv* or machete) made out of the old artillery *Hirchfaengere*, carried in a brown leather scabbard.

Around 1810 the men started to receive a new uniform which consisted of an M1810 shako hat with a black cockade and a small white plume. They kept their orange facing colour, but the coatee was now grey and they appear to have lost their cuff flaps. Their breeches remained grey.

Supply-Train Drivers

These men were not considered proper soldiers, but classed as non-combatants as they were peasants called in locally, normally from the 'reserve' militia class, and using either local civilian wagons or driving military

Plate 56. Danish 12-pdr M1753 Iron Piece, System 'Reitzensteins', on 'Gribeauval'-Type Fortress Carriage M1788/1802

A new 'high', three-wheeled fortress and coastal artillery carriage was designed and approved in 1788 based on the French 'Gribeauval' system, to be used by mainly by 12-pdr guns, both iron and bronze pieces. The barrel was 274cm long including the cascable. They were mounted on a special 'swing sledge', also part of the system. They were in general use from 1802 (Artillery Treatise 1813). Although not shown on the original plans they probably had some wheels or rollers on the rear of the sledge to allow it to pivot freely. These three-wheeled 12-pdr fortress guns often had different types of wheels.They were originally intended to be dismounted and drawn to different places in the fortress on the landward side, as needed. Originally they had spoked wheels to lessen the weight. But this also made the gun more fragile, so sometimes solid wheels were used instead. But the only one preserved in Norway has the original spoked wheels, so these were used, and were probably the norm.

Source: based on a near-contemporary model and drawings found in the Tøjhusmuseet, Copenhagen, now called the Krigsmuseet some original pieces found in Norway, and several full-scale reconstructions in Denmark.

Danish 12-pdr Iron Fortress Piece on a 'Gribeauval'-Type Carriage *c.*1802

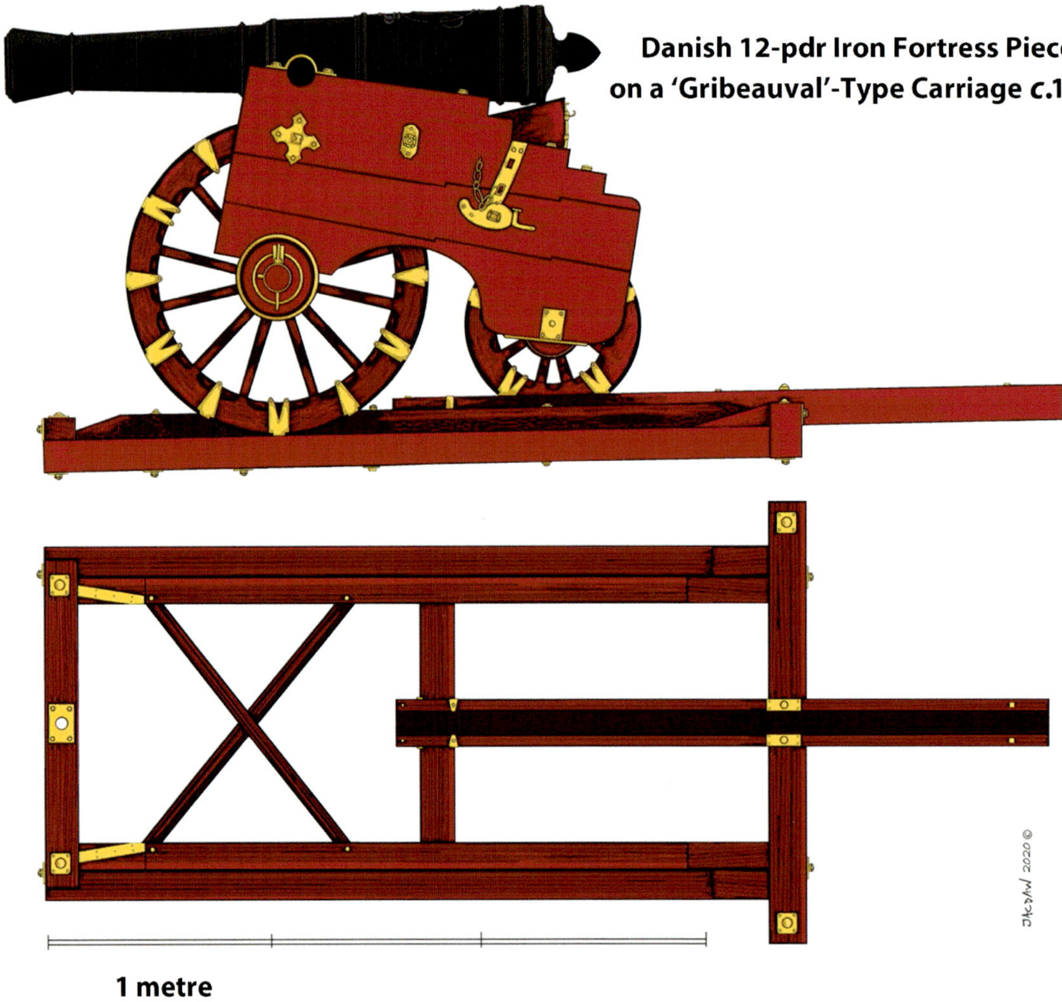

wagons to transport supplies, and in some cases, evacuate the wounded. They had no uniform, but some wore their old Landeværn militia uniforms or other bits of military uniform. They were unarmed.

Other Specialist Units

The Marine Company, Matros Kompagniet, 1813–14

This company was formed to assist the Danish Auxiliary Corps during the campaign of 1813 in bridging, boating, road clearance and general fortification, and for this purpose a special *Matros compagni* (naval company) was raised.

The company had three officers, six NCOs and 180 sailors. These were drawn from two NCOs and 40 volunteers from the *Tømmermænd* (literally 'timber-men' or shipbuilders) at the naval shipyard in Copenhagen; the rest were volunteers found among the 3,300 returning sailors who had been serving aboard the French ships of the line on the Scheldt in Holland. All were to 'Be able to Swim, use an Axe, [be] Young, fit and unmarried'. The corps performed sterling service, both at the Battle of Bornhøved and at the Battle of Sehestedt, were they were divided among the Artillery batteries as 'dragrope men' to help manoeuvre the guns.

Uniforms

The Naval Officers

In 1813 these men still wore large bicorns, more or less fore and aft; they had a gold laced border, tassels and loop holding a black cockade. The officer would have worn a double-breasted navy blue long-tailed coat, lined blue with a red collar and cuffs, a white waistcoat and gold or brass buttons. His fall front breeches were blue with gold or yellow Hungarian knots and a strip of yellow or gold lace down the outer seam and black Hungarian or Hessian boots with gold binding and tassel on the border. His uniform may also have been used without the gold embroidery, but it was not uncommon that officers wore their old uniforms out! Senn indicates that they lost their gold epaulettes and changed to pointed cuffs with cuff rank markings in 1812 as the army. They could be armed with a sabre as sidearm, carried on a black belt with a lion-head clasp, although a contemporary watercolour only shows a dagger with a gold sword knot.

The NCOs would have had hats like sailors with a strap and brass buckle around the base and a black cockade on the side. They wore a plain double-breasted long-tailed navy blue coat with a red collar, and the cuffs had a yellow/gold stripe around each cuff like those of the artillery chevrons after 1812, and brass buttons. They wore a pair of blue or grey fall-fronted trousers and black shoes; short boots were also allowed.

The NCO's sidearm would be the naval version of the M1802 artillery sabre, carried on a black leather belt.

The sailors wore standard naval service dress. They wore sailors' hats, described by a Danish soldier who saw them in camp during 1813, and they were apparently made of woven straw and lacquered black, making them look just like normal hats. They wore a plain, double-breasted, long-tailed navy blue coat with a red collar and blue cuffs and brass buttons. Their fall front trousers were grey or blue and worn with naval shoes in dry weather at least, but some had grey infantry breeches and black gaiters with brass buttons and black shoes instead.

Arms and Equipment

Normally, the men should all have been equipped with a naval boarding axe issued from the naval stores. They also brought other working equipment with them to do their job, so spades could also be used. They did not usually carry firearms, but it was apparently not unusual for some of the sailors to carry privately acquired pistols for self-defence.

The old French grenadier sabre was possibly carried as a sidearm by the Danish Matros compagni. These had apparently been supplied from French stores to the Danish naval personnel manning the French ships on the Scheldt, and the sailors brought them back in 1813.

Musicians

Apparently the company did not have any musicians, but all the officers and the NCOs had boatswain's pipes called *Bådsmandspiber* in Danish, to use for signalling.

Colours

As they were classed as ship's crew, the company was allowed the same colours as a ship. A smaller version of the normal naval ensign was carried as a unit colour, and alongside this a smaller pennant was carried as a secondary (company) colour. Both were carried on white staves with a round white wooden knob as a finial.

An interesting anecdote. A Danish naval officer wrote that when Napoleon inspected the Danish crews serving on board the French ships of the line in Holland in 1809, he was very impressed by the Danish naval ratings in general, but also with the Danish naval uniforms, which were all in dark marine blue and with black hats with shields bearing the name of their ship on it. Napoleon told the Danish officer present that at the moment he was thinking of changing the French naval uniforms (which at the time resembled more or less an army uniform, with shako and all, and it was generally disliked by all). Soon after this all the French naval crews changed into a new uniform closely resembling the Danish uniform (1810). So maybe Denmark's naval traditions served to inspire the new French naval uniforms

Danish Engineer Officers
Danish Sappers
1
1805
1811
1808
Matros Kompagniet 1813–1814
Sapper 1811
2
3
4
not to scale
JACDAW 2019©

Plate 57. Danish Engineer Officers and Sappers

Top, from left to right:
Danish engineer officer c.1805. After an engraving and a watercolour in the Tøjhusmuseet, Copenhagen.
A Danish engineer officer c.1811(sash omitted to show belt buckle and lower part of the coat.
An officer of sappers, 1808
Sapper NCO in 1808 uniform.

Bottom, from left to right:
Sapper in new uniform from c.1811
Matros Company 1813–1814, officer, NCO and a seaman sapper pontoneer in landing dress (with a privately aquired pistol).
1. Faskinkniv M1808 (fascine knife) as carried by the sapper privates. After an engraving and an original in the Tøjhusmuseet, Copenhagen.
2. Bosun's pipe. Drawn fron a model in a private collection. The corp is in brass and the pipe is in copper.
3. Naval Boarding axe.
4. Holstein Naval Sabre converted from an older French or Dutch grenadier sabre, which was probably used as side arm by the Danish Matros Kompagni' They had been supplied, from French stores, to Danish naval personnel manning French ships in the Scheldt, and brought back with them in 1813. After an original in the Tøjhusmuseet, Copenhagen.

Appendix

The Puzzle of the Standards of the Livgarden til Hest (Horse Guards) 1720–1866

By Jørgen Koefoed Larsen

As a general note, the issuing of colours and standards by the 'late kings' was frequent and more the norm than anything special. It was only normal to present new colours to the regiments when the old ones were worn out and in tatters.

Regarding the Royal Horse Guards' standards, I have consulted the only detailed regimental history there is: C.C. von Krogh, *Den Kongelige Livgarde til Hest*, written in 1866. Von Krogh had himself been an officer in the Horse Guards until 1866 and had full access to all their archives and papers. But although he used a lot of energy getting drawings of uniforms, there are none of the standards, and little information is found in the text regarding the appearance of kettledrum banners. Also the archive notes found regarding the surviving standards in 'Tøjhusmuseet'/'The Krigsmuseet', have also been consulted.

Krogh clearly gives a clear date for the ordering and delivery of the 'old set of standards' from 1720, of which four were received (one white and three red, see above). But there is no clear date given for the 1758 standards. There are only two notes from internal correspondence in 1759 one explaining that 'The old standards (M1720), are to be returned for storage at the arsenal (of Copenhagen)',and another that 'The old kettle drum covers are to be given to the widow of the late kettledrummer Petersen, as her widow's pension'. So it was probably these notes that the *Tøjhusmuseet*/The War Museum used to date them as'1758', and I have found no other clear date of issue, but that this must have been done between 1758–1762. However, continuing the research I have found something strange regarding the old M1720 standards, which may point to them possibly being reused later than previously thought: in 1829, in a list and description of the colours and standards then stored in the arsenal of Rendsborg, we find three of the M1720 standards (one white No.044, and two red 046 and 047), together with a set of red kettledrum covers (Nos. 048 and 049).So only one (red) standard was actually present at the arsenal of Copenhagen, and the kettledrum cover was apparently also shipped for storage here, not given to the widow (but perhaps she received a 'parade set'?)But why were they stored in Rendsborg? The Horse Guards were only once present in Holstein between 1720 and 1847, as far as we know, and that was for a very short period in 1762, when two squadrons were sent to join the Danish army stationed on the border waiting for a Russian attack. For the rest of the period they were only ever in Copenhagen. So this does not seem to fit in. But one (red) standard was accordingly missing at this period, apparently in the possession of the Horse Guards in Copenhagen. There was also a note that this standard(No. 045), probably is a 'restored' standard, as it today has a red fringe; the white standard and the other red standards from Rendsborg have no fringes at all, but one (No. 046) red standard has the small remains of a fringe in gold or faded silver! This is probably the remains of the original fringe.

I have chosen to follow the remains of the silver/gold fringe and that Haffner's picture of *c*.1800, is correct in originally showing a silvered/golden fringe.

But accordingly somewhere between 1758 and 1762 four new (all silver/white) standards were issued, together with a set of white parade (No. 501) and red ordinary (No. 121) kettledrum covers. Only one of those in an original state exists today, ref. 118 (ref. 119, from the text at the *Tøjhusmuseet*, has been slightly damaged over the years) and 118 is the one that was drawn in the *Fanebogen* (the book of colours). Originally all four standards had silver cloth embroidered with the royal arms and monogram sewn upon them, and fringes (probably gold or faded silver) on all four sides. That they all were silver conforms to the colours of the Royal Foot Guards (*Livgarde til Fod*) which are also all white in this period. In 1763 the Horse Guards were totally reformed and reduced to only two small squadrons (60 men each). Also Frederik V died in 1763. So when did they actually receive them, and how many? We simply do not know for sure. There was for a short period in 1762, plans for five squadrons, and so an extra standard was needed, which could have meant that the Horse Guards kept one M1720 standard for this use.

But this is only speculation. And the final reduction late in 1762 was for only two squadrons, and it stayed as such until 1842. Again we have no details at all of the use of the standards before 1787 (except that they were present).

The artist Lorentzen painted the standard of the first squadron (chestnut horses) in 1787 (the painting is found in two versions), and here the standard is coloured as mainly gold/dark with a red shield, and gold fringes with streaks of silver. This is not a detailed picture, and the colouring is somewhat doubtful, so probably the standard actually had a silver background and golden fringes. So undoubtedly he has painted the M1758 'silver/white' standard, although it looks very dark and has previously been seen as probably red, at least by me.

The most detailed picture we have of the standards of both squadrons and the kettledrum banner is a picture allegedly painted by the staff officer in the Crown Prince's staff, Haffner, *c.*1800, of the Crown Prince inspecting the Horse Guards. Here we see as expected a white/silver (M1758) standard in the 1st (Liv) Squadron. But the 2nd Squadron clearly carries a red standard! This is puzzling. The researcher T. Snorrason has personally studied the detailed sketches, made during the process of painting, the finished picture in the Museum of Frederiksborg and the picture itself is well-painted with very fine details and there is no doubt that this is a 'official' picture commissioned by Crown Prince Frederik, and painted by an officer who knew the details. So we must trust that Prince Frederik would not have allowed his Horse Guards to be shown with the wrong standards, so the 2nd Squadron (black horses) carrying a red standard in *c.*1800, is probably without a doubt. My theory is based on the fact, that much points to the M1758 standards possibly being somewhat worn by this period, so perhaps the Crown Prince may have wanted to 'spare' the original standards. Also the Crown Prince may, following the issuing of new 'C7' standards to most of the cavalry from *c.*1783, and when he took personal command of the Horse Guards from *c.*1784, have wanted his regiment, like the rest of cavalry to have a 'white standard' for the Life Squadron and a 'coloured standard' for the 2nd Squadron. So as the Horse Guards clearly had a 'spare' (red M1720) in store, he may have wanted to use this also, to spare the rest for parades and special occasions. Between 1792 and 1800 the cavalry were thoroughly modernised, and during much of this modernisation the Crown Prince used the Horse Guards as his own personal 'experimental unit'. But as he himself ordered that there were to be no 'white standards' issued after 1795, the red standard was probably issued between 1785 at the earliest and 1795 at the latest. An interesting date is 1790, when a general reorganisation was carried out, in the cavalry.

As the Horse Guards had one red M1720 standard in the arsenal they were able, without any expense, to use this old standard. That it carried the monogram of Frederik IV was not a hindrance, quite the opposite: it was seen as 'showing respect to a royal forefather'.

But clearly more soon happened. It is clear that somewhere between 1800 and 1825, two of the original M1758 standards and the red set of kettledrum covers underwent a major restoration. In several details this changed the appearance of the standards.

In 1828 the painter Hyllested, in his description of the Danish army, drew the standard bearer of the 2nd Squadron (black horses). What I first noticed is, that at this period the standard clearly no longer has any fringes but only a white cloth border. So from this picture it is clear that the 2nd Squadron in 1828 carried a 'silver' standard (not red any more), but also that the original standard(s), has been remade/restored with a white cloth border on three sides, and had lost their original fringes! This is also clear when looking at one of the two original standards given to the King in 1866 (refs 116 and 117 *Tøjhusmuseet*). After my best estimate most likely this change first occurred after 1808, but before 1828, when the whole army was both reuniformed and reorganised, and several regiments were issued with new standards

As the Crown Prince had become King Frederik VI in 1808, it was now up to him, whether the Horse Guards should have new standards with his monograms. But he had on several occasions stressed the importance of showing respect to his royal ancestors by continuing to use the older standards, so he clearly would have wanted the old standards kept in use. Probably the old red M1720 standard was by 1808 too fragile to be used, and so the red M1720 was put into store for good. Two of the original M1758 standards (Nos. 116 and 117) then had a major repair/ restoration. They were unstitched and taken apart, cleaned, repaired and the two sides stitched onto a piece of heavy white canvas cloth between them, leaving a 4cm stiff white border around the original standard, as a replacement for the fringes. But it is not surprising that the standards originally made *c.*1758 were rather worn by *c.*1808–1828.

But then by chance I realised that there was a 'special edition' made only for the King, of Hyllested's work (today in the Queen's personal library), and that this special edition shows another version of the standard! This version shows a more elaborate standard with golden fringes! This was because, I think, the ordinary version showed the 'ordinary standards' (refs 116 and 117). The King's version showed the 'parade' version, which must tell us that the two best preserved M1758 standards (refs 118 and 119), were kept, but only used on very special occasions. So from somewhere between *c.*1808 and 1828, two 'sets' of the original M1758 standards were in use: an 'ordinary' set and a 'parade' set. Also at the *Tøjhusmuseet* there exists an official drawing of both these restored standards, without a date but probably *c.*1810–1820. In 1842 the Horse Guards were reduced to just one squadron, and so from this year they only used one standard and probably finally retired the 'parade' set (refs 118 and 119) to the arsenal. There exists a painting from *c*.1847, showing one standard still in use, although the details are not so clear as to which of the two models it shows. In 1848 they received two new 'Dannebrog' standards (with the Mantova cross), for 'field and ordinary use', and the two remaining restored M1758 standards were probably only used for parades. When the Horse Guards were disbanded in 1866, the two remaining (but restored) M1758 standards (Nos. 116 and 117), and the restored set of kettledrum covers were presented to the King as his personal property, first displayed at Amalienborg, later at Christiansborg (after 1927), and there they remained until 2019, when they were taken down for storage.

After the disbandment of the Horse Guards in 1866 they were resurrected, on at least two occasions, in 1911 (250th-year jubilee) and in 1936 (275th-year jubilee), with cavalrymen dressed up in original uniforms (all at that time conserved at the *Tøjhusmuseet*), and took part in large parades. In 1936 there is even a colour photograph of the show, and here we see that also one of the original standards (without fringes so either refs.116 or 117) was part of the display!

One of the standards displayed at Christiansborg (refs. 116 and 117), were later drawn for the book *Dannebrog* in 1949. It is a rather speculative painting, and probably much too simple in its details. It may well be that the standards already were rather damaged at this period. It is mentioned in the text that the silver background was in fact nearly blue, but that is a fact also visible on the drawing found at the *Tøjhusmuseet*!

The historical artist H.C. Würgler also used the remade/restored standards on display at Christiansborg (refs. 116 and 117 again) as his model for his plate of the Horse Guards made in the 1980s, but this is clearly not completely right for at least the full period 1800–1815.

In 1985 standard ref. 118 was put on display at an exhibition about the uniforms of the Danish cavalry. It was clearly observed as 'dark brown/reddish' in colour, but with rather blurred details. (only the brown clubs of the two 'wild men' was really clear). This is probably as a result of poor storage, and gold and silver mixing, and as we now know from the 'Fanebogen', ref. no. 118 looked quite different when painted *c*.1900.

To recapitulate;

According to the information from the *Tøjhusmuseet* and found in C.C. Krogh, originally four, then only two silver/white standards of exactly the same design, were issued sometime between 1758 and 1763. Whether the fringes were originally golden or if they were silver and later faded into a yellow colour is open to debate, as both options are possible. Also a set of (ordinary) red and a set of (parade) silvered kettledrum covers were issued in same period.

A very detailed, and clearly an officially commissioned painting, conserved today in the Castle of Rosenborg, allegedly painted by von Haffner, shows the Crown Prince inspecting the Horse Guards *c*.1800, which very clearly shows a white/silver standard in the 1st Squadron, but very clearly a red standard in the 2nd Squadron. Also the kettledrummer has a set of red banners.

This red standard was probably one of the red M1720 standards from the reign of Frederik IV. This were probably taken into service at the earliest 1785 and at the latest 1795 and was probably used until at the earliest 1808 and at the latest 1828.

At some unknown date between 1808 and 1828, two of the original standards were heavily restored for use as 'daily' standards. The 'original' standards were probably used as 'parade' standards until 1842, when they were probably taken into store. The two restored standards were used until 1848, as the only standards, from when they were used as the 'parade' standards.

These were the two standards turned over to the King in 1866, and later on display at Christiansborg Castle and also the standard of the 2nd Squadron painted by Hyllested in 1828. It is clear, that this revised/restored model of standard without fringes, but with a white cloth border in its place, was already in use as early as 1828, and probably had been for some years. Also the drawing found at the *Tøjhusmuseet* seems to confirm this. As stated, this change probably happened sometime between 1808 and 1828, but as we have no firm information, this can only be a qualified estimation.

J.K. Larsen 2020

Bibliography and Sources

Original Sources: Iconographical Sources

Köller, Frederich Ludwig von, a series of watercolours (Kiel: Darmstadt University and Federal State Library)

Ljunggren, Carl Johann, *Minnes-Anteckningar under 1813 och 1814 årens kampagner uti Tyskland och Norge* (Stockholm: 1855)

Lorentzen, Christian August, *Uhlans in Camp 1812–13* (private collection)

Lorentzen, Christian August, *Frederik den 6. kørende til det kongelige teater c.*1811/1813 Kongernes Samling (Castle Rosenborg Copenhagen: with the kind permission of Peter Kristiansen, Curator)

Möller, initial unknown, *Fuldstændige Tabeller over alle den Kongelige Danske og Norske Armee til hörende, regimenters, corpers, batailloners, borgervæbningers og frivillige etc., corpers Corpser Uniform* (Kiöbenhavn: C. Steen forlag, 1810), not to be confused with Waldemar Moller of *c.*1892.

Senn, Johs, Eckersberg C.W., Heuer Wilhelm, Reiter J., *Danske Klædedragter* (København c.1808–1812)

Brockdorff, Schack von, *Den Danske Armées Uniformer c.1806* (Copenhagen: Tøjhusmuseet)

Suhr Brothers, *Abbildung der Uniformenaller in Hamburg seit den Jahren 1806 bis 1815 ein quartiert gewesener Truppen* (Berlin: Staatlicher Museum Kunstbibliothek). These illustrations were published in the 1820s in a book called The Danish Army in Hamburg (1812–1814) Uniform Plates. They were drawn and painted by Christoph and Cornelius Suhr. Only four copies are known to be in existence.

Von Prangen, series of 19 watercolours of Danish soldiers, Glückstadt *c.*1809–1810 (Hamburg-Altona Das Altonaer Museum)

Original Sources: Manuscripts

Kierulf, Herman, *Kalender over samtlige officerer ved den kongelige Danske og Norske Armée ansatte Officeerer og øvrige Beetiente, saavelsom over Borgervæbninger og frivillige corps No. IV* (København: Kongeligog Universitets Bogtrytter, 1811)

Printed Sources

Aagaard, Erik, *Den Norske Hær I Dansketiden-et billedheft* (Oslo Norway: Forsvarsmuseet Småskrift nr. 10, 1992)

Aagaard, Erik, *Det Norske kavaleris standarter* (Oslo: Norsk Våpenhistorisk Selskap Årbok, 2016)

Aagaard, Erik, *Det Norske infanteri faner* (Oslo: Norsk Våpenhistorisk Selskap Årbok, 2017)

Aagaard, Erik, *Tilføyelser og debatt: Krigsskolens faner* (Oslo: Norsk Våpenhistorisk Selskap Årbok, 2018)

Andersen, Kaptajn Willy, *Ingeniøkorpset 1684–1934* (København: Særtrkaf Tidsskrift for Ingeniørofficer, 1934)

Anonymous, *Exerceer-Regler for hesteryg Copenhagen 1806*

Bellander, Erik, *Dräktoch Uniform* (Stockholm: P.A. Norstedt & Söner, 1973)

Blom, Otto, *Ældredanske metal ogjernstykker* [Older Danish Metal and Cast Iron Cannons] (København Danmark: Krigsministeriet, 1891)

Bruhn, Helge, *Dannebrog og danske faner gennem tiderne* (København: Jespersen og Pios Forlag, 1949)

Carman, W.Y., *A Dictionary of Military Uniforms* (London: B.T. Batsford, 1977)

Cassin-Scott, Jack, *Scandinavian Armies in the Napoleonic Wars* (London: Osprey, M.A.A. 60, Long Acre, 1976)

Franklin, C.E., *British Napoleonic Field Artillery* (Stroud: The History Press, 2008)

Eriksen, E. & Frantzen, O.L., *Dansk Artilleri I Napoleonstiden* (København: Tøjhusmuseets, 1988)

Funcken, Liliane & Fred, *L'Uniforms et les Armes des Soldats du Premier Empire*, Tome II (Tournai: Casterman,1969)

Johansen Hauerbach, M.W., *Fanekatalog over Hærmuseetssamling* (Oslo: Utg. Hærmuseet, 1956)

Johansen, Oberstløjtnant Jens, *Frederik VI's Hær 1784–1814* (København: Udgivetaf Generalstaben, Heydes Bogtrykkeri, 1948)

Kannik, Preuben, *Military Uniforms of the World in Colour* (London: Blandford, 1968).

Knötel, Richard, Knötel H., and Sieg, H., *Uniforms of the World* [*Handbuch der Uniformkunde*] (London: reprint, Arms & Armour Press, 1980)

Krogh, C.C. von, *Meddelelser om Den Kongelige Livgarde til Hest, et bidrag til dens Historie* (History of the Royal Horse Guards) (København: Høst & Søns, Kongl. Hof-Boghandel 1886 Kjøbenhavn Lange, P.H.W., *Den danske generalstabs historie* (1889))

Liebe, Poul Ib, *Napoleons Danske Hjælpetropper 'Auxiliærkorpset 1813'* (Copenhagen: Forlaghet Zac, 1968)

Lienhart, Dr., and Humbert, R., *Les Uniformes de l'Armée Française de 1690 à 1894*, Volume V (Saint Aignan: Edition de Leipzig, 1897)

Lars Lindeberg, *De så det ske - Englandskrigene 1801–14* (Copenhagen: Lademann Forlagsaktieselskab, 1974)

Nielsen, Kay S., *Danske blankvåben* (Copenhagen: Forlaghet Sixtus, 1978)

Over, Keith, *Flags and Standards of the Napoleonic Wars* (London: Bivouac Books, 1976)

Petersen Karsten Skjold, *Kongens klaeder. Hærens uniformer og udrustning I Danmark-Norge* (Copenhagen: Tøjhusmuseet, 2014)

Petersen, Karsten Skjold, *Faner og Estandarter I den Danske Haer* (Copenhagen: Tøjhusmuseet, 2016)

V. Richter, *Den danskeland militærestat 1801-1894* (København: bd. 1–2, 1934–1935)

Sandstedt, Fred, *Between the Imperial Eagles, Sweden's Armed Forces during the Revolutionary and the Napoleonic Wars 1780–1820* (Stockholm: Armémuseum, 2000)

Scheel, Heinrich Otto von, *Mémoires D'artillerie, Contenant L'artillerie Nouvelle Ou Les faits Dans L'artillerie Françoise en 1765* (Paris: chez Magimel, 1765). This was the book which was used as a guide for modernising the Danish artillery.

Stilling, Valdemar, *Danske Livregiment til fods, 1 Bataillon 1763–1913* (København, Gyldendalske Boghandel Nordisk Forlag, 1913)

Strøm, Knut Erik, *Norske Borgervæpingsuniformer et Billedhefte* (Oslo: Forsvarsmuseet Akershus, 1992)

Thaulow, Th., *Samsø I krigsårene 1801–14* (Samsø: Boghandler Henri Neble, 1934)

Thaulow, Th. Ernst Mentze and Møller, M. Friis, *Livgarden gennem 300aar* (Copenhagen: Martins Forlag, 1974)

Vaupell, Otto, *Den danske Hærs Historie til Nutiden og den norske Hærs Historie indtil 1814.* 2 volumes. i 3 dele. (København: Forlagtaf den Gyldendalske Boghandel, 1872–76)

Walberg, Erik, *Vapenlexikon Artilleri 1350–1880* (Stockholm: Sveriges militähistorika arv SMHA 2017)

Walbom-Pramvig, B., *Uniformer, Faner og Väben I Den Danske Hærfra 1659 til 1980* (Frederikssund: Forlaghet Thorsgaard ApS, 1988)

Wise, Terry, *Flags of the Napoleonic Wars (3)* (London: Osprey M.A.A. 115, 1981)

Wise, Terry, *Military Flags of the World 1618–1900* (New York: Blandford/Arco, 1978)

Wolter, Hans Christian, *Den Danske Hær I Napoleonstiden 1801–1814. Håndbog om uniformer, faner, udrustning og krigshistorie* (Copenhagen: Tøjhusmuseets skrifter 12. Tøjhusmuseet, 1992)

Magazines & Periodicals

Bruun, Daniel, *Enung Rytter officers Erindringer fra felttoget 1813* (København: *Militært* Tidsskrift, 43.årg. pp.1–30. 1914)

Hoff An. 'Ridendeogkørendeartilleri', *Danske Artilleri Tidsskrift*, 1970, pp.185–194

Hoff An. 'Det ridende artilleri I Danmark', *Danske Artilleri Tidsskrift*, 1970, pp.222–227

Jonsgaard, Möen Ola, *Regimental Distinctions of Norwegian regiments 1807–14* (Oslo: lverumske Skieløber Compagnie, 2014), association publication, limited distribution, members.

Snorrason, Torstein Würgler, Hansen, 'The Assault on Stralsund 1809, Part I', *Tradition* magazine (English), No. 52,pp.22–25, 36–37.

Snorrason, Torstein & Würgler, Hansen, 'The Assault on Stralsund 1809, Part II', *Tradition* magazine (English), No. 53,pp.2–7.

Snorrason, Torstein & Würgler, Hansen, 'The Light Dragoon Regiment of Jutland 1813–1814', *Tradition* magazine (English), No.56, p.33.

Snorrason, Torstein & Wügler, Hansen, 'The Battle of Boden 4th December 1813', *Tradition* magazine (English), No. 64. pp.14–16, p.20.

Wolter, Hans Christian, 'Danish Infantry of the Line and Light Infantry 1803–1814, the Perry achievement', *Chakoten, Dansk Militæhistorisk Selskab*, December 2016, No. 71 årgang nr. 4, pp.10–17.

Thureholm, Ole & Larsen, Jørgen, & Wolter, Hans Christian, 'Danish and Norwegian Cavalry and Artillery 1803–1814', part 1, *Chakoten, Dansk Militæhistorisk Selskab*, June 2018, No. 73 årgang nr. 2, pp.14–21.

Thureholm, Ole & Larsen, Jørgen, & Wolter, Hans Christian, 'Danish and Norwegian Cavalry and Artillery 1803–1814, the Perry achievement', *Chakoten, Dansk Militæhistorisk Selskab*, September 2018, No. 73 årgang nr. 3, pp.4–10.

Uniform Prints

Dr. Peter Bunde. Brigade Uniformtafeln, *Tafel 16 KGR DÄNEMARK REITER- LIEBREGIMENT*, Herzogenrath, Germany 1999

Dr. Peter Bunde. Brigade Uniformtafeln, *Tafel 17 KGR DÄNEMARK REITER-REGIMENT SEELAND*, Herzogenrath, Germany 1999

Dr. Peter Bunde. Brigade Uniformtafeln. *Tafel 18 KGR DÄNEMARK REITER-REGIMENT SCHESWIG*, Herzogenrath, Germany 1999

Dr. Peter Bunde. Brigade Uniformtafeln, *Tafel 19 KGR DÄNEMARK REITER-REGIMENT HOLSTEIN*, Herzogenrath, Germany 1999

Dr. Peter Bunde. Brigade Uniformtafeln, *Tafel 22 KGR DÄNEMARK; DIE INFANTERIE REGIMENTER 1808–13*, Herzogenrath, Germany 2005

Dr. Peter Bunde. Brigade Uniformtafeln, *Tafel 23 KGR DÄNEMARK; LIEBGARDE ZU FUSS 1806–15.* Herzogenrath, Germany 1999

Dr. Peter Bunde. Brigade Uniformtafeln, *Tafel 26 KGR DÄNEMARK LIEBREGIMENT DER LIETCHEN DRAGONER*, Herzogenrath, Germany 2015

Dr. Peter Bunde. Brigade Uniformtafeln, *Tafel 27 KGR DÄNEMARK LEICHTES-DRAGONER REGIMENT FUNEN*, Herzogenrath, Germany 2015

Dr. Peter Bunde. Brigade Uniformtafeln, *Tafel 28 KGR DÄNEMARK LEICHTES-DRAGONER REGIMENT JUTLAND*, Herzogenrath, Germany 2015

Dr. Peter Bunde. Brigade Uniformtafeln, *Tafel 29 KGR DÄNEMARK PRINZ FRIEDRICH FERDINAND DRAGONER REGIMENT*, Herzogenrath, Germany 2015

Dr. Peter Bunde. Brigade Uniformtafeln, *Tafel 33 KGR DÄNEMARK LIEBREGIMENT ZU FUSS DER KÖNIGIN*, Herzogenrath, Germany 2009

Dr. Peter Bunde. Brigade Uniformtafeln, *Tafel 41 KGR DÄNEMARK; INFANTERIE REGIMENT HOLSTEIN*, Herzogenrath, Germany 2009

Dr. Peter Bunde. Brigade Uniformtafeln, *Tafel 258 KGR DÄNEMARK; FUSS-ARTILLERIE*, Herzogenrath, Germany 2012

Dr. Peter Bunde. Brigade Uniformtafeln, *Tafel 259 KGR DÄNEMARK; REITENDE ARTILLERIE*, Herzogenrath, Germany 2012

Internet Sources

<http://napoleon-online.de/suhr.html>, for the plates by Suhr

<https://www.arma-dania.dk/public/timeline/_ad_blankvaben_list.php>(site containing details and photographs of Danish weapons)